WHO ARE WE NOW?

Also by Jason Cowley

Statesmanship: The Best of the New Statesman, 1913–2019
(*Edited and introduced*)

Reaching for Utopia:
Making Sense of An Age of Upheaval

The Last Game:
Love, Death and Football

JASON COWLEY

WHO ARE WE NOW?

STORIES OF MODERN ENGLAND

PICADOR

First published 2022 by Picador
an imprint of Pan Macmillan
The Smithson, 6 Briset Street, London ECIM 5NR
EU representative: Macmillan Publishers Ireland Ltd, 1st Floor,
The Liffey Trust Centre, 117–126 Sheriff Street Upper,
Dublin 1, DO1 YC43
Associated companies throughout the world
www.panmacmillan.com

ISBN 978-1-5290-1778-6

9 8 7 6 5 4 3 2 1

A CIP catalogue record for this book is available from the British Library.

Typeset in Scala by Palimpsest Book Production Ltd, Falkirk, Stirlingshire
Printed and bound by CPI Group (UK) Ltd, Croydon, CRO 4YY

Visit **www.picador.com** to read more about all our books
and to buy them. You will also find features, author interviews and
news of any author events, and you can sign up for e-newsletters
so that you're always first to hear about our new releases.

This book is dedicated to my mother, Lilian.

CONTENTS

[It is] of the deepest importance to try and determine what England *is*, before guessing what part England *can play* in the huge events that are happening.

– George Orwell

Life can only be understood backwards; but it must be lived forwards.

– Søren Kierkegaard

'Do you remember 1969?'

'Vaguely.'

'I loved it. So many things were going on. I don't know what happened afterwards. It really seemed like the start of a new era.'

'It was,' Reacher said. 'Just not the era you expected.'

– Lee Child, *Worth Dying For*

PROLOGUE

On the evening of Thursday, 26 March 2020, at precisely 8 p.m., we went outside during a period of unusually radiant and settled early spring weather that every day was tempting us from our houses even as the government urged us to stay inside 'to protect the NHS and save lives'.

In our quiet road in a market town in Hertfordshire our neighbours stood at open windows and doors, on balconies or in their front gardens. Everyone was applauding. There were whoops and cheers. Pots and pans were being banged together. A firework illuminated the darkening sky. In these early, eerie days of lockdown, when we didn't quite realize how cataclysmic the pandemic would be, here was an expression of fellow feeling among near-strangers – we'd only recently moved into our house – a moment of magical mutuality and togetherness of a kind one seldom if ever experiences outside of a World Cup or Euros summer when England are doing well and nearly everyone you meet seems to be talking about the football.

We came out that evening not because we felt compelled to do so by the pressure of public piety but because we wanted to. We knew that similar scenes were being repeated across the country as people applauded the doctors, nurses and essential support staff working on the front line against a new respiratory virus that was sweeping the land, leaving death and suffering in its wake. A week later, at this same time on Thursday evening, Boris Johnson, the prime minister, though sick with Covid-19, pulled himself from self-isolation to stand applauding at the door of 10 Downing Street. A few days later, he would be in intensive care in St Thomas's Hospital.

That first night of the Great Applause was so affecting because it was so transient. We stood apart and yet we also stood together, and then we waved goodbye and closed our doors again, the strange, unnatural quiet of recent days returning once more. As I made a drink and stood at the kitchen window looking out, I felt unaccountably moved.

I'd been worrying inordinately about my mother, Lilian, who was then approaching her eighty-fourth birthday, and her two elder sisters, Iris and Connie. The three siblings were widows; each lived alone. They were also admirably phlegmatic about the unfolding crisis. I was not. In the early days of lockdown, I would wake with a sense of dread and disbelief: how could this be happening, here and now?

I put this question, rhetorically, to my mother when we spoke shortly after I'd stopped commuting to London and started working full-time from home. She and her sisters grew up in Dagenham, about ten miles east of central London, and had lived through the privations of the Second World War. They experienced food rationing and the Blitz. As we became more used to life under lockdown, I wanted to know how the pandemic compared to my mother's experiences of wartime as a child on the home front. She and Iris were evacuees and they often talked about the dislocating experience of being separated from their parents and about the loneliness of their lives in the Devon countryside where they were billeted with two unmarried women.

As lockdown dragged into a second month, even my mother's resolve weakened a little. 'This experience is worse in a way than the war because you knew who the enemy was and back then we could be together,' she said when I called one afternoon. 'This enemy is invisible and you're on your own.'

+ + +

When we face crises in our lives – the breakdown of a relationship, cancer scares, bereavement – we promise ourselves, as we re-emerge on the other side, if we emerge on the other side, that nothing can be the same again. But the pattern of daily life is re-established. Personal pledges are broken. Habitualism devours our days. We struggle to create space for the kind of self-reflection that is necessary for post-traumatic growth.

When I reflect on that first night of the Great Applause – the weekly 'clap for carers' continued for ten weeks as hospital intensive care units filled with the sick and the dying – I'm sure we experienced something special: a renewed sense of social solidarity. Consider those 750,000 people who responded within a few days to the government's appeal for volunteers to help the NHS as we approached the first peak. The paradox of the pandemic was that, during those early weeks of lockdown, community was being rediscovered through enforced social isolation. It did not last. It could not last. But while it did, the social atmosphere in the country, so markedly different from the polarization and division of the period of the Brexit endgame, offered tantalizing possibilities of how we might live, work and organize society in the post-pandemic world.

+ + +

On the evening of Tuesday, 23 March 2021, at exactly 8 p.m., nearly a year later, we went outside with lighted candles and torches to mark the first anniversary of lockdown and, according to the Office of National Statistics, the death of nearly 130,000 people from Covid-19 in the UK. This was being called a day of 'national reflection' but this time it felt like a top-down, state-directed initiative, not a spontaneous mobilization. On our road only a few people came out and no one stood at doors or windows. The neighbours I spoke to were good-humoured but restless. One of them was carrying a glass of red wine. Everyone wanted to move on, not look back. And they wanted a haircut; we'd been locked down, with all but essential shops closed, since early January.

So much changed in that year of the virus. How were we living and working before it? Who were we and what did we want? Or think we wanted? And – here's the question I put to one of my neighbours as I snuffed out my candle and prepared to go back inside: Who are we now?

PART ONE

1 THE ENGLISH QUESTION

I want us to be a young country again.

Tony Blair, 1995

My mother's eldest sister has lived for more than fifty years in the same modest, end-of-terrace, brick-built house in the west Essex town of Harlow. Constance Scott – Auntie Connie to me – celebrated her ninetieth birthday in spring 2018 and is our family matriarch: she has seen much and borne most. Her late husband served as a commando in North Africa in the Second World War and, common to many of the wartime generation, Connie has a quiet resilience and deep sense of history. She believes in the necessity of shared national sacrifice, as she said to me one afternoon as the Covid pandemic was accelerating, closing down the country, forcing us apart, and inside.

Connie moved to Harlow as a young mother in the early years after it had been established by the Labour government's 1946 New Towns Act, which created eight towns in the south-east. The original village of Harlow (renamed Old Harlow) is mentioned in the Domesday Book. This and other long-established settlements – Potter Street, Parndon, Netteswell, Tye Green, Latton, Churchgate Street – were subsumed by the chief architect-planner Frederick Gibberd into his urban masterplan for the new town; they were built on and around, developed, expanded but not erased or demolished. Even today, Potter Street, where Connie settled and still lives, retains something of the character of a village, on the far edges of the town, close to Junction 7 of the M11 motorway.

I was born in Potter Street and we lived there in a rented maisonette and then a nearby council house for the first six years of my life before my parents bought their first property on a quiet cul-de-sac elsewhere in the town after my father had benefited from a small family inheritance. I was christened in the local church, St Mary Magdalene, which overlooked what we used to call Harlow Common, with its scattered woodland and uncultivated fields where cattle and horses grazed. My first school was a short walk from Connie's house and occasionally on those afternoons when my mother was out or working, Connie would wait for me at the school gates. The local doctors' surgery, at Osler House in the Prentice Place shopping precinct, was close too, across a small, neat park which had its own children's play area: swings, seesaw, roundabout, concrete paddling pool. We could see the imposing black front door of Osler House from the window of our maisonette, situated above a busy bakery in Prentice Place, and it was there that we saw our family doctor, John Meyrick. He was an austere yet respected man with black-framed spectacles, a high forehead and quizzical expression, and he lived in a fine detached private house that pre-existed the new town (today a housing development is named after him in Potter Street). Back then there were still family doctors, which meant continuity of care between doctor and patient was possible: Dr Meyrick knew our extended family well and remained our doctor long after we moved away from Potter Street.

In Frederick Gibberd's original masterplan for the town, each discrete settlement or district had its own self-supporting infrastructure: a shopping precinct (such as Prentice Place), community centre, primary school, pub, NHS health centre, sub-post office, general store, newsagent, fish and chip shop, and so on. But, as with so much of the town, these neighbourhoods were allowed slowly, irreversibly, to decline. Prentice Place was no exception. Over the years when I occasionally passed by, always on the way to somewhere else, everything about the area seemed desolate. The old community shops had gone and with them the spirit of the place. Prentice Place: the very name is resonant because for many of us the deepest structures of identity are bound up with having a stable connection to place. But nowadays Potter Street feels so unfamiliar that it is as if we'd never lived there.

+ + +

In February 2018, the West Essex Clinical Commissioning Group announced that Osler House Surgery, opened in 1955, was closing, leaving more than 3,000 people without convenient access to a local NHS doctors' surgery. There had been no advance warning or process of consultation before residents were sent letters dated 21 February informing them that the surgery would be closed on 30 April. It was a fait accompli. No questions asked and no explanation offered.

Nor were the local Tory MP, Robert Halfon, or the district council consulted before the decision was made. It emerged that the GP surgery was operated by a private company, the Practice Group, which further investigations revealed had responsibility for at least fifty other such practices and healthcare centres in England, as well as 200,000 patients. The ultimate owner of the Practice Group turned out to be a multibillion-pound private insurance company, Centene Corporation, based in St Louis, Missouri. According to press reports, its chief executive earned £18.5 million a year. The company's motto was 'Better health outcomes at lower costs' and the reason given for closing Osler House was one of cost: it was 'no longer financially viable'.

Osler House patients were instructed by the Practice Group to register at other health centres in the Bush Fair and Church Langley conurbations. Neither was easily accessible for Connie and other elderly residents who did not have a car or relatives living close by; to reach the Church Langley Medical Practice my aunt faced an arduous journey requiring her to take four separate buses, at the age of ninety.

I discovered more about what was happening in an email from my wife titled 'Go on, Connie!' I opened it and clicked on the accompanying link to a video: there she was, my aunt, being interviewed outside Osler House. In the news clip, which attracted the interest of the *Daily Mail* and the BBC, Connie is tearful as she expresses her frustration at the decision to shut Osler House.

She was as disconsolate as I'd ever heard her when I called. 'It's an absolute disgrace,' she said. 'The whole thing has been so underhand. Why was an American company running our doctors' surgery? Why was it allowed to close? Why was there no consultation? We're still hoping to reverse the decision – but we are fighting giants. This has broken my heart.'

For all the local and national media interest in the Potter Street residents' campaign – the *Daily Mail* interviewed and photographed Connie, investigated the background to the proposed closure and published an editorial condemning it, and a BBC camera crew visited her at home – the decision was not reversed. Osler House was closed in May 2018. One of the residents who was campaigning alongside Connie told me she felt 'humiliated'. Her humiliation was linked to feelings of powerlessness and dispossession. There was nothing that she, or Connie, or even Robert Halfon MP could do to stop a business decision for which the ultimate responsibility lay with the senior management of a multinational conglomerate in the United States.

From its earliest days Connie had believed in the promise of the new town and in its founding aspiration to dignify working people's lives, not only where they lived but how they lived; more than a million buildings had been destroyed or damaged in east and north London during the Second World War, leaving tens of thousands of people in need of resettlement. She willingly contributed, through a form of local taxation, to the building of the then state-of-the-art town sports centre, which opened in the early 1960s. It had indoor community facilities, as well as a football stadium and a cricket pitch, where Essex played occasional first-class county matches.

Her politics were shaped by the more egalitarian society created by the Beveridge Report, J. M. Keynes's commitment to full employment, the wartime command economy and the social reforms of Clement Attlee's post-war Labour government, with its insistence on patriotic purpose, the common good and reciprocal obligations. The war centralized the state and expanded its bureaucracy. It also took away a golden age of local government and voluntary agency. When considering who we are – not just who owns us – this is important, because in the parable of Prentice Place it was agency that Connie, the people of Potter Street, the local MP and even indeed the town council believed they lacked.

Attlee's political awakening began while he was working among the urban poor of London's East End before the First World War, in which he later served. When he became Labour leader in 1935, and then eventually prime minister in 1945, he longed to remake the social order, to create the 'New Jerusalem', as he described it. Much later, in 1960, he visited Harlow to open the new high-rise town hall. Designed by Frederick Gibberd and located in the Water Gardens in the town centre, known locally as the High because of its elevated location, the town hall was an icon of modernity and progress. The best that Harlow offered.

Connie stayed on in the town long after everyone in our

extended family had moved away, unsettled by decline and spoiled purpose. She stayed on even as friends and long-time neighbours died. She stayed on because she was rooted in a community. She had a profound attachment to place. 'I belong here,' she told me. No one could persuade her to move out of her house in Potter Street, which she'd (somewhat reluctantly) bought from the council after much encouragement from her three daughters. But the closure of Osler House Surgery had 'broken her heart'.

Robert Halfon called it 'a terrible and short-sighted decision'. He is an advocate of working-class, or white van, conservatism – he has called for the Conservatives to be renamed the Workers' Party – and what a mighty lesson the closure of Osler House was, or should have been, to Tories like him. For Connie, it was not only short-sighted but signified something deeper about what George Orwell called the social atmosphere of the country. After the rapid deindustrialization of the 1980s and then, from 2010, nearly a decade of austerity which had led to severe cuts in public spending and the neglect of the public realm, many people were grappling with feelings of dispossession like those residents of Potter Street 'fighting giants'. The closure of Osler House symbolized something important too about the more destructive effects of market-driven globalization, so long celebrated as a panacea by British leaders of the liberal left (Tony Blair) and liberal right (David Cameron). How could Dr Meyrick's old community NHS practice be controlled and closed without consultation by an insurance conglomerate in Missouri? It didn't make sense – except that it did in the context of our national priorities and present discontents.

TAKE BACK CONTROL

Now consider the 2016 European referendum. There's a reason the Brexiteers' slogan – 'Take Back Control' – and their professed mistrust of 'experts' cut through during that fractious, often deceitful campaign: it spoke directly, as the American political philosopher Michael Sandel said to me one summer afternoon on the eve of the poll, 'to people's sense that they no longer had any meaningful say in shaping the forces that govern their lives and believed that their identities and very way of life were under siege'.

At a deep, personal level many people felt they'd lost control over something fundamental in their lives and could do nothing about the cultural disruption and technological and economic shifts destabilizing society. What had gone was a sense of a common ethical life, and its passing was experienced as a profound loss.

The truth about globalization was that it had lifted hundreds of millions out of poverty, especially in China, and created limitless opportunities for educated supranational elites, but alongside the gains arising from an integrated global economy there were considerable losses, even in the more affluent West, especially in the West. And what matters for the purposes of this book is that millions of ordinary men and women believed they'd lost control, or were ignored, or disrespected, or left behind. Encouraged by political ideologues, as well as chancers such as Boris Johnson – who took an outside bet that supporting Leave offered him a pathway to the premiership – when the time came, many millions ignored David Cameron, the youngest prime minister for 198 years, and chose Brexit because this time they believed their vote could make a difference.

In the 2016 referendum people were asked to vote for the status quo and a majority chose the opposite. They wagered on the unknown. They were prepared to bet against the political, legal and business establishment because they believed the status quo was already unsustainable. With 'quiet resolve', as Theresa May, a sceptical Remainer, described it to me when I interviewed her as prime minister, they voted for apparent instability and far-reaching change; David Cameron said Brexit would cost every household £4,300. But the vote to leave was for many motivated less by economic self-interest than an expression of national sentiment: 'We want our country back!'

Millions more – determined Remainers – were horrified by the decision. Instead of reflecting on the sense of grievance that had motivated so many ordinary voters to opt for Leave, or what it was that had been voted against or indeed for, a campaign was launched to overturn the referendum result, as if Brexit voters had allowed themselves to be duped. But Brexit was not simply an expression of frustrated nationalism or post-imperial nostalgia; it also showed politics was being driven by big, bold ideas about sovereignty, community, identity, immigration, security and control. One cannot overstate, in retrospect, just how dramatic and extraordinary the Leave vote was, and it forced the political elite to turn back towards its own country. For all his destructiveness, Trump pulled off something similar in the United States.

For Remainers it was traumatic to discover that so many of their fellow countrymen and women rejected their belief in cosmopolitan democracy and their worldview; nearly two-thirds of all parliamentary constituencies voted to leave, the poorest three categories of the population voted overwhelmingly for Brexit, while 57 per cent of those with university degrees voted Remain (I was one of them, powerfully so, but I understand – and accept – why Remain lost).

And so began the Brexit culture wars in which we were mired for more than three miserable years until Boris Johnson's Conservatives won an emphatic victory at the 2019 general election on a decisive, if crude, pledge 'to get Brexit done', which settled the argument, in England at least, if not in the rest of the UK. Under the leadership of Jo Swinson, the well-financed Liberal Democrats, junior partners in the Conservative-led coalition government from 2010 to 2015, had campaigned to revoke the referendum result altogether. Jeremy Corbyn's Labour had pledged to hold phased renegotiations and ultimately a second referendum. It didn't work out for either party. Labour suffered its worst defeat since 1935, the Lib Dems returned only eleven MPs, and Swinson lost her seat a few weeks after declaring she could be the next prime minister. We had entered a new era and, on Christmas Eve 2020, the United Kingdom finally signed a free trade agreement with the EU. We were out. '[I] did not fully anticipate the strength of feeling that would be unleashed both during the referendum and afterwards,' wrote David Cameron, with comical understatement, in his memoir *For the Record* (2019).

+ + +

What most interested me about the 2016 vote, beyond the economic consequences and the darker forces it had unleashed, was what it revealed about the condition of England. When, in early 2013, David Cameron announced he would, in the event of a Conservative majority at the next election, hold an in/out European referendum, Nigel Farage, leader of the United Kingdom Independence Party (UKIP), said, 'They're coming to play on our pitch now.'

The nation that emerged from the campaign was more atomized and more divided than at any time in living memory: we were passing through the most culturally febrile period for fifty years, and in September 2019 Parliament would be prorogued, unconstitutionally suspended. We seemed to be locked in a struggle over how to define who we were and what sort of place we, and our children, and their children, lived in.

'The Brexit vote and the chaotic debates that followed are proof that some older ideas about England and Englishness, long submerged into a broader definition of "Britain", also retain a powerful appeal,' wrote Anne Applebaum in her book *Twilight of*

Democracy. She neglected to mention that a majority in Wales had voted Leave, and she also underplayed the frustration of the many people who believed that Parliament – and elected politicians from all parties – was attempting to thwart the vote for Brexit, a vote Parliament had granted.

'Brexit was an instruction from the electorate to turn around the ship of state by 180 degrees,' Nigel Farage told me. 'You cannot do that unless you believe in what you're doing. You have to actually, passionately believe in what you're doing. Ignore all criticism, you just have to do it. It's like an act of going to war.'

He spoke of his pride at having mobilized what he called a 'people's army'; UKIP, which first broke through at the 2009 European Parliament elections, won nearly four million votes at the 2015 general election. David Cameron had dismissed its supporters as 'fruitcakes, loonies and closet racists' – a remark as ill-judged as Hillary Clinton's 'basket of deplorables' condemnation of Trump supporters. The deplorables and fruitcakes would have their revenge over Cameron and Clinton.

The referendum, wrote Ali Smith in *Summer*, the final novel in her state-of-the-nation quartet, 'sliced right through the everyday to a bitterness nobody knew what to do with'. Value divides and the culture wars set Remainers against Brexiteers, the old against the young, the cities against the towns, graduates against early school-leavers, the open society against the closed society, baby boomers against millennials, home owners against renters, the north against the south, England against Scotland, the UK against the EU, and so it went on.

The discourse in the unregulated space of social media became ever more viciously polarized. The cultural schisms of the day were over race, trans rights, freedom of speech, immigration, and the legacy of colonialism. Twitter mobs swarmed, denounced, shamed and cancelled. A binary logic prevailed. We were barricaded behind walls of indifference and contempt. One was reminded of W. B. Yeats's 'The Second Coming':

> The best lack all conviction, while the worst
> Are full of passionate intensity.

+ + +

The social problems creating the conditions for Brexit were just as acute in Harlow, a former Labour town and now a Conservative stronghold, as they were in the post-industrial north and Midlands. Harlow has high unemployment, intergenerational inequality, deprived estates, struggling schools and, until recently, a semi-derelict town centre and a hospital rated 'inadequate' and placed in special measures. A large majority of people in the town voted for Brexit (68 per cent), and yet, in another striking example of the spatial inequality that blights much of Britain, it is only a short thirty-minute train journey from Harlow to Liverpool Street Station, the gateway to the gleaming corporate towers and stupendous wealth of the City of London.

My aunt understood all this but, until the abrupt closure of Osler House Surgery, she'd been pragmatic about the decline of the town. Connie valued a particular type of community that had long given meaning to her life and she mourned its passing. 'I have always been happy in Harlow, but when I found out about what was happening to our local doctors, I was so angry it actually made me ill for a few days,' she told the *Daily Mail*.

Ever since the Great Recession, people were experiencing, in many towns and for different reasons, the arbitrary closure of essential community services – doctors' surgeries, child centres and nurseries, libraries, post offices. A fracture had opened up between comfortable and uncomfortable Britain. In the words of the writer and broadcaster Andrew Marr, a 'social revolution' began in the years after the 2008 financial crash, 'when the British state responded by radically restricting spending and, in so doing, greatly exaggerated the gap in life expectations, hope and happiness between the poorest social classes and least invested-in communities, and the rest'.

According to the Marmot Review published by the Institute of Health Equity in 2020, austerity created a 'lost decade' of stagnant wages, stalled mobility and growing inequalities of income and wealth. It examined health inequalities in England and found that, for the first time in more than a hundred years, life expectancy had stalled and even declined for women in the poorest 10 per cent of areas. Between 2010 and 2020, the seven-year gap in life expectancy between the richest and poorest parts of the country had increased to more than nine years for men and nearly eight years for women. The north–south divide had also widened: life expectancy in a deprived area of the north-east was nearly five years lower than in a comparable part of London.

'If you ask me if austerity is the reason for the worsening health picture, I'd say it is highly likely,' said Professor Michael Marmot, who led the review.

The British Medical Association called austerity 'Covid's little helper'.

+ + +

In the summer of 2021 the Taliban recaptured Afghanistan following a humiliating and panicked American-led retreat from the country ahead of the twentieth anniversary of the al-Qaeda attacks of 11 September 2001 which destroyed the illusion of global peace. Shortly after 9/11, Tony Blair delivered a fervent speech to the Labour Party conference. It was a call to arms and action. Britain was heading for war in the Middle East: 'This is a moment to seize. The kaleidoscope has been shaken. The pieces are in flux.

Soon they will settle again. Before they do, let us reorder the world around us.'

A deeper understanding of Afghanistan and Middle Eastern history ought to have made Blair more circumspect about his astonishing ambitions to reorder the world. But he was a young prime minister in a hurry, seemingly energized by his own rhetoric of democratic messianism. Stuart Hall, the sociologist and leading exponent of cultural studies, once likened Margaret Thatcher to one of Hegel's 'historical individuals': her politics and contradictions 'instance or concretise in one life or career much wider forces that are in play'. The same could be said of Blair.

In February 2003 perhaps as many as a million people marched in central London to protest the coming American-led invasion of Iraq. They were heard and seen but ultimately ignored. But just as Blair thought he was winning, the ghosts of his political life blew wilder than before. You could even say that history caught up with him, not least in Iraq and Afghanistan, where Britain became tragically embroiled in America's 'forever war'.

The Iraq protests, the war itself and the growing disillusionment with Blair among leftish voters had one big unintended consequence: it was in those years, in the wider anti-war movement, that alliances were formed and the foundations were laid for the takeover of the Labour Party many years later by the Corbynite left. Another legacy of the Iraq War was a collapse of faith in the political class, exacerbated by the MPs' expenses scandal of 2009, when it seemed to many voters as if our elected representatives at Westminster were all on the make. They were not. But the perception that they were hardened into something permanent.

Meanwhile, the devolution settlement introduced by Blair's government did not kill Scottish nationalism 'stone dead' as Labour's George Robertson, later secretary-general of NATO, hubristically predicted. It galvanized the independence movement, inflamed English grievance and exposed the discontinuities within the creaking post-imperial British state – 'UKania' in the coinage of Tom Nairn.

In 2016, Blair returned to public life after a post-parliamentary career dedicated to serious personal enrichment as a prominent leader of the anti-Brexit campaign. He still believes the arc of history bends towards enlightenment and justice, as he told me.

There was much that New Labour got right, especially during its first term in power as it invested significantly in schools and hospitals and early years education, legislated to eliminate child poverty and concluded the negotiations for the Good Friday Agreement bringing peace to the island of Ireland after so much violence and death. For all his extraordinary self-belief, or because of it, Blair became complacent. He was overconfident and believed in the myth of his own great good fortune, in the inevitability of progress, in his remarkable verbal fluency, in his powers of persuasion. Perhaps the country was suffering from wilful blindness back then, buoyed by continuous economic growth and caught up in the euphoria of Cool Britannia.

An attachment to the nation and the flag is often strongest among those groups who are struggling or feel excluded or scorned, and during the New Labour years, far away from the multicultural cities, increasing numbers of people started self-identifying in surveys as English rather than British. If the question was whether national identities were still pertinent at a time of accelerated globalization, the answer from peripheral England was unequivocally yes.

In his book *The Future of Capitalism*, the economist Paul Collier likens the vote for Brexit to a mutiny driven by stark social divergences. 'Think of the most famous mutiny: on the *Bounty*,' he said when we met. 'What happened to those sailors was that they ended up on an island in the middle of nowhere. That wasn't their objective when they mutinied. They didn't mutiny with a view to the future but because the conditions they were living in had become intolerable. Mutinies are angry reactions to neglect.'

The era of social democratic hegemony that lasted in Britain, broadly, from 1945 to 1970 was 'glorious', Collier said. 'It was when it all came together. We inherited a huge asset – a shared sense of purpose coming out of the Second World War, a sense of common endeavour. But it was a wasting asset that needed to be renewed. And both left and right failed to renew it. We are haunted by what was lost.'

LOST FUTURES

One experience of being haunted is noticing absences in the present, as the cultural critic Mark Fisher wrote. The New Labour era, with its cult of Cool Britannia, can be understood in retrospect as having been haunted by an England that was lost in the shadows, but always present. Something was stirring. England, wrote Jeremy Paxman in *The English* (1998), in which he attempts to define national character, continues to be based in a 'slow to anger' tradition of personal liberty, fair play, tolerance, amazing theatre, good television, choral music, beautiful countryside, intellectual freedom. 'And yet they [the English] remain convinced they're finished. That is their charm.' Paxman spoke too soon: the English were far from finished when he published his book, a year after New Labour took power. England was rising again. Rapid changes in society and a bold reconfiguration of the constitution were nudging the British state towards a reckoning with this submerged English identity. In a 1999 speech William Hague, then Conservative leader, warned his listeners not 'to ignore this English consciousness or bottle it up' because 'it could turn into a more dangerous English nationalism that could threaten the future of the United Kingdom'.

In his book *New Model Island* (2019), Alex Niven writes that the 'most complex and profound facet' of Englishness is its 'hiddenness'. There is a 'void at the heart of all England', he says, which is why 'Englishness is so often felt as a condition of loss'. For too long its regions have been disempowered and its infrastructure – rail links between the northern cities, say, or from west to east – has been neglected. Niven, of Newcastle University, advocates what he calls a new 'radical regionalism', a remaking of the country so that it might more closely resemble something akin to the pre-Norman, Anglo-Saxon heptarchy, the seven kingdoms (or regions, in this reimagining) of the geographical space that was once 'England'.

The problem is that there is no sustained bottom-up demand for autonomous English regions and the creation of new bureaucracies and levels of government. In 2004, the north-east overwhelmingly rejected proposals for an elected regional assembly in a referendum. Today politicians such as Andy Burnham (Greater Manchester), Andy Street (the West Midlands) and Ben Houchen (the Tees Valley) are regional election-winning mayors of national prominence, yet there is not yet a movement for an English parliament. The message from the north-east in 2004 seemed to be that regional politics in England is no simple answer to national politics: it devolves the questions and postpones the answers. Nor is it any less corrupt.

For Ferdinand Mount, a conservative essayist and author, the dominant tone of English discourse is less one of loss than 'one of regret, of nostalgia rather than self-congratulation'. The way to escape nostalgia, as Mark Fisher wrote in 2014, 'is to look for the lost possibilities in any era'.

For Fisher, the present was haunted not by the past exactly but by the lost futures it presaged. Or perhaps, more accurately, we experience a kind of double haunting: we feel the presence of the past that has gone and the future that never happened.

Born in 1968, Mark Fisher grew up in an upper working-class family in the Midlands and went to a state comprehensive school. In his essays and blogs, he celebrated what he called 'popular modernism', the culture that had shaped his early intellectual development: the music press (especially the *NME*); post-punk and pioneering electronic pop bands such as Joy Division, Kraftwerk and David Sylvian's Japan; avant-garde programmes on BBC 2 and Channel 4; art-house and science-fiction movies; Penguin paperbacks; the stories of J. G. Ballard. Fisher studied at Hull University and did post-graduate research at Warwick University, but he struggled to find fulfilling work as an itinerant academic, teaching bored, often demoralized students. 'Ask students to read for more than a couple of sentences and many . . . will protest that they *can't do it*,' Fisher wrote. 'The most frequent complaint teachers hear is that *it's boring* . . . To be bored simply means to be removed from the communicative sensation-stimulus matrix of texting, YouTube and fast food; to be denied, for a moment, the constant flow of sugary gratification on demand.'

Fisher's best writing on music, popular culture and politics was published in small magazines or on his k-punk blog. His breakthrough arrived with the book *Capitalist Realism* (2009), in which, inspired by his reading of Slavoj Žižek, Franco Berardi, Jacques Derrida and Fredric Jameson, as well as his critical engagement with pop culture, he wrote about the spiritual impoverishment of neoliberalism and about a culture of social pain that was affecting education, work and family life. He described 'the widespread sense that not only is capitalism the only viable political and economic system, but also that it is now impossible even to *imagine* a coherent alternative to it'. (He especially disliked what market-driven reforms had done to higher education: the excessive bureaucracy, the form-filling, the box-ticking, the relentless targets.)

Tormented by the 'malign spectre' of depression – he wrote with painful, hard-won authority about mental health issues – Fisher killed himself in January 2017, while at home with his wife and young child in Suffolk. He was forty-eight. At Fisher's memorial service, Tariq Goddard, his publisher and co-collaborator, said that meeting him was a bit like 'joining a band; you shared a sense of purpose before you knew whether you were even going to like each other'.

Capitalist Realism particularly appealed to a generation of millennial students who, after the financial crash, had graduated into a prolonged economic crisis. Some of them became involved in the Occupy movement and student protests over the coalition government's imposition of higher tuition fees. During the New Labour years there had been a significant expansion of higher education – 'So today I set a target of 50 per cent of young adults going into higher education in the next century,' Tony Blair said in a 1999 speech. Twenty years later, around 50 per cent of the UK population attend university, compared to as few as 3 per cent seventy years ago.

Fisher analysed the psychological stresses on a precariously employed, debt-burdened generation of young graduates whose anxieties were increased by their experience of coming to maturity in an age of shrinking security. The future these young people had been educated to expect had been 'slowly cancelled' and this made them seem, for different reasons, as disconsolate as those early school-leavers in the neglected towns who embraced Brexit. 'What should haunt us is not the no longer of actually existing social democracy, but the not yet of the futures that popular modernism trained us to expect,' Fisher wrote, in characteristic gnomic style.

+ + +

What 'lost futures' were being mourned during the Brexit culture wars? In his 1999 conference speech, Blair had expressed confidence that, 'having modernised itself', New Labour was now 'the new progressive force in British politics which can modernise the nation, sweep away those forces of conservatism to set the people free'. Blair set a liberal-modern Britishness against a conservative-traditional Englishness, and thought there could only be one winner. 'We will be a young country,' he promised in a 1995 Labour conference speech.

Or should we go further back in search of lost futures: back to the 1970s and early 1980s, and to the unravelling of the more socially cohesive, less unequal era of the welfare state and post-war consensus – Paul Collier's period of shared sense of common purpose and endeavour – to understand what we have lost and what we might yet aspire to regain?

WHAT IS HAPPENING WITH ENGLAND?

In this book, I ask a simple question: who are we now, after Brexit, in these times, as a pro-independence majority in the Holyrood Parliament marshal their forces in Scotland and the United Kingdom faces the threat of dissolution? I want to answer this question – or at least try to – by asking some other questions about England, the country in which I was born and have lived all my life, and I mean England rather than Great Britain or the UK. Why do so many people believe their Englishness has been suppressed or ignored? What accounts for the stubborn notion that Englishness and loss are inextricable? Where do feminist, ideological and multi-cultural rebellions against established narratives of Englishness fit in? How has immigration shaped what it means to be English? Why are so many progressives uncomfortable about celebrating English nationhood? Why is Englishness associated with reaction and even racism for some?

Spanning the years since the election of New Labour to the Covid pandemic, the book explores how England has changed and how those changes have created the anxious political culture of today. I examine contemporary England through a handful of the key news stories of recent times and explain what they revealed about the state of the changing nation. And in doing so I want to show the common threads that unite these stories, whether it is attitudes to class, nation, identity, race, migration or religion. I contrast the exceptional (the effects of the fast-paced, high-tech world of globalization and the mass movement of people) with the unexceptional or unnoticed (my aunt struggling to save Osler House Surgery in Potter Street).

+ + +

In *The Lion and the Unicorn: Socialism and the English Genius*, a book-length essay completed during the German bombing raids on London in late 1940, the year of Dunkirk and the Battle of Britain, George Orwell wrote that it was 'of the deepest importance to try and determine what England *is*, before guessing what part England *can play* in the huge events that are happening'.

More than eighty years later, we are still struggling to determine what England is, and what part it can play, in the huge events that are happening.

David Cameron's desire to resolve the Conservative Party's divisions over Europe through a single binary plebiscite shattered the kingdom; unresolved tensions from the deep past – the Irish border, Scottish independence, the English Question – returned with a vengeance. The pandemic exposed our pre-existing divisions and racial and social inequalities as never before.

'Everyone understands English,' Jean-Claude Juncker, the former president of the European Commission, once quipped, 'but no one understands England.'

'England' here serves as a synonym for Britain, or the United Kingdom, but Juncker was broadly correct. England is hard to understand – but so are other countries. What he surely meant was that England has its own unique peculiarities and vulnerabilities as the dominant nation in the fragile, post-imperial multinational British state, the only country ever to have left the European Union.

What then is the condition of contemporary England? We know England doesn't have its own discrete political institutions or its own parliament. Devolution has been incoherent and incomplete. The United Kingdom abandoned national capitalism in its restless embrace of free-market globalization, as the historian David Edgerton has written, and no other country of comparable economic power has allowed so many of its utilities, strategic assets, so much of its national infrastructure and so many of its iconic brands, companies and football clubs to be sold off or captured by international speculators. Too much wealth and power are concentrated in London and the south-east. Too much power is still centralized at Westminster. If the Scots and Welsh define themselves in part against England, the English, when given the chance, defined themselves against Europe. Yet the English are also internally divided: regionally, spatially and between social classes. What holds the nation together?

'Where's England?' Donald Trump asked in August 2019. 'I asked Boris [Johnson], where's England? What's happening with England? You don't use it too much any more.'

One wouldn't expect Trump to understand the difference between England, Great Britain and the United Kingdom, but he had unintentionally asked the right question.

What *is* happening with England?

PART TWO

2 CROSSING BORDERS

Richard had night sweats and bad dreams. In these dreams his feet were submerged in quicksand and he could feel himself sinking. Or he was up to his neck in water. Or his lungs were filling with water. Sometimes he saw a woman on a foreshore, in a long, dark coat, her face covered by a scarf, and she was calling out to him as he walked across the sands. Sometimes he woke with the word 'mother' on his lips and would find his wife asleep beside him and the house quiet. He was sure, in these recurring dreams, a woman had called out to him in a warm, familiar voice, but not his wife, and she'd used another name, his real name. He never used to be called Richard. He used to be called Li Hua, and this is his story.

THE JOURNEY

Li knew very little about England before leaving his home village in China, beyond what he'd read about and seen on television – and yet he already made of it in his imagination something magnificent and welcoming. When he thought about England, he imagined a light shining as if from a city on top of a distant hill. In the early negotiations with Mr Chang, the local gangboss who was part of a network smuggling Chinese workers to Western Europe, North America, Australia and Japan, Li was told the journey would take only a few weeks and that, at the end of it, he would be guaranteed work in a factory or restaurant. He would be reunited with his wife as soon as he'd found somewhere of his own to live in England, he was told. The gang – Li called them 'snakeheads' – demanded an initial cash payment (the equivalent back then of £10,000) and it was explained to him that he would be going via Moscow, and from there he would fly direct to London. Further payments would be required in the months ahead, and the full debt would have to be repaid when he was settled in England.

To fund the first payment, Li borrowed money from his uncle, who had borrowed money from a cousin. A man who worked for Mr Chang had taken Li's passport because, he was told, he would need a visa to enter Russia. One morning Li received a one-way train ticket to Beijing; the time of his departure was near. He felt uneasy the night before he left the village in Fujian Province, as if he had an emerging fever. He was reluctant to leave his wife and their young son behind on the farm, with only his parents and siblings to support them. But he knew if one day he and his wife were to have more children of their own, as they wished, and if these children were to have a better life, he had to go.

On the morning of his departure, Li held on to his wife for a long, silent time. She was crying and he wiped the tears from her face. He kissed her on the forehead and pulled her into a tight embrace. He recalled this last, warm embrace in the lost, lonely months that followed.

+ + +

When he arrived in Beijing, Li was greeted by a sullen, officious woman who spoke briskly in an unfamiliar dialect. She said he would stay in the city for several days until his visa was approved. He was now part of a group of twenty other workers, all from Fujian Province – 'the Fujianese' as they were known – and they were all on their way to England. They were taken to a hostel, where they slept and ate and were free to come and go. Within a few days, the visas arrived and the Fujianese travellers boarded the Moscow flight.

One of the group immediately took control when they arrived in Moscow, and led them through immigration controls and, on the other side, to a car park where there were several vans waiting. They were ordered into the vehicles and their passports and money were taken away. They were driven to a low-rise apartment block on a Soviet-era estate in the suburbs of Moscow, what Russians call the sleeping districts of the city. There Li would share a room with twelve others in the subdivided block. They were given duvets, water bottles, coffee and cigarettes, but there were no beds or pillows; they slept on the concrete floor.

Europeans and Russian-speaking men controlled the house. Most of the time they smoked, drank beer and vodka, talked on their phones or watched pornography, football and other sports. When the windows were closed, the smell inside the rooms was rancid and at night Li was kept awake by the sound of coughing, snoring and groaning – and sometimes by the sound of men who cried in their sleep and then said nothing. One Chinese woman in the house told him she'd been raped; she left the room one evening and returned many hours later with her face swollen and bruised. She was inconsolable when Li reached out to her. 'Please no, please no,' she said.

+ + +

For the next several months, stretching into the summer, Li Hua remained in Moscow, in the same room, in the same block. He spent slow, empty days fantasizing about escape. The residential apartment block had a shabby courtyard and they were allowed to sit in it or walk around it; sometimes the room in which they slept was locked from the outside, and Li would stare at the walls, willing his mind to empty. During this period, he was convinced one of the Fujianese men in the house had died; no one said what happened to the body. He felt ashamed at his passivity and helplessness. When he complained, he was told he was free to go, but where would be go? 'Once you're in, you are in,' Mr Chang had said to him.

+ + +

One morning Li and some other men at his breakfast table – breakfast was served in sittings of six – were told to pack their rucksacks and prepare to depart: they were going to Ukraine.

They set off in vans later that evening and Li slept fitfully for much of the long journey. Some time the next afternoon they stopped close to a lake in what was presumably Ukraine. They were given water and sweet biscuits and ordered to follow their guides across fields and over hills. Carrying rucksacks, they walked for several hours until they reached a road junction, where several trucks were parked, apparently waiting for them. The white European drivers never looked at their faces or into their eyes. From there, after more hours on the road, they arrived at a derelict farmhouse, where they stayed for at least another week. Each day they were given a single baguette, some hard cheese, coffee or sweet tea and a bottle of water, and each night they slept on the floor in a small, fetid room. At night, Li heard mice or rats scurrying beneath the floorboards and in the rafters above.

The next stage of the journey required Li and another Fujianese man to get into the boot of a large car; they were covered with blankets. They were told not to make any noise or to speak because they would be crossing the border into Slovakia.

When they stopped, many hours later, and the boot was opened, they were told they'd arrived.

+ + +

They were given water and more bread and sweet biscuits and soon afterwards were on the move again. Their next stop was some kind of hostel, and they were given rice and fruit to eat. There were no beds, however, and they slept huddled on the floor in a narrow upstairs room, where there were more Chinese men already waiting, introverted, subdued. On two occasions, they were driven in small groups to the distant German border but it was considered too dangerous to cross, and so they reluctantly returned.

After so long away from home, Li felt dejected and deeply humiliated. 'I did not want to carry on, and yet I had no choice but to carry on,' he said. He had no passport or identification papers, no money, and he was in debt to the gangmaster back home in China. He never knew for sure which country he was in – Ukraine, Slovakia, the Czech Republic, Germany . . . Sometimes when he could not sleep because of the heat and humidity and the noise, he withdrew into his own memory palace and wandered among its rooms. He pushed at doors and they opened on to different scenes from his life: at school, on the farm, alone with his mother, in bed with his wife.

As the weeks passed, he was allowed to go for short, supervised walks. He could occasionally use a mobile phone to make brief calls to his family in the village. These were charged at one dollar per minute and were strictly monitored. Li was given a pre-prepared statement to recount: there had been a 'realignment of expectation' and the overland journey was taking 'much longer than expected' because they were working to pay their way. He listened helplessly as his wife pleaded for him to come home, to give up; during one call he heard his mother crying in the background and his father's agitated voice. 'Ask Mr Chang about England,' Li said. 'Ask him about my job.' And then the line went dead, as it always did after a few minutes, as if a switch had been flicked or a cable cut. The next time he spoke to his wife, she said that Mr Chang wanted another payment; it was overdue. 'I will send more money,' Li said, and his wife asked him to come home. 'Why are you doing this?' she said.

+ + +

One afternoon Li and two Fujianese workers were squeezed into the back of a car; they were on their way to another hillside location, close to the German border. After another drive they were led by guides through dense woodland until, at the roadside, they saw two parked cars. 'Welcome to Germany,' one of the Chinese drivers said, in English, using a faux-American accent.

They were taken to a house on a residential estate; inevitably it was full of more Chinese workers. Li was given some green tea, white rolls and vegetable soup, and was then sent to wait in an upstairs room with many others. One of the men started beating his fists against the door when he heard it being locked from outside, demanding to be let out. And perhaps he was heard because not long afterwards police officers arrived at the house. It seemed another trap had been set for them.

The workers were rounded up and transported in groups to a detention centre, and so began another period of idleness and drift. Li adapted to the new routine and rituals of life inside the centre: regular hot meals, exercise in the grounds, a pillow and proper bed to sleep on. He had his hair cut, he saw a dentist and doctor, he began to feel less exhausted and slowly he gained some weight. His lips stopped splitting. The metallic taste of blood in his mouth faded. Once a week he was allowed to call his wife at home in the village. Some mornings he woke early and forgot where he was or what had happened, and then he remembered.

Li's debts were accumulating. How safe were his family in the village? If he escaped, or tried to escape, if he did not pay or could not pay, or never returned, or even died, would they be hurt – or, worse, killed?

One afternoon, during a meeting with a German official, Li was told he would be released the next day but must leave Germany immediately. The official did not care where he went as long as he left the country. He was given a number to call, some euros and identification papers. That same day Li received a call at the centre and was told he would be collected early the next morning by a Chinese-speaking driver.

The next morning the man arrived, as had been agreed, and Li was driven to a bus station. He was instructed to take a long-distance bus to the Netherlands; someone would collect him on the other side of the border.

Li was in Western Europe now, the man said; people could move freely and borders could be crossed easily, *no questions asked.* He would be all right.

He was on the move again, passing through towns he would never know, through countries to which he would never return. His mother, a devoted Catholic, had impressed upon him from a young age that he must pray, and every day now Li prayed. He believed his mother was praying for him too, though she knew nothing of his real plight. What sustained him? It was this: he believed he was surrounded by a protective wall of prayer. Nothing could break it down or break him down.

In Holland he was taken to another house, where he was greeted by more Chinese men just like him, lost, emaciated, some of them stinking and sick. At the end of each day, the gangboss in the house would tell them what to do next and what they should expect. From Holland they moved to Belgium and then to France, in small groups, in small rooms, bearing the mark of men's smudge and sharing men's smell. Li did not know these fellow travellers, but he knew he was getting closer. *You are close to the end now*, Mr Chang, or someone claiming to be him, had said.

He'd been travelling for a year, perhaps longer, and though he prayed dutifully, as his mother would have wished, Li was spiritually exhausted and profoundly alone. *The journey will only take a few weeks*, he had been told back in China. Sometimes he recalled what his father used to say to him as they worked together on the farm – that he must be independent, that he must strive to *live a good life*. Protect his son. *Don't beg*, his father had said. *Never beg. Don't expect. Don't give in.*

He had not given in.

LONDON CALLING

The final phase of the journey was across the sea, across the English Channel; Li was very close now, closer than he'd dared imagine when he was at the German detention centre and resigned to being deported to China. One evening he and a group of Chinese men from the house in France where they'd been staying – fifteen of them – were waiting by the side of the road close to a port. In his pocket, Li carried a piece of paper he'd been given by the gangboss, on which was written an address in London's Chinatown, his final destination.

On this occasion, as they waited at the roadside, a large canvas-covered truck pulled up. A ladder was dropped down from inside and a Chinese man jumped down and urged Li and the others to climb in, quickly, without hesitation. As the last of them was ascending the ladder, the truck abruptly shunted forward; the last man clung on to the ladder, his legs dangling like a trapeze artist's, before he fell. As the truck pulled away, Li peered at the forlorn figure in the road, receding from view. He was on his knees, beating the road with gloved hands.

Inside the truck, amid the crates and wooden pallets, Li felt something like relief, if not yet hope, because already the truck was shuddering to a stop. He could hear voices outside, and reasoned they were at the border. The men murmured to one another inside the truck; they'd been told to huddle together beneath the blankets left inside for them. 'Quiet now,' one of them whispered, as the canvas covering was pulled partially open from outside; torchlight pierced the darkness and Li closed his eyes and held his breath.

The check was merely cursory and soon they were moving again, the throb of the engine keeping Li awake as they travelled through the night. It was getting colder inside the truck – the men huddled together like children for warmth – and he imagined ice forming on the walls and even in the tangles of his hair.

Did the driver know the cargo he carried?

+ + +

It was light outside the next time the canvas covering was pulled back, and there they were, revealed, in all their helplessness and vulnerability. Someone shouted, 'Run!' – and they did, chaotically, in different directions. It was another trap. Li had been told to look out for the white cliffs and green fields of England. There were no white cliffs or green fields. The men were rounded up and taken by uniformed officials to a nearby detention centre, where they were photographed, interviewed and fingerprinted. Li stayed there for two days and nights, and, when he wasn't being ignored or fed, he was asked, through a translator, where he was from and what he planned to do in England. What did he want and expect? Why had he come? Li kept saying the same thing: he wanted to work and had a job in London.

On the third day, Li was released, with new British identification papers – name, age, country of origin. He was given a phone card and a permit that allowed him to travel on a train to London. He was on the move again.

+ + +

Chinatown was not a town: just some pedestrianized streets, busy with people, the hustle of traders and tourists, many languages spoken, shoppers all around. Buildings were decorated with Chinese symbols – dragons and lanterns – and Li could read the street signs because they were written in Mandarin, as well as English.

The address he'd been given turned out to be the location of a small, multipurpose supermarket. A Chinese man received him warmly, and without surprise, introducing himself as Mr Wei. 'I've been expecting you,' he said. They talked for a while about Li's journey; Mr Wei said he had shown 'great fortitude' and that he should worry no longer because there was good work for him 'in the north'. Li would have his meals provided and share a house with other Chinese workers in Liverpool. He was given a coach ticket, the address of the house in the city and some money so that he could pay for a taxi when he arrived. Perhaps for the first time since leaving the farm, Li felt something close to happiness. 'I am here now,' he said. Mr Wei rested a heavy hand on his shoulder, in reassurance and friendship. 'God bless you my good man,' he said.

ON THE SANDS

The room in the terraced house in the Kensington area of Liverpool was much like all the others: cold and damp, foul-smelling, locked windows, frayed carpets, rotten floorboards, everyone sleeping on the floor. The workers shared one putrid-reeking bathroom in which the lavatory water ran black. There were cluster flies crawling on the windows but so sluggish were their movements that it was as if they craved only extinction.

Some of the workers in the house were also from Fujian Province but there were other men from the north of China.

The next day, Li was driven from the house to Morecambe Bay on the Lancashire coast. 'Welcome to the office,' the foreman said as the minivan pulled up in the village of Hest Bank. By now, it had been explained to Li exactly what was required of him in his role as a cockle-picker and that it would take most of the day, from morning light to early evening darkness, to fill just one of the orange nylon bags he'd been given with cockles. These were small edible saltwater clams found buried in sediment. In Morecambe Bay the cockles were not dredged but hand-picked, as they had been for centuries, and they were sold in bulk as seafood, especially to continental markets.

Li had never encountered a landscape such as this before and he surveyed the vast flatness of the bay. He recalled images of the limitless empty spaces of the Gobi Desert and wondered, again, how he'd ended up here, by the sea, on these sands, in winter. This is not how he'd imagined England: isolating, crushingly cold, so alien. He looked towards the distant hills but there he saw no shining light to encourage him.

Li was given a pay-as-you-go mobile, waterproofs to wear, a black beanie hat with an LED light attached, as useful in the winter darkness as a miner's Davy lamp was underground, and boots. He pulled the beanie down tight over his ears against the hardness of the weather: the ripping winds, squally showers and the oppressive cold. Each worker was given a short-handled rake and Li was shown how to use it to sift the sands, extracting the cockles when he could find them, and being moved further along when he could not. But mostly he found it easier to dig in the dirt with his bare hands as he worked in the area of the bay around Warton Sands. He was fascinated by the bilaterally symmetrical heart-shaped shells of the cockles, firmly closed and ribbed to the touch, and wondered how the fleshy substance inside would taste.

Through the day his back ached as he scrambled and raked for cockles; he was convinced permanent damage had been done to his lower spine from travelling in car boots on unmade roads, and working on the sands only made the pain more persistent.

By mid-afternoon, it was already getting dark, and yet they were being urged further out across the monotonous flatness of the wet sands, following the retreating tides, with the fells and the moors beyond, and the lights of the surrounding towns visible in the gathering distance.

+ + +

Chinese workers had started appearing on the sands the previous year. Local fishermen received them with suspicion and hostility and controlled certain key sites, forcing the despised Chinese pickers further out into the bay in search of more distant cockle beds. What was peculiar, in retrospect, was that local people had seen the cockle-pickers come and go, they knew they were out there, but the authorities chose not to see them. They were just shadows on the sands.

Morecambe Bay has the largest expanse of intertidal mudflats and sandflats in the United Kingdom and is the confluence of four principal estuaries: Leven, Kent, Lune and Wyre. The sands are submerged at high tide, and when the sea is out in the bay they are crosscut with continuously shifting river channels. These channels, combined with treacherous quicksands, deep hollows and fast-moving incoming tides, are why there has been an official Queen's Guide to the Sands since the sixteenth century. Every twelve hours and twenty-five minutes the tide comes in at a rate *swifter than a galloping horse*, as the locals say.

Before the Furness railway link opened in 1857, crossing the sands at Morecambe Bay estuary provided the most direct route from mainland Lancashire to North Lonsdale (now part of Cumbria). The journey by horse and carriage was hazardous. There were drownings and disasters. In 1847, nine young people were returning from a fair in Ulverston to Cartmel when the fisherman's cart in which they were travelling overturned in a hollow. The water closed in and everyone drowned.

THE LAST MAN

They had stayed too long on the sands. Now the tide was rushing in and Li was being ordered back to the minivan. Water was surging along deep channels, isolating the cockle-pickers and cutting them off from the foreshore. They hurried towards the van as the driver was attempting to start the engine. He turned the ignition but it did not move: the wheels spun and churned in the mud. The water was rising fast as they clambered into the van; the foreman, sitting beside the driver in the front passenger seat, started shouting obscenities, his panic palpable. The driver thrust the gears into reverse and pressed down hard. The engine roared but the wheels did not turn.

Li could see nothing because of the darkness but he could feel the pressure of the rising water outside. Someone opened the doors and seawater surged into the vehicle: dark, salt, hard, cold. Li forced his way out and attempted to climb with some of the others onto the roof. But he fell back into the water and tried to wade-push against the currents, but they were too strong and he tumbled backwards. Salty water flooded into his mouth and lungs. He resurfaced, gasping. He found he could stand again, his head and shoulders above the water-line. He held his mouth tightly shut and reached for the phone in his pocket but it was saturated and wouldn't switch on. People were screaming around him, and one man was desperately shouting in English: 'Sinking water . . . Many, many sinking water . . .'

Li removed the waterproofs that were weighing him down, and the clothes beneath. He had no idea in which direction to start swimming. Towards the lights that ringed the bay, but which ones, and where? He tried to swim, but was hit by a wave, turned on his back, and swept along in a channel of rushing water. This was it . . . he came to rest on a raised bank and, with incredulity and relief, felt the ground beneath his feet again. Firmer ground, much firmer. He could stand without immediately sinking into the sands. He stumbled, waded, and then simply stood still, breathlessly, the water seething all around.

He couldn't see the vehicle, nor hear human voices. The faraway street and house lights seemed as remote and meaningless to him as the impossibly distant light from dead stars. He thought about his mother and how she used to pray every day and how she'd urged him to do the same. He prayed, but he felt forsaken. He'd been in England for only a few days. And this was his first day as a cockle-picker, his very first day of work on the sands.

Why would God do this to me?

He'd always done as he was asked. He'd followed his father's advice – work, don't ask, work, don't beg. Was this his reward? To die in the sea: the shame of it. Perhaps he'd died already, and yet, even if this was the end, he could find nothing hopeless in having lived. He felt as if he were already mourning the end of his own life. He remembered something, from somewhere: *In the midst of life we are in death.*

He believed his mother's spirit was with him in the water. She would look after his wife and their child, he knew that. His mother was praying for all of them. The hope he had carried in his heart like fire all the way on the trans-European journey was dissipating.

The near-naked man sank to his knees in the freezing water . . . but hold on . . . there was brightness, a radiance that lifted him. In the black sky above, he heard a loud disturbance, the sound of something harshly mechanical, the thwack-thwack-thwack of what he realized was a low-flying helicopter, its searchlights probing the waters. He waved his hands and shouted out but he could not be heard above the wind and the noise of the engine. The helicopter circled above, pulled away, but returned, its searchlights scanning the water in a restless arc. *His mother was praying.*

Li jumped up and down, his arms outstretched and held aloft, as if in manic celebration. There was a golden halo of light – he was saturated in this light – and he felt a sudden, all-enveloping warmth, as if a safety blanket, or heatsheet, had been wrapped around his bare shoulders.

'I thought I saw God in the water,' he recalled. 'The feeling at that moment is very hard for me to explain. I was alive again.'

THE PARABLE OF THE COCKLE-PICKERS

One summer afternoon in 2010 a human skull was found half-buried in the sands near Silverdale on the Lancashire coast by a guide leading a group of walkers across Morecambe Bay. Teeth were taken from it and DNA tests confirmed that it was the skull of Liu Qin Ying, a thirty-seven-year-old woman who, together with her husband, had drowned when they were trapped by incoming tides on the sands of Morecambe Bay on the night of 5 February 2004. They had been searching for cockles far out on Red Bank, two and a half miles from the foreshore near Bolton-le-Sands. Their thirteen-year-old son, Zhou, who had remained in southern China, was orphaned that night.

Liu Qin was one of seventy undocumented immigrant Chinese workers staying in four rented houses in Kensington, Liverpool.

She and many of the others had been smuggled in on a container ship; triad-affiliated gangs moved them from the Liverpool docks to the houses they controlled. One of Liu's fellow workers, Guo Bing Long, a former subsistence farmer in China, made at least two phone calls as he struggled in the water. First, he called his family in Ze Lang village, San Shan town, Fuqing city; his wife and their two infant children, a son and an adopted daughter, were asleep and he spoke to his parents. He told them he was up to his neck in the sea and he asked them to pray for him. Next, he called the emergency number 999; a female operator answered. The call was recorded and, when you listen to it, you can hear people crying and screaming as Guo Bing Long, in desperation, shouts, in English: 'Sinking water, many sinking water . . . Sinking water, sinking water . . .'

After receiving the harrowing call from their son, Guo Bing's parents woke his wife and together they waited for another call which never came. Guo Bing Long was twenty-eight when he died and, after his body was recovered, family photographs were found in his well-worn wallet and a white metal cross around his neck. A year later his mother committed suicide.

Most of the cockles were picked and processed for export to European countries and the Chinese workers were paid as little as £5 per 25 kilos of cockles picked – or more accurately raked – scandalously below the market rate. Many of them were from rural or coastal villages in Fujian Province and their motivation for risking their lives was to work and send money home to their families in China. On the night of the disaster the leader of the gang, Lin Liang Ren, a Chinese national who lived in Liverpool, the so-called gangmaster or gangboss, had ignored warnings from local fishermen about the severe weather forecast and imminent high tides.

Morecambe Bay locals know all about the dangers – the sudden tidal bores, the submerged channels, the quicksands – and that night the Chinese workers were trapped by fast-rising tides in the winter darkness. The workers were islanded, far from the foreshore, and the water just kept on rising around them. 'The tide crept up behind them,' recalled Cedric Robinson, the long-time official Queen's Guide to the Sands. 'You can't hear the tide out there when there's a wind. They were circled, there was nowhere to run.'

Later a second group of Chinese cockle-pickers were found huddled together on the foreshore. Like their unfortunate colleagues, they were carrying forged fishing permits and had been issued with fake national insurance numbers. Among the group was Lin Liang Ren, the gangmaster, and his closest associates. During police questioning, Lin and the workers each initially told the same risible story: that they were on the foreshore for a picnic, in the darkness of deepest winter. It quickly became obvious to detectives that Lin Liang Ren was not one of the abused: he was in control and the others were terrified of him.

A Royal National Lifeboat Institute hovercraft searched the sands the next day and, eventually, what was described as a 'sea of bodies' was discovered. Twenty-three Chinese workers drowned or died from hypothermia that night, including the foreman who led the way across the sands and had slept in a separate room at the house. The last man alive in the water was thirty-year-old Li Hua, and he was rescued after being located by a search helicopter's thermal imaging camera. He was naked above the waist and standing in water on Priest Skear, an expanse of raised land, covered at high tide. Skear: from the old Norse 'sker', meaning rock in the sea. Li Hua's survival was described locally as the 'miracle' of the sands. 'The Devil's beach' was how one Chinese newspaper described Morecambe Bay in the immediate aftermath.

+ + +

The inquiry into the tragedy was the largest ever undertaken by Lancashire Constabulary. DNA samples were collected and taken by police to southern China so that they could be matched with relatives of the dead. The cockle-pickers were paid in monthly cash payments which were deposited in high-street bank accounts. Most of the money was transferred to accounts in China as debt repayment. The workers were left with very little for themselves and their families, which forced them to work even longer hours, sometimes at night.

Lin Liang Ren was convicted of multiple counts of manslaughter and served six years of his sentence before being deported to China. The court was told that he had 'cynically and callously' exploited the cockle-pickers and played the tables at nearby casinos while they laboured on the sands. His much younger girlfriend and a cousin were also convicted of breaches of immigration law and of perverting the course of justice. His cousin's pregnant English girlfriend, Janie Bannister, from Merseyside, gave evidence against the gang; on the night of the tragedy she'd called the coastguards to alert them to the unfolding disaster. 'I've got a lot of Chinese boys in Morecambe Bay,' she said, 'and they are stuck because they are cockle-pickers. They have to get out . . . The water, it's around their waist.'

Among the 'boys' were three women.

Early in the investigation some of the Chinese workers from the second group found huddled on the foreshore disappeared from an asylum centre. They were tracked to London's Chinatown but there the trail went cold. The police slowly won the trust of some of those who did not flee, however, and they began to open up about their ordeal.

Li Hua, the lone survivor, gave evidence at the trial, under a witness protection scheme organized by Paul Francis, a now-retired detective sergeant. Li spoke in court from behind a screen so that he could not be identified. Paul believes that more than twenty-three Chinese workers might have died in the water that night. 'The prosecutions were based on the number of corpses discovered,' he said. 'There could have been more. They were illegal immigrants; we had no idea how many were in the country.'

Before the Morecambe Bay investigation, Paul Francis had arranged witness protection for killers ('the people who pulled the trigger first') and members of organized crime gangs. Li Hua and the cockle-pickers from the second group were different. 'They were good people,' he recalled. 'They wanted legal work and to pay their taxes. They didn't want to come to Britain to rip us off. For Li, living on pennies a day at home, it was a simple business decision. He could come to the UK and work for ten to fifteen years and with the money he earned he could build five houses in Fujian Province. For him, the cost of coming to the UK was £30,000 – he thought he could make that in nine months. The main focus was to repay the debt. They have to pay half up front in China and the other half over a period. That's why they couldn't walk away – if they don't repay the debt to the snakehead gangs, their family in China will get it. They're captured. They are slaves.'

Paul asked me if I knew Morecambe Bay and I said that we had family living nearby in Silverdale and that, even on benign summer days, we'd always approached the sands with extreme caution and humility.

'In summer,' he said, 'you can stand in the middle of the bay: you've got the peaks of the Lake District, this beautiful expanse of water, you've got a promenade that's just been modernized, a nice art deco hotel – to look at, it's beautiful. And yet every day these gangs of Chinese were coming in and the whole community just ignored it: the police, the local authority, health and immigration services. There were hundreds of them. Why did we allow it to happen? We all knew they were there. Why didn't we do something about it? It seems to be the British way: until someone thumps you on the nose, you don't sit up and take notice.'

The police investigation was led by Mick Gradwell, also now retired. 'The crime scene was 120 square miles, there were vehicles and bodies and evidence in Morecambe, Liverpool and elsewhere,' he said. 'I'm a Lancashire lad, used to dealing with crimes in Lancashire, not international organized crime gangs and human trafficking – it's not what you expect, not on the landscaped shores of Morecambe Bay. You're thrown into investigating international organized crime gangs, snakeheads, triads, international human trafficking. We dealt with the people who were responsible for the deaths on the night. But we did not make any dent into these wider criminal gangs who traffic people around the world.'

Gradwell explained how the gangs operated in 'plain sight':

'Tens of thousands of illegal Chinese workers were living in England,' he said. 'Building up hidden communities and building a life below official recognition. It was horrifying to discover what was going on in this country.'

In 2003, Geraldine Smith, the Labour MP for Morecambe and Lunesdale, wrote to the Home Office warning of the danger the 'currents and quicksands' posed to migrant workers in Morecambe Bay. In a perfunctory reply, a Home Office minister said immigration services had too few resources to investigate. *Too few resources*: we would hear this refrain, or excuse, again and again, in the years to come, as one of the most pressing moral concerns of our times was simply wished away: mass migration, legal or otherwise.

ENGLAND'S DREAMING

One morning, during the pandemic, Li Hua and I had a long conversation. He still lives in the UK, runs a restaurant and owns a house in which he lives with his wife, two grown-up children and one grandchild. His original dreams of England have been fulfilled, but not in ways that he could have ever imagined. He speaks little English and so also joining us on a Zoom call were Irene, a translator, and Paul Francis, the retired police officer who'd organized Li's witness protection and created a new identity for him.

Li has returned to Fujian Province only once since 2004; he recalled that, when he used to work on the family farm, his father would give a large proportion of their produce to the state as a form of taxation. 'Everything has changed now in the village and farmers don't have to pay the food tax,' he said with a chuckle. It was only in 2012 that he finally repaid the outstanding debt to the gangmaster in China.

Li, Paul and Irene had a lovely, relaxed intimacy: the mutual trust was hard earned. Li was reluctant to use Zoom because he was suspicious of downloading software onto his laptop. At one point, his wife appeared alongside him and waved into the camera. 'Hello, hello everyone!' she said.

'Paul has treated me so well, given me so much support, mental and physical,' Li said. 'He helped bring my wife and child to England, and took care of us as we got to know the people, the climate, the life. Paul is always in our hearts.'

Li was wearing a black leather jacket, a low-necked black T-shirt, and his hair was spiky and cut severely short above the ears. He was physically much heavier than when he was lifted from the water that night, emaciated, traumatized, suffering from hypothermia.

'Li, it's good to see I'm not the only one putting on weight in lockdown!' Paul quipped, and we all laughed.

Li dreams often about that night in the water – the terror he experienced and the hopelessness. He has panic attacks and night sweats.

He spoke directly to, and through, Irene, who could not always understand what he was saying because of his dialect.

'The horror is imprinted on my mind and I can't get rid of it totally,' Li said. 'I have many, many nightmares. I'm trying my best to forget. I try every day not to let it bother me, to bother my work. But the shadow is always there: it keeps bothering me. I didn't realize I was the only survivor until I was in the ambulance later that night. I asked about the others. Where were they? What had happened to them?'

They were searching for them, he was told.

The Chinese foreman had led them out on the sands and demonstrated how to rake for cockles. 'We were not warned about the tides, never once,' Li said. 'We were exploited by the snakeheads. I understand they wanted to make their money, but they should have shown humanity. We have our families too. We were promised proper legal work. We never expected to end up on the seashore picking cockles. When one is desperate, hungry, lack of sleep, you will take any job to escape from hunger and a restless mind. They exploited our weakness: we were not familiar with English law. Our fate was in their hands. We had nobody to depend on, we knew no one who could speak for us. We were under their control. I'd just arrived the day before. I desperately needed to find work to fill my tummy. In Liverpool I found the house and was given food and a blanket: we all slept on the floor. I was sick the next morning – but sick or not sick, you just had to pick the cockles. The more we pick the more we can earn. The tool was not efficient. Each bag must be as full as possible with cockles, right to the top, tight.'

Li's tone darkened. 'They should have carefully watched the time, the tide table, the sea. They should have told us in advance when the tide will be high. They should have prepared us.'

I asked about his vision of God, the halo of golden light in the water, and Irene stopped translating and lowered her head as if distracted by something. There followed silence. She removed her spectacles and lifted a handkerchief to her face, wiping her eyes and nose. I realized she was crying and, for a while, no one spoke. Li moved slightly to one side so that most of his face was now obscured from the camera. He lowered his head and raised his hands to his eyes: he too was crying, but silently. After a long pause, he talked about what he had hoped for.

'In my dreams England was beautiful and big,' he said. 'Peaceful and friendly.'

He had thought about little else but the forthcoming journey as he worked on the farm in China. It wasn't escape he sought from the drab, repetitive tasks in the fields or from his family – his parents, three siblings, his wife and their young child – but rather a more secure and prosperous future for all of them. 'I knew England is democratic system,' Li said, speaking through Irene. 'People are protected to live in peaceful and respectful environment, citizens have freedom to speak. Police will catch the bad guys. Everyone can find a job they can do. Or wish to do. My wish was to live in a country like England. I was determined to make that wish come true. Our village was so poor, finding work to survive was nearly impossible. Our house was damaged and the farm could not keep us all surviving. The soil was bad, worn out. I was told by snakeheads I would have a job if I worked hard. If I'd stayed in China, been stuck in China all those years, we would be a bunch of miserable, unhappy people depending on a tiny farming income to feed our unhappy, miserable family.'

But perhaps he had suffered too much.

'Had I known I'd be in that horrible accident in Morecambe Bay, would I have left? No. I would not have come. But now I feel blessed. Fate brought me to England and kept me alive in the water. When I was picking cockles, before the water came in, I promised to myself I would one day find my own job, without link to snakeheads.'

He looked directly into the camera, leaning forward just a little. 'And, you know, I did that.'

Li Hua often thinks about other victims trafficked into slavery, suffering in plain sight as the cockle-pickers did. He mourns the dead whose stories briefly become news whenever their bodies are discovered in lorry parks or in sealed containers, or when they fall from the undercarriage of an aircraft, or when they drown while trying, in small boats, to cross the English Channel. He thinks of all the nameless people he shared rooms with and crossed borders with. He thinks of those he slept alongside in the room in Moscow and the room in Liverpool – the people who died on the sands. Even at his most despondent, Li believed he would reach England and would one day be free – until that night, when everything seemed lost.

Then he saw God in the water.

FREE MOVEMENT

The Morecambe Bay tragedy is a parable about borders and about loss – of home, of identity, of agency. It is also a parable about wilful blindness: from Blair to Cameron, the governing elites of Britain turned away from the effects of uncontrolled migration and the exploitation of people by traffickers and smuggler gangs, as if they wished they weren't happening. As national leaders they knew they lacked control – or were losing control – but rather than levelling with the public, they kept on making bogus promises about capped net migration targets and British jobs for British workers. Under their leadership Britain became embroiled in foreign wars – in Afghanistan, Iraq, Libya – while other more pressing domestic matters were neglected. They equivocated while Nigel Farage agitated and mobilized his people's army.

By the time of the Brexit referendum, uncontrolled migration, modern slavery, the worst refugee crisis in Europe since the Second World War and legitimate freedom of movement within the EU were wilfully conflated by the hardest Brexiteers and their media cheerleaders to create a kind of moral panic. Anti-immigration sentiment energized the most toxic extremes of the anti-European movement.

The year of the Morecambe Bay tragedy was also the year in which ten new countries joined the European Union; eight had been part of the former communist Eastern Bloc, the so-called A8 (accession eight), the Czech Republic, Estonia, Hungary, Latvia, Lithuania, Poland, Slovakia and Slovenia. Of the existing member states in 2004, only the UK, Sweden and Ireland chose not to impose 'transitional controls' restricting incomers from the A8 states.

The New Labour government's provisional forecast was that as few as 5,000–13,000 migrant workers per year would arrive in Britain from Eastern Europe. In the event, over the next few years, with Germany, France, Italy and Spain imposing the maximum seven-year transition controls to restrict freedom of movement, more than a million Eastern Europeans came to Britain. Annual net migration rose inexorably. By 2012, there were estimated to be 700,000 Polish people alone working in Britain. Bulgaria and Romania joined the EU in 2007, and this time the New Labour government imposed seven-year transitional controls on the two new accession states. By 2019, 427,000 Romanians were reported to be living in the UK.

The economic crisis in the eurozone and sharply rising youth unemployment in southern Europe were also push factors driving large numbers of European workers to Britain, which – because of its flexible labour market – became what the writer Helen Thompson calls 'the employer of last resort' for the EU. All the while, the population level was rising sharply. In 2021 official figures revealed that, from 2012 onwards, net migration was in fact 43,000 higher each year than official estimates had said. 'Britain 2004–2019 is a textbook case of how to lose public trust on migration,' the political scientist Matthew Goodwin has written, because for many voters, particularly those who voted Leave, immigration 'seemed to encapsulate the failure of a remote political class to respond to their concerns'. The unanswerable question is this: had the Blair government introduced transitional controls in 2004, would Brexit have happened?

'We live in a world in which people move more easily between countries than at any time before,' wrote Ivan Krastev.

> And it is becoming almost impossible to distinguish
> between migrants and refugees. In a world defined by
> rising wealth inequality between states and within states,
> where social media enables people to peek at the ways even
> the most distant others live, migration has become the new
> revolutionary force. This is not the twentieth-century
> revolution of the masses, but a twenty-first-century exit-
> driven revolution enacted by individuals and families . . . A
> simple crossing of the border into the EU is more attractive
> than any utopia.

+ + +

In 2000, George Walden, a former diplomat and Conservative government minister, published *New Elites: A Career in the Masses*, a polemical book examining what he considered to be the liberal populism of the New Labour years. A revised edition was published during the pandemic. According to Walden's updated figures, 'In 2004, the non-UK-born population was 5.3 million. By 2018 it was 9.3 million – just over 14 per cent of the total population – of whom 3.6 million were from the EU and 5.7 million from outside.'

Resentment was concentrated among those most likely to suffer directly from immigration, whether economically or from pressure created on housing, schools, the NHS, or among older people unsettled by rapid demographic change.

'BBC managers helped bottle up discontent by avoiding discussion of the issue on the corporation's news programming,' Walden wrote.

> Repressed anger frequently focused on Muslims, whether for cultural or racist reasons or fears over terrorism, and because non-EU migrants were the majority. Hence a huge paradox. In the 2016 referendum many voted Leave in the belief . . . that Brexit would stem immigration from all sources. In this sense Dominic Cummings' slogan to 'Take Back Control' from Europe was a lie: Britain controlled non-EU migration.

This is true but, as we have seen, the desire for 'control' was about much more than the issues most people associated with Brussels. It was about loss – the sort of loss experienced by my aunt and her friends in Potter Street, Harlow, and in many other small towns.

In 2010, David Cameron's Conservatives had been elected on a manifesto pledge to reduce net migration to less than 100,000 a year. It was an unrealistic, and dishonest, target. Cameron knew, just as Gordon Brown knew before him when he pledged in his first conference speech as the new prime minister to create 'British jobs for British workers', that it could never be achieved under freedom of movement and residence rules – a cornerstone of the European citizenship bestowed upon citizens of the EU's member states by the 1992 Maastricht Treaty.

When the treaty was signed, Ruud Lubbers, the Dutch prime minister and one of its architects, was convinced the British pro-

European elites were not being honest about what greater EU integration entailed. 'It was as if the makers did not dare to tell the truth,' he said.

+ + +

In the years after Maastricht, the arrival of many hundreds of thousands of Eastern Europeans in Britain was welcomed by the business community as a net benefit to the economy; most of them were working and paying tax. 'But it evidently benefited some more than others: employers more than workers; the middle classes more than the working classes,' wrote Robert Tombs. 'Between 2005 and 2007, 540,000 incomers found jobs, and 270,000 British workers lost them. For many people, this was the most tangible consequence of EU membership, and larger numbers started voting for the United Kingdom Independence Party.'

None of this was inevitable. Not only could successive British governments have reduced immigration from outside the EU, they could have raised wages and reformed the labour market, which was far more flexible than in any other EU member-state, as well as introducing restrictions on residence (as in Germany or France). This, coupled with improved vocational and technical training, would have reduced the substantial demand for skilled labour from the EU. UK governments had scope for action that they chose not to use.

In 2003, David Goodhart published an essay titled 'Too Diverse?' in *Prospect* magazine, of which he was founding editor. The essay explores how in the author's view greater diversity had undermined social cohesion and solidarity in Britain and he argued that too much immigration was weakening the consensus on which redistributive welfare capitalism depended: the so-called progressive dilemma. Without reciprocity and shared obligations, there could be no stable social contract.

After the Morecambe Bay tragedy, Goodhart's essay was widely discussed; it was also misread as an anti-immigration diatribe. It was not. What it did was raise questions about the conflict, as Goodhart later explained, between rapidly increasing diversity and the solidarity and trust required to sustain a generous welfare state. A divide was growing between younger liberals, who embraced the opportunities of globalization, and conservative-traditionalists who feared its destabilizing effects. These do not have to be opposing sides and should never have been allowed to become so.

'My essay was not an essay on mass migration,' Goodhart recalled. 'It was, rather, a tentative exploration of the boundaries of people's willingness to share in modern welfare states.'

In 2016, after the vote for Brexit, Goodhart published a timely book, *The Road to Somewhere*, in which he described a binary divide in society between 'Anywheres' and 'Somewheres'; between a highly educated and mobile group who valued autonomy and diversity and who dominated our politics, and a more rooted, less well-educated group who valued security and familiarity. Somewheres 'feel that their more socially conservative intuitions have been excluded from the public space in recent decades', Goodhart wrote, and this resentment has 'destabilised our politics and led to Brexit and Trump'.

Nigel Farage is by temperament and lifestyle an Anywhere and yet he paradoxically mobilized Somewheres to his great cause. Through his blokeish banter and relentless, single-minded determination he did more than any other politician to create the political conditions for the European referendum. He too considers the year 2004 to be a significant turning point in the story of modern Britain: EU enlargement and the failure to impose transition controls resulted in the largest unplanned migration in British history and, inevitably, a populist backlash.

'The European Union and immigration had ceased to be an

issue before 2004,' Farage told me. 'It was the mistake of letting in the former communist countries. Many in UKIP said to me, "No, no, don't do that, you mustn't do that. They'll call us all the names under the sun." I knew that touching the immigration issue was going to be very difficult. But I think the impact that had on me, the family, all of that was bad. And frankly . . . the only thing that upsets me about it is that, had it been wilfully and overtly a racist message, I might have deserved some of it. But it wasn't. It never was. It never, ever was. For me it was a logical argument about numbers, about society and control.'

Behind the scaremongering and xenophobia was a material reality of everyday hardship and neglect that Farage and his allies exploited and rival politicians from the two main parties ignored or simply wished away. From 2010 onwards, people's anxieties about immigration were compounded by stagnant wages, spending cuts which weakened public services – primary schools, maternity units, doctors' surgeries, libraries, social care, and the public realm – just as the population was rising fast. By the time of the referendum, annual net migration was running at 330,000. That David Cameron chose to hold it during the 2015–16 European refugee crisis merely reinforced how detached this smoothly insouciant, risk-taking, self-confident charmer was from the realities of most people's everyday lives. Michael Portillo, a former Conservative minister and a Brexit supporter himself, described Cameron's decision to call the referendum, and then to lead such a complacent campaign, as the 'greatest blunder ever made' by a British prime minister.

Migration was 'the new revolutionary force of the twenty-first century', Ivan Krastev wrote and Cameron's premiership would be swept away by it.

It was as if the makers did not dare to tell the truth.

+ + +

If the story of immigration from 2004 to the Brexit referendum was one of political mismanagement, false promises, missed targets and careless disregard for public opinion, Brexit and the end of freedom of movement have led to a cooling of the immigration debate. But another world most of us would rather not think about continues to thrive – the world of the smugglers and their victims. Trafficked people are everywhere around us, labouring in plain sight – in high-street nail bars, 'Thai' massage parlours, textile factories, restaurant kitchens, sweatshops, warehouses, and abattoirs. Or they're lost in the shadow economy, in marijuana farms and brothels. Some of them are dying, without passports or identity papers, without dignity, as the cockle-pickers did in Morecambe Bay.

Pham Thi Tra My was a twenty-six-year-old woman who was found dead alongside thirty-eight other Vietnamese people, aged between fifteen and forty-four, in a refrigerated lorry container parked at Purfleet Docks in October 2019. Two people-smugglers, from Romania and Northern Ireland, were found guilty of thirty-nine counts of manslaughter; two lorry drivers were also found guilty of illegally conspiring to transport Vietnamese migrants from northern France to southern England.

The young woman's family had paid the equivalent of £30,000 for her to be smuggled to England, where she was promised work in a nail bar. Her salary would be £1,600 a month in what her family believed was a safe and hospitable country. Like Li Hua, she expected to work hard to repay her debts in good time. As she suffocated in what became a sealed tomb – the temperature inside the lorry container had risen to 38.5 degrees Celsius in transit across the Channel – Pham Thi Tra My sent text messages to her mother:

'I'm sorry mum. My path abroad has not succeeded. Mum, I love you so much! I'm dying because I can't breathe. I am sorry, Mum.'

The young woman died as if in a state of self-forgetting: in her final moments she must have been thinking not principally of herself but of her mother and the family she would never see again. Her texts were not enraged but gently regretful, resigned; she wanted to apologize.

Pham Thi Tra My did not have a passport or identification papers, and so she also texted her home address in Vietnam. She must have hoped her body and phone would be found so that she could be identified. She must have hoped with her last thoughts that her body would one day be returned to her family in Vietnam. Pham Thi Tra My is buried in her hometown of Nghen, in Can Lôc, a rural district of Hà Tinh Province.

+ + +

People trafficking is the dark shadow of globalization, driven by the ceaseless demand for cheap, complicit labour – too often unregulated migrant labour – to power the world's quest for perpetual growth and innovation. To understand who we are today is also in part to understand the unstable foundations on which our globalized prosperity is built. Before he set off from China, Li Hua imagined England as a shining city upon a hill whose beacon light pulled freedom-loving people everywhere towards it. For many migrants guided by that light but manipulated and exploited by gangsters and traffickers, England turned out to be a place of darkness.

'We didn't know about the snakeheads, gangmasters and illegal immigration until then,' Chris Turner, a Lancashire coastguard who was working in Morecambe Bay on the night of the tragedy, said. 'We didn't know people were living thirty to a house, with no furniture, just mattresses.'

The Chinese cockle-pickers were working in plain sight. We should have known.

If they were ignored in life they have not been forgotten in death and their story has attracted the attention of filmmakers and artists: Nick Broomfield, Isaac Julian and Daniel York Loh. Those frail, dark-clad figures in their beanie hats out on the sands haunt our imagination not only because of what their tragedy revealed about modern slavery and people smuggling but because it goes on. It has never stopped.

'I just wish our British government and immigration services could pay more attention to what is happening at the borders where human trafficking and smuggling take place,' Li Hua said to me. 'Who is looking out for these people – people just like me?'

NEVER LET ME GO

Li Hua was alone on Priest Skear, an expanse of raised land surrounded by sea water. He could hear nothing but the wind and rain. Earlier, as the tide surged in, he'd dropped his phone and watched as it was swept away in the fast-moving currents. Now what was this? He heard voices and searchlights penetrated the darkness. They were coming for him – he knew they would come for him. He waited, and he waited . . . but the lights were fading now; the voices growing softer, quieter, as if they were moving not towards him but further away. Would he die out here on the sands, without hope, like a dog? He felt the shame would outlive him. He tried to move his arms but it was as if they were straitjacketed at his side. He was shouting . . . they must not go . . . they must come back . . . they must not leave him here, *in the sinking water, the sinking water* . . .

'My love?'

He opened his eyes as his wife pulled him close. He was perspiring – night sweats again – and his T-shirt was soaked through.

'Nightmares,' she said.

She placed a gentle, restraining hand on his forehead, stroked his hair and wiped the tears from his eyes.

'You are safe,' she said. 'We are safe. We will never let you go.'

He understood and his panic subsided. Yes, he understood, and he also remembered – who and where he was. His name was not Li Hua. It was Richard. He was not going back. He was never going back.

3 THE TOWN THAT WEPT

His name was Loren Marlton-Thomas. He was a bomb hunter. As a corporal from 33 Engineer Regiment, the Sappers, he was based at Carver Barracks in Wimbish, Essex, close to the old Quaker town of Saffron Walden, and that summer he had one of the loneliest and most dangerous jobs on the tour of Afghanistan. He was the leader of an advanced search unit in Helmand province and his mission, as part of the NATO command combating the Taliban insurgency against the United States-backed government in Kabul, was to track down improvised explosive devices (IEDs), which were maiming and killing British soldiers. Nearly one hundred of them had died over recent months.

Corporal Marlton-Thomas relished the fierce challenge of his work and was proud that his interventions saved lives – the lives of his comrades, as well as of Afghan servicemen and local civilians. But he had no illusions: he understood the dangers as he led his unit along the rough tracks and wadis of Helmand. The IED hunters were admired for their rare courage: where they went, others could follow, even into the Valley of Death, especially into the Valley of Death, as the area between Sangin and Gereshk was known.

+ + +

Waking early on this Sunday morning, Loren felt the familiar churn of anticipation in the pit of his stomach. This was what his body was telling him: he was going out on patrol again. The Taliban and the armed drug cartels were an omnipresent threat, elusive, implacable enemies; IEDs were being used indiscriminately not only to kill British soldiers but to weaken their resolve. The previous Sunday he'd been interviewed by BBC television for a Remembrance Sunday programme and he was cheered to know that his brother, Fraser Marlton-Thomas, the Queen's senior footman, and their mother Anne were watching back in England.

The day's task was to clear a path in the area around Gereshk, in the vicinity of Patrol Base Sandford. It was named after Lance Corporal Paul Sandford, who had been killed by a sniper in 2006; he was twenty-three. The base was located ninety minutes from Camp Bastion, Britain's largest overseas military base.

What was Corporal Marlton-Thomas looking for as he moved through the stark, monotonous landscape? He was searching for disturbances in the parched soil, trackside irregularities, mounds and broken surfaces – markers of unusual human activity. He moved slowly, meticulously, his men following close behind. They knew one false step could be fatal and their leader was acutely aware of the anxiety that comes with combat.

It was autumn 2009 and for the twenty-eight-year-old Loren, who'd grown up in the persistent rain and damp of the north-west of England, it felt like a fine summer day in Lancashire. In the peak summer months in Helmand, in the dusty, arid landscapes of the Upper Garesh Valley especially, the temperatures rise above 38 degrees Celsius, and the soldiers have no choice but to endure the heat.

Even on this November day, Marlton-Thomas could feel the sweat gathering beneath his helmet and body armour and pooling in his armpits. He could sense the dry heat rising and it was as if he could also hear the silence around him, so intense was his concentration as he scanned the surrounding landscape, alert to every possibility and sound. Just behind him was the ATO team (ammunition technical officers) who defused the explosive devices his unit discovered.

That day the clearance team was led by Warrant Officer Ken Bellringer of the Royal Logistics Corps, who had spent several weeks training in the test lanes at Camp Bastion. So far on this tour they'd defused three main types of IED – the time-delayed device, the victim-operated device and the command-initiated, remotely detonated device.

Marlton-Thomas felt secure in the convoy of armoured vehicles that had set out from base camp, but out on foot patrol, leading from the front, with the ATO team tracking behind, he simply did not know: the uncertainty had its own strange, thrilling intoxication. Sometimes he liked to think of himself as an explorer in some undiscovered land. He was going where others could not, a path-finder, a path-maker, clearing the way ahead. Out there the Taliban insurgents were everywhere and nowhere. He felt as if they were watching him and they were waiting. He knew they wanted him to die and the British and Americans to leave in abject defeat and humiliation. But where were they?

Like all Sappers, Corporal Marlton-Thomas was a multi-skilled tradesman: soldier, combat engineer, accomplished blacksmith. He'd previously served on two operational tours, in Northern Ireland and Iraq. No one had made him join the army as a sixteen-year-old, straight from school. Originally, he'd wanted to be an infantry soldier but his late father Chris, a civil engineer, persuaded him to join the Engineers, so that he would have a trade to call on for the rest of his working life.

When he was at home, with the family, Loren never talked about his experiences on patrol; he never mentioned IEDs and bomb hunting. He wanted to protect his wife, as well as his brother and mother, from the reality of what he did, from the extremity of it, the true dangers. He didn't want them to know – and he couldn't really explain, in any event – just how it felt to be out in front, alone, in the gathering silence, when the boundary between life and death was membrane thin. There were long, silent days when he was sure he could hear blades of grass moving in the faintest of breezes.

On this six-month tour, Corporal Marlton-Thomas knew what was expected of him and all who were deployed alongside him on Operation HERRICK 11. He offered constancy, expertise, determination, vigilance. His wife at home in Essex said he was 'army-barmy'. His friends and comrades called him 'Loz' or 'MT'. His mother called him 'my Loren'. Fraser called him 'my brother'. He was a Sapper and searcher. Leader and team player. He was a bomb hunter.

+ + +

Warrant Officer Ken Bellringer was moving methodically along a narrow irrigation channel through a churned-up field when Marlton-Thomas, just a few metres ahead, abruptly stopped. He seemed agitated; he twisted and turned. What was it? What had he found?

'Mate,' Loren called out. 'I'm stuck. Really, I'm stuck!'

Bellringer chuckled more out of nervous surprise than amusement when he heard this. Stuck – how could he possibly be stuck? He edged closer, expecting to discover that his comrade's feet were submerged in thick mud but he couldn't quite process the sight before him: Marlton-Thomas seemed to be standing in a rabbit hole, and yet he could not move his feet. On closer inspection, Bellringer saw that the hole had unnaturally straight edges; no rabbit or wild animal could have made it. With mounting alarm, he realized what had happened: Marlton-Thomas had stepped on, and was trapped in, an IED. There was still time to act but not much, because the device had been disturbed; they were in what the army classifies as a Category A situation. 'A category A situation is where EOD [explosive ordnance disposal] operations commence regardless of the risk to the operator's life,' Ken Bellringer recalled. 'We're told if there is nothing you can do, and you know categorically a device is about to go off – imagine it's a movie and you can see the timer counting down – then you're supposed to make an excuse and get out of there yourself, perhaps say you're just going to get a piece of equipment.'

Ken Bellringer chose not to get out of there; he stayed on. He searched for a wire to the device but there was nothing. He knew the IED had been disturbed but it could just as easily have malfunctioned. He would not leave his comrade behind. He would get him out of there. He reached under Loren's arms and prepared to lift him by the elbows.

'Here we go,' Bellringer said.

+ + +

Warrant Officer Ken Bellringer sustained catastrophic injuries to his lower abdomen. His legs were blown off above the knee; his pelvis and testicles were shattered; muscles were ripped apart in his arms and he lost fingers on each hand. The next day, having been stabilized and put into an induced coma at Camp Bastion, he was flown to England and transferred to the Queen Elizabeth in Birmingham, the hospital where servicemen and women wounded in Afghanistan were treated. Bellringer, who had a wife and two school-age children, was considered to be the most severely wounded British survivor of the Afghanistan war: years of hospital treatment and suffering, psychological and physical, lay in wait for him.

'I was thrown through the air but when I landed, I had no pain,' he recalled. 'I kept my eyes shut. I think something in my head was telling me I didn't want to see the damage – I knew instinctively that my legs had gone. The last thing I remember was someone in the helicopter taking hold of my head and saying: "We've got you, you're safe."'

+ + +

Loren Marlton-Thomas was blown into a nearby canal, where he lay undisturbed below the surface of the water until the next morning when a search team of divers found him. At the inquest into Loren's death, it was revealed that an order to abort the day's mission over concern that signals from soldiers' radios could trigger IEDs was never received by his unit. If that message had got through, he would have stopped, but he carried on. A bomb hunter to the end.

+ + +

It was Sunday evening and Fraser Marlton-Thomas was in his room at Buckingham Palace – 'the office' as the Royal Family call their London residence – when he received a message asking him to contact his cousin James, a lieutenant colonel in the army air corps.

'When I was asked to phone James, I immediately thought something had happened to Nanna [his grandmother],' Fraser said. 'Then he told me. I said, "Fuck off, James – he's not dead. It's Loren. No one's going to kill him." I'd only seen him the week before on television. He looked fit, tanned, happy. How can it be? I'd just seen him. I put the phone down. I said to my friend: "My brother's dead."'

The next day the Queen came to see Fraser. 'She was very sympathetic. She was so sorry. He was one of her soldiers, and he was my brother.'

BRING BACK THE BODIES

Loren Marlton-Thomas was a cousin of my wife, Sarah – his parents, Anne and Christopher, were guests at our wedding – and we heard about his death in a phone call from Sarah's uncle, Paul Marlton. A few days later we watched televised coverage of the repatriation of Loren's body through the Wiltshire market town of Wootton Bassett. There was a second hearse carrying Rifleman Andrew Fentiman, a Territorial Army soldier who had been shot and killed on the same day as Loren, while out on foot patrol near Sangin. The repatriation ceremony had special significance because it was the hundredth to pass through the town.

The two soldiers' bodies were flown into RAF Lyneham in Wiltshire early on the morning of 20 November, where Fraser, Anne, Nicola and other members of the Marlton-Thomas family were waiting. The bodies were taken from the plane to a chapel at the base. 'We went to see the coffin and were given time to say a few words to Loren,' Fraser recalled. 'I remembered how he and our father Chris loved tinkering with engines, always busy doing something.'

From Lyneham the hearses carrying the Union flag-draped coffins of the two soldiers were driven to the John Radcliffe Hospital in Oxford, passing en route through Wootton Bassett, where townspeople, many formally and sombrely dressed as if for a funeral, were lining the long, narrow high street in what had become a familiar ritual of public mourning. The cortege stopped at the town's war memorial and there Anne laid flowers on the roof of the hearse carrying her son's coffin. The bell in the fifteenth-century St Bartholomew's Church on the high street tolled solemnly. 'It was lovely what people did coming out to mourn,' Fraser said. 'It all started with one person and grew and grew, and in the end the whole world knew about this little English town.'

+ + +

The repatriations through Wootton Bassett began in April 2007 because of an accident of geography: the town is directly on the route from RAF Lyneham to the special armed forces department of pathology at the John Radcliffe Hospital. The runway at RAF Brize Norton was under repair and so the fallen soldiers were being flown into Lyneham instead.

The first repatriation through the town was of two young soldiers killed on patrol in the vicinity of Saddam Hussein's former presidential palace in Basra, in south-eastern Iraq, where the British were struggling to contain a Shia insurgency. Ballistic evidence suggested that both soldiers were killed by the same sniper using the same weapon. A few days later, four more British soldiers were killed by an IED just outside Basra, and they too were repatriated through Wootton Bassett.

The first corteges did not stop on the high street and were noticed perhaps by only a few members of the local branch of the Royal British Legion; no one can recall for sure who was there that day. But soon something unusual was happening in the town, and more and more people were coming out to honour the soldiers as they passed through. Even when Brize Norton reopened, the repatriations continued through Wootton Bassett for a period, and the grieving families also started coming into the town itself; it was as if the whole town was weeping.

Before too long visitors from elsewhere were arriving on 'repat' mornings; there were collection tins for military charities in nearly every shop and pub window. Foreign media began turning up as well to report on these ceremonies of mass mourning, just five miles from Swindon. The repatriations caught the attention of President Obama, who said 'the small British town of Wootton Bassett' represented 'the best of British character'.

Reverend Canon Thomas Woodhouse, chaplain of The Queen's Chapel of the Savoy within the Duchy of Lancaster, was vicar at St

Bartholomew's Church throughout the years of the repatriations. 'In the early stages there was no plan – the whole thing was so ad hoc,' he told me. 'I don't think anyone can truly claim credit for starting it. People will try to, but lots of people had the same idea at about the same time. Even the tolling of the church bell as the cortege passed was an accident. It just happened that a repatriation was taking place on a Monday when we had bell ringing and that day someone just decided to toll the bell. It's a long, narrow high street and it rang as if into a silent cavern – the sound just ricocheted. Afterwards, we realized it was amazing. And thereafter at every repatriation, as the cortege approached the church, the bell would toll until it had passed and was leaving the town.'

+ + +

The British are committed to acts of remembrance. Nearly every village and older town across the realm has a memorial to the dead of the two world wars. Wherever the British have been and settled in the world, they have left behind gardens of remembrance in the form of the Commonwealth War Graves Commission's cemeteries; the Falklands War marked the first time in Britain's military history that the bodies of British soldiers were repatriated. As the military historian John Keegan has written, the dead of the British Empire and Commonwealth of the two world wars are buried in 134 countries, from Algeria to Zimbabwe. The Commission maintains as many as 2,000 cemeteries throughout the world and cares for 23,000 individual graves or plots in non-military cemeteries. The Commission also commemorates the many hundreds of thousands whose bodies were never recovered or were found but could not be identified. A central belief of English identity, John Keegan wrote, is that 'England is a garden, and that to be English is to be a gardener; that in life they are best at home in a garden; and that, in death, a garden is where they belong.'

The repatriation ceremonies in Wootton Bassett were quite different from the more familiar, grand, dignified state-organized services of national remembrance for all rather than individuals. The Wootton ceremonies did not come from orders of the state and did not take place in churches or gardens of remembrance; they happened spontaneously, in public, in the high street. Until 2000, the town had a memorial hall rather than a cenotaph; the stone war memorial – raised hands carrying the weight and burden of the globe – was built following local fundraising efforts and would become the focal point of the liturgy of the repatriations.

What we witnessed in Wootton Bassett during those four years of the repatriations was nothing less than an act of national commemoration. But it was unofficial, of the people and for the dead soldiers and their families; political leaders did not come to the town and the Royal Family were not represented on the high street. 'No one organized it, no one requested it,' the Royal British Legion's former national president, Lieutenant General Sir John Kiszely, said. 'It happened because it was the right thing to do.'

Every repatriated man and woman, of all faiths and none, was treated the same as they passed through Wootton Bassett, but there were moments of difference. The families of dead Gurkhas would place flowers directly on the coffins rather than on the roof of the hearses as the cortege paused at the war memorial, and they would also sing. On one occasion, when a military dog-handler was repatriated, hundreds of people brought their dogs into town in solidarity. 'It was so silent in the town during repatriations you could hear people's footsteps. On this occasion the silence was broken by barking dogs,' Thomas Woodhouse said.

'What happens in Wootton Bassett is not a revolution and does require co-ordination, but it is still a spontaneous mass movement,' wrote the historian Hew Strachan. 'If the prime minister needs evidence of "big society" in operation, this might be it. However, he may also have cause to regret it rather than to welcome it. Publicly grieving the dead while the war is still going on has the potential to create problems for policy. The government fears its potential impact on public support for a conflict whose rationale has never been secure.'

Hew Strachan said that Britain had no grasp of how to mourn the soldier who had died in a war that was discredited by defeat, as the French and Germans had, or in a war that was considered unjust, as so many considered the Iraq War to be. 'The meaning of Wootton Bassett is freighted because, for all the political neutrality of its acts of commemoration, they mark a politically contentious war.'

CULTURE WARS

In early January 2010, a group called Islam4UK announced that it would stage a demonstration in Wootton Bassett. The group's leader, Anjem Choudary, was planning to parade empty coffins through the town to remind the British of the Muslims 'murdered by merciless' coalition forces in Iraq and Afghanistan. If you wanted to spark a race war this would be how.

Islam4UK was in effect another incarnation of al-Muhajiroun, a militant Islamist network. Other related names used by the group included Al Ghurabaa, Muslims Against Crusades, Shariah4UK, Call to Submission, Islamic Path, the London School of Sharia and Need4Khilafah.

A former Wootton Bassett mayor and councillor Chris Wannell spoke for many locals when, alarmed that the town itself was becoming a source of contention and a site of political conflict, he said, 'We don't do what we do at Wootton Bassett for any political reason at all, but to pay our respects to those who have given their lives for our freedom. We are a Christian country and a traditional old English market town who honour very much our Queen and country. We obey the law and pay respects to our servicemen who protect our freedom.'

Al-Muhajiroun ('the emigrants') was co-founded by Anjem Choudary and Omar Bakri Muhammad in the 1990s. Omar was a Syria-born Muslim Brotherhood preacher who, after his expulsion from Syria, lived in Beirut, where he joined Hizb ut-Tahrir, which agitates for caliphism, for the creation of a caliphate in the Middle East under sharia law. Later, after being expelled from Saudi Arabia, Omar was given asylum in London. There he set up a branch of Hizb ut-Tahrir – today the group is most active in the English Midlands – and then, after he split from it, he created al-Muhajiroun just as the Balkan wars and the atrocities in Bosnia were radicalizing a generation of European Muslims.

Unlike Omar, Anjem Choudary was born in England, in 1967, the son of a market trader of Pakistani heritage. He dropped out of medical school and then studied law at Southampton University – he was there around the same time as me – and after his embrace of Salafism, he would appear as a robed, bearded, and bespectacled antagonist in political discussions on British television. For Choudary, a passionate advocate of instituting sharia law in Britain, Islam was at war with the secular West and with the *kufr*, or unbeliever: there could be no compromise in this clash of civilizations. He was imperious and articulate and, because of his legal training and mastery of counter-terrorism laws, he seemed untouchable – until one day he wasn't. He was finally convicted, under the Terrorism Act 2000 for inciting his followers to join Islamic State in Syria and Iraq. He was sentenced to five and a half years in prison in 2016 and was released on licence in October 2018.

Before the 11 September 2001 attacks on New York and Washington, DC, and the London bombings of 7 July 2005, in which fifty-two people died in coordinated early morning suicide strikes carried out by four young British Muslims on public transport, Britain had been considered a safe space by, and for, Islamist dissidents and radical preachers. An unofficial 'covenant of security' is assumed to have existed between Muslim groups and the British authorities in the 1990s: the dissident preachers, many of them exiles from persecution in Arab states, were free to proselytize and recruit, so long as there were no attacks on British targets from within Britain. As in the Victorian period when Karl Marx worked in the great Reading Room of the British Museum and Pyotr Kropotkin wrote for the anarchist-communist journal *Freedom*, revolutionaries and dissidents relished the liberty and anonymity of life in the metropolis. So this was the climate in which al-Muhajiroun flourished in the late 1990s and into the 2000s, becoming an incubator for terror, right up until the London suicide attacks on three Tube trains and a double-decker bus; a quarter of convicted terrorists in Britain are reported to have been linked to the network.

The New Labour government initially showed little interest in and understanding of al-Muhajiroun's activities and its malign intent, and the group was deemed by the intelligence services MI5 and MI6 to be an inconsequential, even eccentric threat, clowns rather than criminals. It was much more than that: Mohammed Sidique Khan, the Leeds-born leader of the London bombers, trained at a terrorist camp established by the Pakistan branch of al-Muhajiroun in the North West Frontier Province.

By late 2009, al-Muhajiroun was using yet another name, Islam4UK – the original group had finally been banned in Britain in 2008 – and the Wootton Bassett repatriations provided an ideal opportunity for Choudary to mobilize. Among those provoked was Tommy Robinson, a recidivist, football hooligan and de facto leader of the English Defence League (EDL). Aggressive nationalists, thriving on a sense of victimhood, EDL activists were self-styled defenders of the embattled English nation, as they saw it, their main enemy being the alien presence of Islam in Europe. Which explains why, on a cold, snowy day in early January, the EDL staged a pre-emptive counter-demonstration against Islam4UK in Wootton Bassett.

With frozen slush on the pavements, a couple of hundred EDL members congregated at the town's war memorial. Some of them wrapped themselves in a giant cross of St George, the national flag of England since the early modern period, as if seeking both its affirmation and protective warmth. They spent the rest of the afternoon on a desultory pub crawl, their movements tracked by police officers. In many ways it was a comically low-key provincial event, more Monty Python than political protest, and yet it hinted at something darker: rising antagonism between English far-right nationalists and radical Islamists, and it was being played out on the high street of a quiet market town in rural southern England, the countryside so central to a particular cherished vision of English national identity. England as a garden.

+ + +

Robinson's birth name is Stephen Yaxley, but over the years he has used nearly as many aliases and pseudonyms as al-Muhajiroun: Stephen Yaxley-Lennon, Andrew McMaster, Paul Harris, Wayne King, Stephen Lennon, as well as Tommy Robinson, the *nom de guerre* by which he became widely known. He grew up in Luton, one of only three white British-minority towns in the UK, according to the 2011 national census. His mother worked in a bakery and his adoptive father at the local Vauxhall car plant. He was bright but distracted and inattentive at his state school. 'I never studied, and I still breezed the exams,' he said. His first job was as an apprentice aircraft engineer at Luton Airport, one of the few local employers offering skilled apprenticeships and structured training. He was a Luton Town supporter and gravitated towards the club's hooligan fringe, hanging out with the hardcore firm Men in Gear. Robinson was later jailed for drunkenly assaulting an off-duty police officer.

On his release from prison, he worked as a plumber and opened a tanning salon, and all the time he was becoming more preoccupied with nationalist politics. He studied the Quran and briefly joined the neo-fascist British National Party. After founding the English Defence League, because he was angered by the activities of Islamist groups in Luton, notably al-Muhajiroun, he organized various anti-Islamic street protests around the country. He formed alliances with European groups such as Pegida (Patriotic Europeans Against the Islamization of the West) in Germany and the Bloc Against Islam, which had emerged out of the Czech Defence League. Robinson, who has a sleeve of patriotic tattoos on his arm, cites his formative political influences as being the murder by an Asian gang in Luton of Paul Sharp, a friend of one of his uncles, and a march against the British Army by Islamist militants through the town centre.

In November 2018 he was appointed as an adviser to UKIP by its leader Gerard Batten (the party had moved even further to the right in the post-Farage era). By this time, Robinson had become something of a folk hero to the global alt-right. He had more than one million social media followers and his own YouTube channel, which he successfully monetized through adverts and appeals for donations. He was endorsed on social media by Donald Trump Jr, the then-US president's eldest son. According to the British political writer Jonathan Rutherford, Robinson was a fighter in a class culture war. 'He is a tribune of that working-class white identity – although he'd probably not like the white identity bit. He's for them, and of them, and who else is?' Rutherford later moderated that view. 'At that point, he could have gone either way,' he said. 'But because of his ongoing war against Islam, he turned very dark.'

In 2018, Robinson was permanently banned from Twitter for violating its rules on 'hateful conduct'; in 2019 he was also banned from Facebook and Instagram, drastically limiting his reach and reducing his earnings. He was declared bankrupt two years later.

+ + +

Fearing greater unrest, and possible violent clashes, in and around Wootton Bassett, the Labour government responded to the proposed Islam4UK march by banning Anjem Choudary's group under new legislation outlawing the 'glorification' of terrorism. 'Wootton Bassett has a special significance for us all at this time, as it has been the scene of the repatriation of many members of our armed forces who have tragically fallen,' Prime Minister Gordon Brown said in a statement. 'Any attempt to use this location to cause further distress and suffering to those who have lost loved ones would be abhorrent and offensive.'

In an article for the Cambridge University student paper *Varsity*, Beth Staton, who'd grown up in the town, complained that it was being romanticized, even mythologized, as a kind of arcadian English idyll. It was nothing of the kind:

> I've lived in Wootton Bassett for twenty years, and seen several repatriations . . . The town has reached the point where it cannot be removed from politics. Wootton Bassett is a typical English town; my home is a place of interesting people, dodgy politics, and tacky high streets, not a benign embodiment of little England. We cannot succumb to this lie; if it becomes entrenched in national consciousness, it threatens to breed a destructive and sinister hatred.

In the event, the Islam4UK march never happened but the controversy surrounding what might have happened delighted Choudary: it had 'successfully highlighted the plights of Muslims in Afghanistan globally' he said, and he promised the group would rise again on 'another platform with a new name'. For Tommy Robinson, the EDL rally in Wootton Bassett was one more step along the road that would eventually see him back in prison, but not before he'd inspired and empowered a new generation of nationalist white supremacists.

For Reverend Woodhouse, the aborted Islamist protest march had one big benefit: it served as a 'powerful expression of unity', bringing together local Christian churches and the Wiltshire Islamic Cultural Centre. 'The repatriations were about the deaths of all people, not just some, because all deaths in war are tragic,' he said. 'It doesn't matter what nationality or creed you are. Until that point there hadn't been an easy way of having a cross-religious conversation in the town and we ended up with much closer links.'

THE WORLD IS WHAT IT IS

In the years after the invasion of Iraq and that country's descent into perpetual conflict, you longed to turn away from the truth of what was happening in the region, to wish it wasn't so. You wanted to turn away from the images of suffering and the carnage, the endless suicide bombings and sectarian bloodlust, the displacement and exile of millions of people, the harrowing loss of life. The destruction of the Baathist state created chaos and the ideal conditions for insurgency to flourish. 'Following Saddam's fall, Iraq became a theatre of revenge, each murder inspiring another and then another,' wrote the American war correspondent Dexter Filkins. 'Sometimes it felt like the sounds of bombs and the call to prayer were the only sounds the country could produce, its own strange national anthem.'

Through all of this, and because of their roadside vigils, the people of Wootton Bassett, in their modest, dignified manner, made sure we would not turn away. They made sure we recognized the human cost of reordering the world, of trying to impose Western values on those who would resist them. They made sure the returning dead servicemen and women were not left to expire offstage, unacknowledged by all except those who loved them most. As the corteges of the repatriated passed along the Highway for Heroes, as it became known, and as the months went by, the Wiltshire town started to be a destination, even a place of pilgrimage. In October 2008 an armed forces parade was held in Wootton Bassett. *Question Time*, the BBC's flagship current affairs programme, broadcast a special edition on the Afghanistan war from the town. Prince Harry, in a private capacity rather than as an official representative of the Royal Family, attended a Remembrance Day service at St Bartholomew's – many of those in the church did not even know he was there, so low-key was his presence. Prince Charles, together with the Duchess of Cornwall, also came to the town to bless the flagpole (a recent gift) and to lay a wreath at the war memorial. Princess Anne, honorary air commodore of RAF Lyneham, was a visitor. Others were less welcome – Nick Griffin of the British National Party turned up but was received with indifference.

And the bodies kept coming home. I sometimes thought of these dead soldiers as the returning ghosts of Britain's foreign policy misadventures, haunting our unquiet present, their fate a poignant testament to the sacrifice of duty but also to the fraudulent ways in which the war in Iraq had been prosecuted and conducted. Publicly grieving the dead while the war was going on did pose problems for policy, as Hew Strachan wrote. In time public support for the wars (but never the troops) collapsed. The soldiers themselves protested that they were being sent inadequately equipped into combat zones.

Shortly before he was killed, Andrew Fentiman from Cambridge, who was repatriated alongside Loren Marlton-Thomas, posted an internet blog in which he revealed he and his comrades had not been issued with the required protective equipment. 'We are still waiting on these new body armour and helmets that were promised to us,' he wrote. 'You would have seen the story splashed all over the news, they said they would be ready for us but we hope they will arrive soon.'

By the time the equipment arrived, it was already too late for Rifleman Fentiman.

+ + +

In July 2016, seven years after it was commissioned, the Chilcot Inquiry (named after its chairman Sir John Chilcot) into the Iraq War concluded, in a 2.5 million-word report, that the British armed forces had been humiliated in Iraq because of inadequate strategic planning before and after the invasion. The dismantling of an entire state had created zones of anarchy. The regime of Saddam Hussein had not posed an urgent threat to British interests at the time of the invasion and there had remained peaceful alternatives to war. The Blair government had been too certain in its judgement that Saddam possessed weapons of mass destruction and the intelligence reports which it used to make its case for war were flawed. The safety and the effectiveness of British combat troops were compromised by serious shortages of vital equipment, and the military was overstretched because it was embroiled in unsustainable parallel operations in Iraq and Afghanistan.

None of this offered any consolation to the family of Corporal Loren Marlton-Thomas. 'My mother has never got over it,' his brother Fraser told me. 'A mother should never bury a son. How can you? I can't get over it either. But I saw it from a different angle. He was doing his job. Where did the courage come from? I don't know how he did it. He started so young it was built in him.'

+ + +

Sometimes when I watched news reports or read about the repatriation ceremonies during those years, I was reminded of Robert Lowell's poem 'Waking Early Sunday Morning'. Lowell, a pacifist, had participated in the march on the Pentagon in Washington, DC, in 1967, to protest the Vietnam War. On the eve of the march, he read the poem, which contains some of his finest lines, to an audience of anti-war protestors. In the graceful, elegiac final stanza, the poet envisages future generations being caught up in endless foreign conflicts because America was doomed by its great power and sense of manifest destiny to fulfil the lonely role of world's policeman. Lowell urges us to pray for the young people who are destined to die in future wars, as indeed thousands of troops would die in the decades to come in America's 'forever war'.

Loren Malton-Thomas had woken early on that final Sunday morning of his life in Helmand province, and as a dedicated soldier he'd died in a foreign war in a land his country should have known better because of its imperial history in South Asia.

During his final year in power, Barack Obama discussed the moral limits of American power and used a pointed phrase to describe his worldview: 'tragic realism'. In a *New York Times* interview, he cited the opening to V. S. Naipaul's novel *A Bend in the River*, set in an unnamed African country which the reader assumes is the Democratic Republic of Congo (DRC), formerly Zaire: 'The world is what it is; men who are nothing, who allow themselves to become nothing, have no place in it.'

Obama said he reflected on the meaning of that sentence and Naipaul's uncompromising vision when 'thinking about the hardness of the world sometimes, particularly in foreign policy, and I resist and fight against sometimes that very cynical, more realistic view of the world. And yet, there are times where it feels as if that may be true.'

Like the philosopher-theologian Reinhold Niebuhr, who deeply influenced his thinking on foreign policy, Obama acknowledges the existence of evil in the world but also the difficulties and dangers inherent in confronting it. As a young politician, Obama opposed the Iraq War because he understood the risks of attempting to impose, through violence and conquest, Western values of freedom and democracy. He understood the need to show humility in the exercise of power.

Great power carries the burden of great responsibility and demands the necessity of restraint – perhaps at times far too much restraint in the case of Obama's response to the Syrian tragedy. In the absence of a strategy on Syria, the Obama administration laid down its red lines against the use of chemical weapons. When the Assad regime transgressed by ordering a chemical weapons attack on rebel-held Ghouta in the suburbs of Damascus in August 2013, killing hundreds, Obama seemed frozen. US equivocation opened the way for Putin's Russia to become, over time, the dominant foreign power in Syria and the Assad dictatorship did not fall. Sometimes the absence of war has nefarious consequences, and this is surely what Obama meant by tragic realism. *The world is what it is.* It resists being reordered.

+ + +

In his response to the Chilcot Inquiry, Tony Blair accepted responsibility for the failures of Allied post-invasion planning but staunchly defended the original decision to invade and occupy.

With his voice hoarse and weakening, he was described as resembling a 'broken man' by some commentators during the press conference at which he replied to Chilcot. Yet when we met not long afterwards, in his London office, Blair was anything but broken: he insisted to me that the arc of history bends towards progress and enlightenment. He expressed no regrets for taking Britain to war in Iraq, and for facilitating the fall of Saddam.

For Blair, the 11 September attacks had been a profound shock but also an opportunity for Britain to redefine its role in the world. He used the horrific attacks to leverage influence over the new Bush administration and, as he saw it, to draw the world's one essential superpower away from hermit security.

'Every American president I've ever dealt with has always come to power with an essentially domestic programme,' Blair said. 'And all of them have ended up, because this is America's inevitable role in the world, being highly engaged in global affairs.'

I asked Jeremy Hunt, when he was foreign secretary in the May government, what Blair had got so wrong in Iraq. Hunt described what happened as a profound breakdown in trust. The Iraq War was a disaster, he said, a lesson in humility and the limits of Western power. 'It was not just a foreign policy misjudgement but a breach of trust, because Blair used his presentational skills to persuade people of something that turned out not to be true, namely the existence of weapons of mass destruction.'

Once again, a covenant between the people and the political class had been broken – a pattern repeated over the last twenty years. As George Eliot put it, 'What loneliness is more lonely than distrust?'

The governed were losing trust in the governors.

THE LAST SOLDIER

One summer day, Lieutenant David Clack of 1st Battalion The Rifles (1 Rifles) was leading his team on patrol around the village of Dactran in southern Afghanistan. The next day a *shura*, or consultation, was scheduled to take place with tribal leaders. As the patrol approached the village it activated a roadside IED. Lieutenant Clack – 'Clacky' to his rugby-playing friends – was killed and five of his men were injured. A graduate of Exeter University whose family lived in Woodford Green, on the Essex/north-east London borders, David Clack had been commissioned into the Rifles on completion of his officer training at Sandhurst. Aged just twenty-four when he died and engaged to be married, he was a young leader of exceptional promise and had been an officer for less than a year. On 18 August 2011 he was the 167th, and last, British soldier to be repatriated through Wootton Bassett.

A couple of weeks later, a sunset ceremony was held in the town to mark the end of the repatriations at RAF Lyneham – it was the day before the runway was decommissioned – and their return to RAF Brize Norton, across the county border in Oxfordshire. Members of the Royal British Legion, many visiting from other branches, lined up around the war memorial and raised their standards; a lone trumpeter played; Laurence Binyon's poem 'For the Fallen' was read aloud by a veteran; the Union flag, flown at half-mast on repatriation days, was lowered from its pole and removed; and as many as 5,000 people of all ages gathered on the high street for the sombre ceremony, which was televised nationally. Among the crowd, unnoticed by most, was Prime Minister David Cameron, 'not officially there but just loitering at the back', as Thomas Woodhouse described it.

At the end of the sunset ceremony, Reverend Woodhouse collected the Union flag and took it back to the church. There it was blessed overnight on the altar before being transferred to Carterton, a town in the prime minister's Oxfordshire constituency.

'The flag was given to me and that evening it was like Moses [and the Red Sea], the crowd just parted before me as I walked in silence to the church,' Thomas Woodhouse recalled. 'The final ceremony released us: we didn't ask to do what we did, we stepped up and nothing had gone wrong. It was an extraordinary period but one of the strengths of the town is that we just get on with getting on. Life didn't stop but the repatriations became a crucial and unexpected part of our lives. We were witnessing at first hand, and responding to, people in deep mourning. Any conversation about the rights and wrongs of the wars happened behind closed doors – because the focus in those moments were the grieving families. We just accessed it at our own level and nobody did anything that could be perceived by the outside world as cashing in.'

For this reason, he delayed a much-needed redecoration of St Bartholomew's, which would have required a fundraising campaign, until after the runway at RAF Lyneham had been decommissioned and the repatriations through the town ended.

+ + +

A few months after the sunset ceremony the town was officially renamed Royal Wootton Bassett, the first to be honoured with the prefix 'Royal' for a century. Lyneham was finally closed as an RAF station at the end of 2012. Two years later the Cameron government ceased all combat operations in Afghanistan, though a contingent of British troops stayed on as part of a transnational NATO mission engaged in diplomatic, logistical and humanitarian activities for another seven years until the final, chaotic US-led retreat. By the time Trump left the White House, the United States had squandered in excess of $2 trillion on its military operations in

Afghanistan and 2,448 American service personnel had died, with nearly 21,000 injured. As many as 69,000 Afghan soldiers as well as 47,000 civilians had also died in the conflict. The Taliban had offered an unconditional surrender in December 2001, which the Americans rejected. By 2021, Afghanistan was a fully-fledged 'narco-state', the world's largest producer of illicit heroin, and the Taliban controlled much of the opium trade.

Towards the end of his first hundred days in the White House, Joe Biden announced that, ahead of the twentieth anniversary of the al-Qaeda attacks of 11 September 2001, all US troops would be withdrawn from Afghanistan. The conflict was never intended to be a 'multi-generational undertaking', he said in a televised address, and it was 'time to end America's longest war . . . time to end the forever war'.

There was nothing but doubt in his expressions of confidence and his tone betrayed the reality on the ground: the Taliban had as many as 75,000 full-time fighters and hundreds of Afghan soldiers were being killed every month. The Taliban had not been defeated and its leaders were emboldened. The Americans were preparing to cut and run, which in the event they did, resulting in the instant reconquest of the country by the Taliban and the creation of the self-styled Islamic Emirate of Afghanistan, ruled by sharia law. As the Islamist group's fighters closed in on Kabul, the remade Afghan state was revealed to be a fiction and President Ashraf Ghani and other national leaders simply fled to the airport, abandoning the country and its people to their dismal fate, including many who had worked alongside the Americans and their NATO allies.

This was a profound humiliation for the United States and the Biden administration and total defeat for the hubristic Western project of 'nation-building'. 'In Afghanistan no one feels capable of stopping the movement of history, with all its struggles and calamities,' wrote Bruno Maçães as he prepared to leave Kabul a few days before it fell to the Taliban on 15 August 2021. 'This is a country ruled by fate and for the last 20 years, fate, with all its randomness, has been manufactured in the United States.'

Today the former site of Patrol Base Sandford is an opium farm; more than half of the opium in Afghanistan is cultivated in the fertile areas around the Helmand River. Sangin is the de facto capital of the illicit trade and fields of opium poppies flourish where Corporal Loren Marlton-Thomas died after his boots became trapped in an IED and Warrant Officer Ken Bellringer refused to abandon him.

What did Loren die for? We can say this for sure: he died leading from the front, in a land he could never know nor understand.

+ + +

One cold, cloudy spring afternoon I wandered alone along Wootton Bassett's high street. With the exception of St Bartholomew's Church and the Grade-II listed museum, with its distinctive tapered oolite columns, formerly the town hall, the town is an unremarkable mix of pubs (there are a lot of them, reflecting its distant past as a staging post on the Bath to London road), fast-food restaurants, charity shops, hairdressers, chemists, more traditional outlets such as an independent butcher, greengrocers and newsagents, and towards the bottom of the hill, on the road out to Lyneham, an infant school, a Methodist church and some older residential housing. Further up the hill, I paused outside the entrance to the tatty town council offices. On display in a bay-window were some of the many gifts received by the council on behalf of the town during the repatriations – commemorative shields, a NATO plaque, a framed score from the Royal Marines, a soldier's hat. These were the only mementos I could find in the high street of the extraordinary events in this most ordinary of English towns.

It had been another world back then – before Brexit, of course, and the pandemic – and yet, in many ways, we still live in the long shadow of the Iraq and Afghanistan wars. The legacies of those wars inform how we think about Britain's role in the world and how we think about our armed forces, and they tell us something important about who we were back then and who we are now. For England is a country in which the soldiers themselves, 'our boys and girls', have never been more esteemed and our armed services never more trusted – and this at a time when people were losing trust in politicians. (According to the 2019 Hansard Society's Audit of Political Engagement, the military was the institution most trusted to act in the public interest.)

The conviction that Iraq was a 'bad' war has hardened since the repatriations through Wootton Bassett ended: we like our soldiers but increasingly we don't like sending them into harm's way. In August 2013 the House of Commons rejected the Cameron government's proposal to take substantive military action against the Assad regime in Syria after the chemical weapons attack in the Damascus suburbs, the moment Obama's red lines were crossed. The vote 'reflects the reality that Britain and the rest of Europe are neither able nor willing to play a substantial role in these other regions that will define the twenty-first century', lamented Richard Haass, a senior US diplomat.

'I get it,' David Cameron told the Commons after he lost the Syria vote. This was not simply an admission of political defeat by an exasperated prime minister: it revealed something deeper about the anxieties of elites in this new, emerging era. Britain's role in the world was changing again. We were not who Tony Blair had believed we were or who Cameron wanted us to be. We were entering not exactly a new age of isolation but our horizons were narrowing. No politician dared now speak of reordering the world or of becoming 'actively involved in other people's conflicts'.

+ + +

In 2006, General Sir Richard Dannatt, Chief of the General Staff of the British Army, warned in a newspaper interview that, through lack of care and investment, the Labour government was undermining the 'military covenant' between the nation and its armed forces over issues such as soldiers' pay, conditions, accommodation and equipment. Blair discussed whether to sack the general after his intervention, but he knew public opinion was turning against him over the number of casualties incurred in wars perceived to have no clear purpose or definition of victory. In his interview, General Dannatt had called for the withdrawal of British troops from Iraq. He knew the mission had failed.

'The original intention was that we put in place a liberal democracy that was an exemplar for the region, was pro-West and might have a beneficial effect on the balance within the Middle East,' he said. 'That was the hope. Whether that was a sensible or naïve hope, history will judge.'

History has already judged – and we get it!

The ultimate meaning of the Wootton Bassett repatriations remains ambiguous, however: the ceremonies of mourning venerated the dead soldiers without ever seeking to celebrate or claim as just the wars in which they died. The military was becoming increasingly politicized and British society more militarized – England footballers started wearing red poppies on their national team shirts, for instance, and the names of the fallen were read out weekly in Parliament – but the public was more reluctant than ever to support war-fighting interventions.

Britain had been humbled and chastened: we were three years

away from the Brexit vote. Small wonder then that Cameron mingled at the back of the crowd during the sunset ceremony rather than speak from the podium. For him, as for Blair, it must have felt like 'never glad confident morning again'. Or perhaps that realization finally arrived for Cameron on the morning after the European referendum when he resigned outside Downing Street, bringing an abrupt end to his six-year premiership. 'I was absolutely clear about my belief that Britain is stronger, safer and better off inside the EU,' he said. 'I made clear the referendum was about this, and this alone, not the future of any single politician, including myself. But the British people made a different decision to take a different path.'

At the end of the short address, Cameron, who had made no preparations in the event of a vote for Leave, turned his back on the assembled media and hummed a tune to himself as he went back inside 10 Downing Street, which he and his family would soon be forced to vacate, his political career finished.

+ + +

One warm afternoon during the years of the repatriations, Reverend Woodhouse was leading an outdoor communion service for three hundred children at a church primary school, just off the high street, when a low-flying RAF Globemaster C-17, a transport aircraft used for operational and humanitarian missions in Afghanistan, appeared above Wootton Bassett. He fell silent and turned to peer up at the brilliant blue sky. The children also fell silent and watched as the plane gracefully followed the line of the high street as it prepared to land at RAF Lyneham. 'I just stopped the service and I said, "We are just going to turn and look at the sky."' We just watched this plane come across the town and out of sight into Lyneham knowing that about an hour and a half later a body would come past the school.'

The service continued but the prayers were affected by what

they'd seen, the majestic Globemaster in a cloudless summer sky.

'I wonder now if any of those three hundred young people remember that moment as I do, and whether it has had any lasting effect on them,' Thomas Woodhouse said. 'It was serendipity – the plane coming in to land at just that moment, everything so still – and incredibly moving.'

A soldier's final journey: to come home to England.

4 THE IMAM OF FINSBURY PARK

By the time he returned to his first-floor office, Mohammed Mahmoud could feel the hunger gnawing at him. It was around midnight on a humid June night during the Islamic holy month of Ramadan, and as imam of the Muslim Welfare House in Finsbury Park, north London, he had just finished leading tarawih prayers. Dressed in a white tunic and flip-flops, his short beard neatly clipped, he had more prayers to lead before he ate again just before dawn. He was making some tea in his office when an Algerian man he recognized from the congregation appeared at the door. He was highly agitated: 'You must come,' he said to the imam, 'you must come now.' Mohammed, who was born in Egypt but had lived most of his life in London, could not quite understand the Algerian man's Arabic dialect, but he seemed to be saying something about a knife attack outside; stabbings and street fights were common in this area of Finsbury Park.

What if someone attacks me with a knife? Mohammed asked himself as he followed the man downstairs and out onto the Seven Sisters Road. What he saw there was like something from a hallucination: there were bodies scattered around a crashed white van, concrete bollards had been knocked over, and some of the fallen were screaming in pain while others were silent, possibly dead. One man appeared to be trapped under the vehicle and another, presumably the driver – Mohammed later discovered his name was Darren Osborne – was being restrained, his face pressed down on the pavement. Mohammed understood immediately that this was not the scene of an accident. It was a crime scene.

He stooped to assess some of the injured, but as he did so an onlooker dropped to his knees and struck Osborne in the face; others began kicking out at him. *This is chaos*, Mohammed thought. *It must not continue.* He rose to his full height and spontaneously shouted: 'Stop! No one touch him – no one. No one!'

Iqbal, one of his oldest friends, was now close by – they'd known each other since they were boys and had been praying together earlier in the evening – and Mohammed asked him to use his phone to record what was happening as the crowd thickened and surged. He knew what it would mean for his community if Osborne was killed by a vengeful mob, and he did not want anything to be misunderstood or misrepresented. He knew how his fellow Muslims would be portrayed – 'as if they were hyenas, hyenas out for blood'.

+ + +

The final ten days of Ramadan are the most blessed of the year for Muslims when prayers can go on all through the night and worshippers come and go, seeking the mercy of Allah. Finsbury Park is seldom quiet or at rest even in winter but the heat of high summer as well as Ramadan prayers had drawn even more people out onto the streets than was usual on a Sunday night in June: worshippers from the Welfare House and the nearby five-storey Finsbury Park Mosque mingled and chatted, or loitered waiting for dawn prayers to begin, or were in nearby cafes eating and drinking ahead of the long fast of the daylight hours. The Finsbury Park Mosque was once notorious as a centre of Islamist radicalization under the leadership of Abu Hamza al-Masri, the jihadi-Salafist preacher now serving a life sentence for terrorism offences in the supermax ADX Florence Prison in Colorado.

Earlier that day Darren Osborne had driven to London in a hired van from Cardiff, Wales, where he lived (though he was English). He had planned to attack a pro-Palestinian Quds day march, which the Labour leader Jeremy Corbyn was expected to attend, as he had done the previous year. As a recent convert to the cause of Tommy Robinson and the English Defence League, Osborne believed the British authorities no longer cared about ordinary white people, and that Corbyn and Sadiq Khan, the Labour mayor of London, were apologists for Islamic extremism. The night before Osborne left for London, he visited a local pub for a drink, and there he ranted about 'killing all the Muslims'. As he left the pub, he issued a cryptic warning: 'I'm going to take it into my own hands.'

Osborne had been obsessively watching *Three Girls*, a BBC television drama series about the abuse of vulnerable underage teenagers by a British-Asian street grooming gang in Rochdale, Lancashire. Nine men from the gang were, after much police neglect and incompetence, eventually convicted of sex trafficking, rape of children and other offences. Osborne mentioned their crimes in a note explaining his desire to avenge recent attacks by Muslim terrorists in London and Manchester. He did not expect to live beyond that evening, and so left the note in the hired van to be read in the event of his death. Muslims, he wrote, were 'rapists' and 'feral' and they were 'preying in packs, hunting our children'.

The Rochdale case, and others similar to it involving Muslim Asian grooming gangs in English towns, had been used by Tommy Robinson in his videos and online propaganda. 'There is a nation within a nation forming beneath the surface of the UK. It is a nation built on hatred, on violence and on Islam,' Robinson wrote in a message to supporters.

Just after midnight, Osborne was watching from the van as a

bearded man, Makram Ali, a worshipper from one of the nearby mosques, collapsed from a suspected heart attack close to a bus stop in Finsbury Park. Several fellow Muslim worshippers hurried to his aid – he was still conscious – and they provided an ideal target: Osborne pressed his foot down hard on the accelerator and drove straight at them. The van mounted the pavement at the junction of Whadcoat Street and Seven Sisters Road, close to the Muslim Welfare House and ninety metres from the Finsbury Park Mosque. The impact was immediate. Afterwards, as Osborne emerged from the van, he raged about wanting to 'kill all Muslims'. 'I've done my bit,' he shouted, as if he were a combatant in a war – perhaps he thought he was. 'Kill me,' he pleaded as he was bundled to the ground. 'Kill me.'

It was then that Mohammed Mahmoud appeared in the street. He understood very quickly what was happening and responded to the logic of the situation.

'I'm the imam of the mosque. Everyone get back and no one touch him,' Mohammed ordered.

The imam was aged only thirty-one but because of his charismatic leadership, the distinction of his scholarship and the power of his example, he had unified the Muslim Welfare House behind him. A protective ring of human security formed around Osborne on Mohammed's orders. With the support of several wise elders from the mosque, he pushed back against the thickening crowd that was trying to close in on Osborne. He demanded the crowd's restraint.

'This man will be handed over to the police unscathed. Nothing must happen to him,' Mohammed said.

'He wants to kill Muslims,' some of the men he'd led earlier in evening prayers shouted.

'He drove straight at us.'

'He wants to kill us.'

'He wants us to kill him.'

By this time, two police officers had arrived at the scene; a passing patrol car had been flagged down and emergency services alerted. Mohammed took the hand of one of the officers, a young man daunted by what confronted him. He was guided towards Osborne, whose thick hair was dishevelled, his face bruised and swollen. Mohammed had one objective – to make sure Osborne survived. Nothing else mattered. 'You need to take this man away now, before something happens to him,' he said.

As more police arrived, Osborne was led through the febrile, ever-growing crowd to a patrol van and, without resistance, he climbed into the back of it. As the doors slammed shut, Osborne smirked and waved at onlookers like some small-time celebrity.

Mohammed felt overwhelming relief as the van pulled away.

He made his way slowly back to the Muslim Welfare House, not yet behind a police cordon. He felt suddenly exhausted and wanted only to pray.

The director of the mosque, Ahmad Khaloufi, said to him, 'What are we going to do now?'

'What can we do but pray?' Mohammed said. 'Let's pray. We can talk all night, but talking is not going to change anything.'

The prayers that followed were the most intense and emotional of that entire month of Ramadan, and the pre-dawn meal that followed was just as sombre. The atmosphere inside the mosque was unusually silent and serene. 'You could hear a pin drop that night,' Mohammed said. 'And it was very calm, very tranquil. A few women were scared, they didn't want to leave the mosque, and we said, "Okay, we'll keep you in."'

Later that morning, after dawn prayers, Mohammed received a call from an old university friend named Asif. He wanted to know what had happened outside the mosque. 'Oh, nothing much,' the imam said quietly.

THE ENGLISH BERSERK

June 2017: the month of Theresa May's snap general election, when support for Corbyn's Labour surged – 'Oh, Jeremy Corbyn,' his admirers chanted throughout the campaign, to the tune of the White Stripes' 'Seven Nation Army'; when Remainers still believed they could derail the Brexit train; when the Tories lost their hard-won majority at the polls and held on to power as the largest party in a hung parliament, now dependent on support from Northern Ireland's Democratic Unionist Party (DUP); when seventy-two people, many of them originally migrants to Britain, lost their lives inside their own homes in an inferno at Grenfell Tower in west London, in one of the richest districts in the one of the richest cities in the world. It was a demoralizing period, inflamed by three lethal jihadi terror attacks, the worst in Britain since the London bombings of 7 July 2005.

The first attack preceded Theresa May's decision to call a snap election. On the afternoon of 22 March, Khalid Masood (his birth name was Adrian Russell Elms and he was a fifty-two-year-old convert to Islam) drove an SUV into pedestrians on the south side of Westminster Bridge and Bridge Street, killing four of them and injuring more than fifty others. He followed this atrocity by crashing the vehicle into a perimeter fence outside Parliament before stabbing to death Keith Palmer, an unarmed police officer who had confronted Masood as he came through the Palace of Westminster's Carriage Gate. Masood was shot dead by an armed response officer. In a message written before the attacks but discovered after them, Masood explained he was engaged in jihad and would avenge British military interventions in the Middle East. Andreea Cristea, a Romanian tourist, was struck by the SUV on Westminster Bridge and knocked into the River Thames; she died from her injuries two weeks later.

The second attack was carried out during the election campaign by Salman Abedi on the night of 22 May. The twenty-two-year-old blew himself up in the foyer of the Manchester Arena as people were leaving an Ariana Grande concert and their family and friends were arriving to meet them. Twenty-two people died in the suicide attack, including children and teenagers, and hundreds more were injured. The youngest victim, eight-year-old Saffie-Rose Roussos, survived for an hour after being injured in the blast but never received the appropriate medical treatment – such as the tying of tourniquets around her legs – that might have saved her. The little girl died because too much blood leaked from her wounds.

Abedi's younger brother Hashem was later jailed for fifty-five years, a record for a determinate prison term, for the role he played in planning the heinous crime. The Abedi brothers, who had assembled their own bomb in a rented flat, were born in England and lived in Elsmore Road, Manchester; their father, a political radical associated with the Libyan Islamic Fighting Group, had left Colonel Gaddafi's Libya in the 1990s. Hashem Abedi was in Libya and, after eventually being extradited to Britain, showed no remorse and even refused to leave his prison cell to give evidence during his trial. Salman Abedi claimed to be a supporter of Islamic State (IS, or Isis) – the brothers used one of its manuals to make their bomb – but he was not a returnee from war zones in Syria or Iraq.

The third attack was on the night of Saturday, 3 June, in central London. Pedestrians were rammed by a van on London Bridge, after which the driver and two accomplices embarked on a murderous stabbing rampage in nearby Borough Market. Here was yet another manifestation of the indigenous English berserk. The obligatory shouts of *Allahu Akbar* were heard. Eight people died, excluding the three Islamist assassins who were shot dead by police. It emerged later that Khuram Butt, a British Muslim and one of the killers, had links to al-Muhajiroun, the militant jihadi network.

+ + +

Islamist terror in Britain has a long tail. The three murderous attacks of the summer of 2017 – 'bound together by the single, evil ideology of Islamist terror', as Theresa May put it – backlit the Finsbury Park outrage, in which Makram Ali, a fifty-one-year-old father of six, died and nine others were injured. Darren Osborne, himself a father of four children, was convicted of murder and attempted murder and sentenced to life in prison. His long-time partner called him a 'functioning alcoholic' and said he'd been self-radicalized on social media and seemed 'brainwashed', 'totally obsessed' as he disappeared into a long, dark tunnel of conspiracy and loathing. Sentencing Osborne, Justice Cheema-Grubb said, 'Your use of Twitter exposed you to racists and anti-Islamic ideology. In short, you allowed your mind to be poisoned by those who claimed to be leaders.'

As he was led away from Woolwich Crown Court after being sentenced, Osborne said: 'God bless you all, thank you.' His work was done, as he saw it, and he was still alive, an outcome he'd not expected when he accelerated towards the group gathered around Makram Ali.

DEAD MEN CAN'T SPEAK

There was a reason why Darren Osborne was not killed that night as he had fantasized: violently, grotesquely, gloriously, becoming a martyr for his cause. And that reason was the intervention made by Mohammed Mahmoud – who 'chose to respond to evil with good', as the judge at Osborne's trial remarked. The noble imam of Finsbury Park chose life over death, and the rule of law over mob rule. If Osborne's aim had been to 'create divisions and hate between communities', to provoke his own killing through his own murderous deeds, he had 'failed', said Commander Dean Haydon, the head of counter-terrorism at the Metropolitan Police. He failed because Mohammed Mahmoud had the clarity of thought and courage to say, 'Stop! No one touch him – no one. No one!'

The people stopped and the people listened. Less than a month after the Manchester Arena bombing, Mohammed's intervention was an act of supreme grace under pressure. He recalled, 'I'd never before felt suspense and tension and anxiety like that from a group of people.'

The Muslim community of Finsbury Park had been stained by association for too long because of the crimes of Abu Hamza, the former imam, and those who followed him and acted on his commands. Those stains were washed away by Mohammed Mahmoud.

'I did think the worst would happen – that the man would be killed,' Mohammed said. 'I remember the words in my head: "Dead men can't speak". I wanted him to answer for what he did.'

He remembered the mass casualty attack by an Islamic State death squad, sent from Syria, on the Bataclan theatre in Paris in November 2015. 'They were all killed, the perpetrators. I have no doubt they were the perpetrators, that they did it. But I always want to know what are you going to say if you're in the dock, if you're stood in court. If you blow yourself up, you're in a thousand pieces, so no one can understand what led you to this, who were you listening to, were you recruited, are you part of a cell? I've never said this before but those things were going through my head in those moments that night.'

+ + +

News of the Finsbury Park attack travelled fast, and the next morning the media descended on the area, and so did Jeremy Corbyn – the two mosques were in his parliamentary constituency – and Sadiq Khan, the London mayor, and Theresa May, the prime minister.

Mohammed Mahmoud was oblivious to all this, he told me, because he was asleep. When he was woken by his wife – 'She was like, "Hamed, come on, get up, your brother and sisters are on WhatsApp saying the *Evening Standard* want your picture." I was just like, "I'm exhausted!" "Quickly: Jeremy Corbyn's at the mosque." I was like, "What are you talking about?" I'm half-asleep, and I said, "It's all right, it will just all blow over." She said, "Come on, Theresa May's at the mosque now. They're speaking about you on the news." I said, "What's going on, what's going on?" I took the first ironed robe I could find, the white one, and I prayed. Then I went into the mosque and they said to me, "Don't you know? Everyone's speaking about you. You need to go and make a statement to the press." I went outside and I saw the press, the line outside the Arsenal shop: there were almost a hundred of them, reporters and cameramen. I kept saying, "I didn't do anything really," and the others said, "No, no, you have to come, you have to come."'

The next day Prince Charles also came to Finsbury Park to meet the 'hero imam', as Mohammed was being called, and he carried with him the good wishes of the Queen. 'The Queen has specifically asked me to tell you how shocked she was by what happened, particularly as the victims were worshippers who had been attending Ramadan prayers – and Her Majesty's thoughts and prayers are with you all.'

+ + +

I first heard about the attack when I woke on the morning of 19 June, which happened to be my birthday. It was dismaying that, in this summer of roiling social and political turmoil, another terrorist attack had occurred – and in the neighbourhood of the Finsbury Park Mosque. I'd monitored the rise to national prominence of the mosque after it reopened at its present site in 1994; I used to walk past it on my way to Arsenal matches at the old Highbury stadium.

I could never understand why Abu Hamza, who became its imam in 1997, was allowed such freedom to conspire and incite hatred. Perhaps a 'covenant of security' existed after all and was more than merely media speculation. 'No doubt that human life is based on conflict,' Abu Hamza, who relentlessly preached Islamic jihad, said in one television interview. 'This is what we see today and is confirmed by the conflicts which arose between sects, countries and groups. No rights or principles can be respected, accepted or imposed except through the use of force.' The Islam of Abu Hamza was not a religion of peace.

I read a lot about Mohammed Mahmoud over subsequent days because his intervention that Ramadan night changed the narrative of that summer of terror and took us in a different direction. I was reminded too of a line from an Edmund Blunden poem about the Western Front:

God bless us all, this was peculiar grace.

THE SECRETS OF THE BEEHIVE

By the time I met Mohammed Mahmoud, he had become the senior imam at the East London Mosque on the Whitechapel Road, the oldest mosque in London and the largest in Britain. With its golden dome and minarets, and its multiple extensions, it has become one of the East End's most distinctive landmarks. It was a quiet midweek winter afternoon and I was shown around the mosque and two adjoining buildings, the London Muslim Centre and the Maryam Centre. Another adjacent building, the Zakat Centre, was previously the Fieldgate Street Synagogue, the last active synagogue in Whitechapel, before it was sold to and absorbed into the complex in 2015. I was shown the mosque's seven rooftop beehives, home to as many as 400,000 bees. A chapter of the Quran is devoted to bees and they are revered in Islam for the healing qualities of their honey, for their constancy, teamwork and benevolence. I was introduced to Sufia Alam, founder of the Muslim Women's Collective and manager of the Maryam Centre, where women can gather and pray. She wore glasses, a hijab (her face was uncovered) and, in a breezy east London accent, talked about the challenges confronting British Bangladeshi women in the area. Her parting words to me were direct but well-intentioned: 'We are here because you were there. You will have to learn to live with us – because we aren't going anywhere. England is our home.'

Dressed in a long white Arab-style *thawb* Mohammed came to see me straight from leading afternoon prayers and we sat in his cramped office eating dates. His old university friend Asif, who does media work at the mosque, joined us; he and Mohammed had an easy familiarity as they bantered and reminisced. Mohammed has a strong north London accent and a relaxed, engaging, idiomatic conversational style.

Born in Egypt, Mohammed came to London with his parents as an infant; his father studied part-time for a PhD at Imperial College while also running a Kodak Express shop, developing and printing photographs. They lived on the Six Acres Estate, off Fonthill Road, just behind the Muslim Welfare House in Finsbury Park, which Mohammed said 'was really where I lived'. His parents were devout, conservative Muslims and home life was structured around worship and education; Mohammed did a degree in biology at University College London, which was where he met Asif and other close friends who today form his trusted social network.

Mohammed said that, until the attacks of 11 September 2001, he knew nothing about the activities of Abu Hamza at the Finsbury Park Mosque, which his parents avoided, perhaps because they were aware of its associations. 'That's when I realized there were other ideologies: violent ideologies, and some people subscribed to those ideologies, loosely, and some were all for them.'

Murderous terrorist attacks carried out by jihadis have led to Islam being misunderstood as a religion of intolerance and violence, he said. 'During my childhood and adolescence, and into my twenties, the only mention that Muslims would get in the media was through terror-related incidents. The only known imams were the notorious three, Abu Hamza, Abu Qatada, Omar Bakri – that was it. We're still reeling from their influence. The reality is that most people in the UK will not have a meaningful engagement with a Muslim in their lifetime; Muslims are mostly concentrated in London and the big cities. People don't get to see Islam up close, they're afraid to engage with Muslims: that's the reality.'

In the years after the July 2005 London bombings, Mohammed observed how people's attitudes hardened against Muslims. He was provoked sometimes in the streets and verbally abused on public transport: he was called a terrorist, or suicide bomber, or 'you Taliban'.

'These things etch away at someone's heart and, bit by bit, it can break you – as it broke some people – or it can make you – sorry for the cliché, but that's the truth. It can make you by causing you to stand up and want to do something about it. I obviously share a name with the Prophet Mohammed (Peace Be Upon Him) and it pains me that people who are named after Him carry out these attacks. His name is synonymous with Islam, and every time I read in the paper that even a normal crime – fraud, bank robbery, a burglary – has been committed by someone called Mohammed or Ahmed, it pained me so much. I wished I could do something to truly represent my religion.'

I asked if he felt despair.

'I felt frustration, but not helplessness, because I realized you can always do something. You have neighbours, you get public transport, you can help people, you can do charity work, you can clean up outside your home: there are a million things you can do to serve your society and truly represent your faith, not for the sake of it being to market or advertise your religion, but because that's the right thing to do.'

He believes Muslims are continually being forced to 'overcompensate' in their public behaviour, and even in their private conversations, because in wider society they are perceived 'almost as social pariahs'. This saddens and frustrates him.

'Many Muslims feel you can't even joke without people taking it the wrong way,' Mohammed said. 'Any joke. It could be a joke about women, so then we're misogynistic oppressors of women. Dark humour, black comedy, is off-limits for us. You have to do the overcompensation. If you're a Muslim, you're already viewed with suspicion. Your words will be interpreted to have the worst meaning possible. We police our language, even when no one's listening.'

Asif interjected. 'We honestly even police what we say on WhatsApp! We do this to get used to not speaking like that in public; to accustom ourselves to not making these remarks or these jokes in public.'

Mohammed mentioned a Muslim acquaintance who had left the East End to live in Essex – what he called 'deep Essex, white Essex'. One day he asked this man why he'd chosen to leave. 'Do you know what this guy said? That he wanted to remember he was a minority. That struck me. His whole life had been spent in east London, Docklands and the East End, and he said living here, he forgot he was a minority, because he could go an entire day without speaking English. And that's the case for many areas in the UK where people may go their entire day without needing to speak English.'

+ + +

I mentioned the success of several notable books which argue that Europe is dying – from migration, from the rise of Islam, from self-loathing, from a reluctance to defend Western values and civilization. In their pessimistic analysis, the declinist intellectuals who write these books seem to understand something important about the forces driving our age of anxiety, but they also provoke bewilderment and hostility. The reactionary French thinker Eric Zemmour, for instance, is well known for his book *French Suicide*, which provocatively attacks liberal elites for, as he sees it, destroying French identity and warns that civil war is coming if it has not arrived already. In *Germany Abolishes Itself*, Thilo Sarrazin, formerly a man of the left, denounces the country's immigration policies and its failures to integrate a growing Muslim population; it sold over a million copies. Douglas Murray's *The Strange Death of Europe* has done similarly well in Britain. For Murray, Europe has allowed itself to become 'a home for the entire world' while losing 'faith in its beliefs, traditions and legitimacy'.

Behind the success of these bestselling books lies more than simply cultural pessimism. The rise over recent years of populist nationalist parties and movements – UKIP, the Sweden Democrats, the Front National (now the Rassemblement National), Alternative for Germany – reflected a widespread belief that ruling elites deliberately restricted discussion about the cultural effects of uncontrolled migration. 'The world is coming to Europe at precisely the moment that Europe has lost sight of what it is,' Murray writes. 'And while the movement of millions of people from other cultures into a strong and assertive culture might have worked, the move-ment of millions of people into a guilty, jaded and dying culture cannot.' Europe will 'not be Europe and the peoples of Europe will have lost the only place in the world we had to call home'.

Murray is a prominent ultra-conservative thinker but the popu-larity of the declinist narrative lies in part in its fusion of left and right, though crucial differences remain. Sarrazin is a German technocrat and former social democrat. In France, Michel Onfray, author of *Decadence: The Life and Death of the Judeo-Christian Tradition*, is a former supporter of the French Revolutionary Communist League and creator of a tuition-free People's University. Alain Finkeilkraut, the socialist son of a Holocaust survivor, has long been a proponent of multiculturalism. Yet his book *Unhappy Identity* – another declinist bestseller – contends that Islamic separ-atism is fundamentally incompatible with French culture and fosters anti-Semitism.

Hatred of or discrimination against Jewish people is of course not only an issue of urgent concern in France: it is widespread across Europe. In Britain, sections of the left formed anti-Zionist alliances with Islamist reactionaries, and the Corbynite leadership of the Labour Party was found by the Equality and Human Rights Commission (EHRC) to have tolerated anti-Semitism among members and activists. Responding to the publication of the EHRC report, Keir Starmer, elected leader in April 2020, spoke of a 'day of shame' for Labour and apologized to the Jewish community.

The declinist narratives – and attendant fears of civilizational decline – were popular in the years following the financial crash, especially during the European refugee crisis, because they spoke not only to people's economic worries but also to their deeper concerns about the strengthening presence of Islam in Europe. So how might we distinguish between objective, analytical predictions of cultural decline and the invocation of civilizational decay to express more mundane insecurities? Will the prophecies of the declinists come to pass – Murray's vision of Western suicide, of a jaded and dying European culture – or are they sublimated uncertainty, morbid symptoms of an age of upheaval? Or is something else in play, something bound up with the crisis of liberalism itself?

For Mohammed Mahmoud, pessimism about the growing Muslim presence in Europe is based on a wilful misunderstanding of Islam, which he emphatically rejects is a threat to secularism, liberalism and the open society. His alternative vision is one of peaceful coexistence of religious and secular cultures, under the rule of law. He rejects forced assimilation or, its opposite, state sanctions against religious symbols and an aggressive assertion of *laïcité* as in France.

'My overwhelming feeling is that I wish people could see Islam as it really is,' he said. 'The media is incredibly influential: TV and cinema and magazines and papers, the more coverage of positive role models, and just regular Muslims, the more normalized they are, because the reality is that we are not normalized in the media; we are not normalized in the eyes of the public. There are things that can be done to change people's perceptions, but communication, through all of its methods and all of its means, has to be utilized entirely.'

When he was growing up in Islington, Mohammed was not 'really conscious' of ethnic divisions. 'It was only when I left the borough that I saw how other minority groups, Muslims as well, lived – how some of them were very inward-looking, because of the stresses on them. But everybody wants to communicate and everybody wants to understand and to be understood. You're taking the easy solution if you just stick with your own. But I understand how it happens. There has been a self-ghettoization of the Muslim communities, partly due to pressures on them to remain inward-looking and insular. Growing up, I didn't feel that there were mechanisms in place to allow you to integrate. I grew up in a very conservative and religious household, and when I went to school and then college, I didn't find the same environment I found at home. The religious values were at risk. You find who you are, as they say, and it narrows down your group of friends and your circle of friends.'

+ + +

In September 2012 Mohammed and his wife and their two young children moved to Cairo so that he could study sharia at Al-Azhar University. The Mubarak military regime had fallen after sustained domestic protests, part of the wave of uprisings that swept across the Middle East and North Africa during the Arab Spring. The Muslim Brotherhood were now in power after Muhammad Morsi won a narrow victory, on a small turnout, in presidential elections, the first democratic elections held in the country. The Brotherhood were doctrinaire Islamists not democrats, however, and quickly began to shape the state in their own image.

Mohammed and his family left Egypt after only nine months, returning to London two weeks before the Morsi regime was toppled in a military coup in July 2013. Living in Cairo, he had missed London desperately, far more than he could have ever imagined, and he'd discovered the truth of where he belonged: in England.

'I have never felt homesick like that in my life, ever. I used to force myself to think about something else so I could stop thinking about London,' he recalled. 'We missed everything about the UK. Everything! I missed walking on a pavement. I missed crossing the road without fear, without imminent threat to my life. I missed queues. Oh, how I missed queues! No one queues like we do. I missed public transport. Public transport here is a luxury, even the bus network, compared to many other countries in the world. And obviously the NHS. If this country had nothing but the NHS, it would be enough for somebody to want to live here and stay here. Everything about it, from the selflessness of staff and doctors and nurses, the hours that they work, the great service – and it's free.'

We met a few weeks before the first national lockdown and, as the virus spread, his comments seemed even more pertinent in retrospect.

'I missed this country so much, and decided never to leave it, when I came back,' he said. 'I've performed pilgrimage – the minor pilgrimage and major pilgrimages, but you can't live there. You can't live in Mecca or Medina, and I definitely wouldn't live in the Gulf. I'd visit anywhere in the world, but I wouldn't live anywhere but here.'

Living for that short period in Egypt enabled Mohammed to resolve a crisis of identity that had disturbed him: was he a British Muslim or a Muslim living in Britain? To whom and to what did he owe his ultimate loyalty – the British nation or the *ummah*? Where did the imam of Finsbury Park truly belong?

'It was a real struggle – "Who am I? What am I? Why am I here? How long will I be here?" I wrestled with these questions for so long,' he recalled. 'I would find myself on one end of the spectrum and then move to the other, and then move again. But for us, now, I'd say – for people who are Islamically educated – it's actually not a huge issue and it's not a struggle. Yes, this country has a colonial past. Yes, they stripped the natural resources of many countries and left them barren, and many people are here because their countries of origin have nothing to offer them, but now that we are here, we're not going to be leeches; we're going to contribute, because that's what a human does. And a Muslim is definitely not supposed to be a consumer: a Muslim is commanded by his faith to contribute and to produce and to give back and to build and to construct, for everyone. Not only for his own kind, but for everyone.'

He recalled the parable of the prophet Joseph (or Yusuf), the son of Jacob, also a Muslim prophet. Joseph was born in Cannan and his great gift, even as a child, was that he could interpret dreams. But one day his brothers, who were envious of their father's love for Joseph, cast him into a well, where he was found by a passing caravan and sold into slavery. He was bought by the chief minister, the Aziz, of Egypt. He was later falsely accused of sexual harassment and imprisoned. Meanwhile, the King was being troubled by strange, disturbing dreams; in one dream seven emaciated cows consumed seven plump cows. What did it mean? One of the King's servants, who had met Joseph in prison, recalled his gift; Joseph was summoned and was asked to interpret the King's dream: he prophesied that it meant seven years of plenty would be followed by seven years of famine that would consume the land, apart from what had been harvested and preserved. The King listened and understood that his dream was a warning: preparation is all. Joseph was pardoned, his innocence was reaffirmed, and he was given a position of authority so that he could help Egypt prepare for the famine to come.

'What I take from this,' Mohammed said, 'and this is not story time, is that Joseph could have said, "You made me a slave: why should I do anything for you?" But despite all of that, he saved an entire country from drought, and Egypt was the major civilization and power at that time. He not only saved a country, he saved all of their neighbouring countries as well, which relied on their economy. Afterwards, his family came, because obviously the drought had not struck Egypt only, and he gave them residency in the country. His family became part and parcel and fabric of society because people said, "Yes, you know what, he contributed. He didn't just contribute, he saved the entire country."'

Joseph served Egypt though he was not of Egypt or born in Egypt.

'I think the same way that Prophet Joseph does: that this country has its sins and it has its good deeds, and every country is the same. I am not going to withhold my services or withhold the good that I can offer because of the sins of the country. And the sins of who? The sins of the grandfathers and great-grandfathers? What portion of blame can ever be given to those who committed no crime, except that they are from the lineage of so-and-so who went and colonized countries?'

+ + +

We discussed the British Muslims who were attracted to the murderous utopianism of Islamic State – despite its millenarianism, its barbarism, its public executions, its grotesque show trials, its commitment to endless war. 'For Muslims who hate the group, the Islamic State's claim that there is no god but God, and Muhammad is his prophet, is a statement of faith that forces a painful admission: the Islamic State is a Muslim phenomenon,' wrote Graeme Wood in *The Way of Strangers: Encounters with Islamic State*. 'Wicked, perhaps; ultraviolent, certainly. But Muslim, by definition.'

Mohammed listened to me as I paraphrased Wood and then repeated quietly that there was no Islamic utopia on Earth. He then digressed to speak more generally about the effects of Islamic terror on Muslims and non-Muslims in Britain. It was his duty 'to reassure people we're not a threat', he said. 'Unfortunately, there are so many terrorist attacks in Europe, but after one attack, it may have been the Charlie Hebdo attack, I was on the bus in London and a woman was staring at me, petrified. Petrified. And I know, I can read people's body language. And I thought to myself, "How can I reassure her?" And everything I did, a movement of my arm, adjusting my collar, everything I did made her scared. When we got to Angel, I needed to get off the bus. I walked towards the door, where she was, and she ran away. She fled for her life, literally. And that struck me more than any other time before, because I realized then that I have to do more to reassure people that I'm not a threat. I shouldn't have to do that. But I have to do it. I began to sympathize with other groups, especially young black men. There's nothing they can do, they're just black, and some people look at them and view them with suspicion. And it makes you empathetic and sympathize with other groups and to draw parallels and realize how much we have in common with each other.'

I brought up the case of Amira Abase, Shamima Begum and Kadiza Sultana, the three Bethnal Green schoolgirls who, without warning, disappeared one day during the half-term holiday in February 2015. Soon afterwards CCTV footage emerged of them passing through security at Gatwick Airport, dressed in brightly coloured jumpers, long winter coats and sneakers: they were on a one-way journey to Raqqa, the then de facto capital of Islamic State. Travelling without parental or adult escorts, the girls flew on Turkish Airlines to Istanbul. There they had a half-day wait before taking a long bus journey to the Turkey–Syria border. With the assistance of smugglers, they crossed into Syria, into a land ravaged by religious sectarianism and civil war. They were heading for the hermit kingdom from where few returned.

The girls had grown up close to the East London Mosque and at school were admired for their intelligence and decency. Why did they go? What motivated them to become jihadi brides at such a young age? What were the push factors?

I mentioned conversations I'd had with Tasnime Akunjee, a criminal defence solicitor who represented the girls' families after they first disappeared and is known at the mosque, where he does pro bono work. When we met, Akunjee too had mentioned their motivation for leaving. 'We talk about the attractions of Britain for

immigrants – about pull factors – but what are the push factors?'
he said. 'Why do you think the girls wanted to leave?'

I put the same question to Mohammed Mahmoud.

'I wouldn't start with the push factors,' he replied, 'although
they definitely need to be considered. But many people idealize
other Muslim countries, where the call to prayer is heard and the
mosques are open. They assume that there are Islamic utopias
outside the UK in Arab countries and Muslim countries. But they
don't exist.'

Then he said something surprising.

'In truth, Britain is more Islamic than most Muslim countries.'

The most Islamic country in the world?

He smiled.

'It is more Islamic because it allows freedom of worship,
because it allows freedom of preaching, it allows freedom of
expression, it allows you to build houses of worship,' he said. 'The
reality is that many Muslim countries, for political reasons, maybe
you're allowed to worship but you're not allowed to preach,
maybe you're allowed to preach but you're not allowed to build a
mosque. If you build a mosque, you're not allowed to preach what
you like – you have a pre-written sermon given to you that you are
bound by and you're not allowed to stray from. So, this country, if
praying in a mosque and building a mosque and preaching and
converting people, let's say – we're not going to shy from the fact
that Islam is a religion that preaches and conveys its message and
wishes for others to adhere to it – if that's what defines a Muslim
country, then the UK is more of a Muslim country than almost all
Muslim countries we have. This country hasn't banned the head-
scarf, hasn't banned religious symbols, and we're no worse off
because of their existence at all.'

It was time for Mohammed Mahmoud to lead evening prayers.

THE CALL OF THE CALIPHATE

Once Tasnime Akunjee, the families' solicitor, established that the Bethnal Green girls were in Raqqa, it 'became a waiting game'. He travelled to the Turkey–Syria border and opened negotiations with smugglers and other networks as he sought to locate the girls. A social media campaign was launched, #callhomegirls. 'We knew the girls were going there to get married, and the death rate is pretty savage for combatants and that sort of shock might cause them to reassess – and we were right. Within a year, Kadiza realized that what she'd done was not what she wanted.'

Kadiza, who wore thick-framed glasses, had access to a phone and sent private messages, via Instagram, to her sister in London and occasionally they also spoke. Their exchanges were through necessity cryptic because Kadiza feared her communications inside the caliphate's oppressive surveillance state were being monitored. Her Canadian-Somali husband had been killed in combat (she was expected to remarry) and, a widow at the age of just sixteen, she felt desperately alone.

Kadiza recalled her last night at home in London, before her departure, when her favourite younger niece had come to stay and they danced together and wore matching pyjamas. Kadiza had slept alongside her mother that last night – her father was dead – comforted by her warmth, the rise and fall of her breathing. Early the next morning Kadiza told her mother she would be spending the rest of the day at a local library as it was the half-term break. She never came home.

For the Bethnal Green girls, the embrace of extreme Islamic conservatism amounted to a perverse form of countercultural rebellion. They rejected the orthodoxies of the hyper-individualistic, pornography-saturated, social media-fixated teenage popular culture that surrounded them in London. One of them spoke of wishing to leave behind an 'immoral society' and, shortly before her disappearance, Amira tweeted, 'I feel like I don't belong in this era.'

The girls wanted to remake their lives, to be freed from the interference and demands of their school and immediate families. They wanted to experience a greater sense of togetherness and they wanted to go their own way. They certainly did that and embraced a religious culture that glorified a different kind of nihilism. The girls escaped their predicament not by abandoning the restrictive cultural inheritance into which they were born but by going deeper into it; they could not get out so they mined the place they were already in.

'Sometimes teenagers operate on the basis of stereotype,' Akunjee said. 'They take one look at their family history, who their sisters and parents marry, how they did that, and they may feel they don't have agency in their own futures.'

The girls took control of their own futures all right but forfeited whatever agency they believed they had. Look at the CCTV footage of them passing through security at Gatwick Airport – so bright, so hopeful, so promising. They were children really and were responding to the siren call of the caliphate by embarking on an awfully big adventure. What they couldn't know was the future they'd imagined for themselves was already lost. The world as they once knew it was irrecoverable. There was death in this business of Islamic state-building.

+ + +

As she plotted her escape, Kadiza could trust no one in Raqqa. Before leaving for Syria, Amira, active on social media, had tweeted a hadith about friendship. 'If you are three then let not two engage in conversation excluding the third.'

Amira once said that she and Kadiza were so close they were 'like twins'. But now Kadiza was alone, and desperately afraid.

Her planned escape, organized by Tasnime Akunjee and inter-mediaries in Syria, was aborted, however, when a young Austrian woman, the daughter of Bosnian refugees who'd made *hijra* to the Islamic State, was discovered attempting to leave Raqqa. Her punish-ment was to be sadistically murdered in a public stoning. 'Isis was a Stasi state, everyone reporting on everyone,' Akunjee said. 'After the Austrian girl was beaten to death, Kadiza basically lost her bottle.'

Akunjee had previously arranged for another British woman to leave IS territory. 'She actually escaped from a second-floor window and climbed down a pipe. There were a bunch of children watching her, and they were cheering her on. Back then, there were little organizations, little groups of people who purely on a humanitarian basis were helping people to get out, decent people. A lot of them are unfortunately dead now.'

Since returning, this woman has been sectioned in a psychiatric hospital.

+ + +

When we first met, Akunjee was convinced that the three Bethnal Green girls were dead. Kadiza had died in a Russian air strike, he said. Eyewitnesses claimed to have seen her body being pulled from rubble, and around the same time the messages to her sister ceased. Akunjee assumed something similar had happened to Shamima and Amira.

Little was known of the fate of a fourth girl, Sharmeena Begum (no relation to Shamima), who was also a pupil at Bethnal Green Academy and a close friend of the three lost girls. In December 2014, after a period of turmoil at home – her young mother had died from cancer and her father had remarried in bewildering haste – she had travelled to Syria to join Islamic State. Soon after arriving there, Sharmeena called her father in London to tell him that if she died there she would 'go to my mother'.

In the weeks after her mother's death, Sharmeena had started visiting a local mosque in Whitechapel, and there she fell under the influence of some older women, doctrinaire Salafists. Salafism is an uncompromising movement within Sunni Islam that advocates returning to the moral and theological practices of the first three generations of Muslims, the so-called ancestors. Sharmeena could speak basic Arabic and started to read jihadi literature; she encouraged her friends, the other Bethnal Green girls, to follow her example by embracing a more austere, fundamentalist form of Islam, and they all started to dress more conservatively, wearing headscarves and long skirts over their trousers, and they watched IS propaganda videos on the internet.

'The girls were schooled into it by the first girl who'd gone,' Akunjee told me. 'It's all about the friendship circle and that bond. The psychology around teenagers is that their friends are everything and their families are nothing.'

After Sharmeena left for Syria, counter-terrorism police visited Bethnal Green Academy to interview Shamima, Kadiza and Amina, but their families were never told the girls were a flight risk, nor that their friend Sharmeena was already in Syria. The three girls were sent home from school with official letters which their parents never received. Kadiza's sister later found her letter folded into a book, by which time five other girls at the school had been barred from travelling overseas by a High Court judge. Who, if anyone, was grooming them all was never established.

One of the first British women to travel to IS territory was Aqsa Mahmood (also known as Umm Layth), a twenty-year-old Muslim of Pakistani heritage from Glasgow. For a time, she was a prolific blogger, posting pro-IS propaganda on Tumblr and Twitter, and both Sharmeena and Shamima contacted her.

+ + +

In February 2019, Akunjee was astonished to be called by *The Times* after its renowned war reporter Anthony Loyd, in a remarkable scoop, found Shamima Begum in al-Hawl refugee camp in north-eastern Syria. Thousands of civilians – the majority from IS families – had been gathered in the camp after they'd fled the besieged town of Baghouz in eastern Syria, the last redoubt of what was left of Islamic State.

'I'm a sister from London. I'm a Bethnal Green girl,' was how Begum introduced herself to the man from *The Times*.

Shamima was malnourished, traumatized and pregnant with her third child (her first two children had died). She'd married Yago Riedijk, a Dutch convert to Islam and jihadi fighter, less than two weeks after arriving in Syria. 'My family wouldn't help me get married in the UK and the way they showed family life in IS was pretty nice,' Shamima later told the BBC. 'Like the perfect family life, saying they'd take care of you and take care of your family. And that was true. They did take care of me and my family at first but things changed after that.'

Together with thousands of other civilians, Begum had fled what was left of IS territory, now under relentless aerial bombardment from US, NATO and Russian war planes, because of her late-stage pregnancy. She was among an exodus of burka-clad women and their children from a desert hellscape of bomb craters, collapsed buildings, dead bodies and burned-out vehicles. The women were transported in open cattle trucks to the camp, which had limited medical facilities and contaminated water supplies. Later, when she was questioned by *The Times*, Begum claimed that two of her friends from London, Sharmeena Begum and Amira Abase, were still alive but had chosen to stay on in Beghuz, to the end, even as the caliphate crumbled to dust. If true, they would have died in the final onslaught as the Syrian Democratic Forces (SDF), a mostly Kurdish militia, and coalition special forces took control of the territory.

Not long after Shamima Begum was found, she was relocated to another camp, al-Roj, in north-eastern Syria, also controlled by the SDF. She was moved there after death threats were made against her by other women in al-Hawl camp. Akunjee visited al-Roj but was prevented from seeing Begum, who was mourning her baby son: the child had been born healthy but died from pneumonia ten days after his birth. Children were reported to be drinking water from worm-infested tanks in the camp. Akunjee blamed the Conservative home secretary Sajid Javid for the baby boy's death – Javid had stripped Begum of her British citizenship – and, at that point, still hoped to bring her back to London. When she was first discovered in al-Hawl camp, Shamima spoke of her wish to 'come home' to London – such a telling phrase for one who'd chosen to live for four years among the zealous true believers of the caliphate. In the event, she could not come home: her British citizenship was revoked and she was designated a national security risk.

A British subject cannot be legally stripped of their citizenship if it renders them stateless, but the government argued Begum was not stateless because she was through her father also eligible for Bangladeshi citizenship. This was rejected by the Bangladesh government, which denied she was a dual national and said she would face the death penalty for terrorism if she ever entered the country.

'I wasn't born in Bangladesh, I've never seen Bangladesh and I don't even speak Bengali properly, so how can they claim I have Bangladeshi citizenship?' Begum told the BBC. 'I have one citizenship . . . and if you take that away from me, I don't have anything.'

In February 2021, the Supreme Court unanimously ruled that the British government had not breached Begum's human rights when it removed her citizenship, rendering her a citizen of nowhere. I asked Akunjee, the Begum family lawyer, if anyone still cared for Shamima in London. 'She has a mother who loves her, and she has her closest sister,' he said. 'But that's pretty much about it. The father's in Bangladesh – he was not really part of the picture of the family for a long time, long before these events. There are other sisters, but they're not on the scene.'

GOING UNDERGROUND

As I made my way from the East London Mosque to Whitechapel Tube Station, passing the Royal London Hospital, originally the London Infirmary, I was reminded of an old family story about one of my maternal ancestors who had died, probably from a heart attack, on the steps outside the hospital on the morning of his release after a long convalescence. He was a stevedore in the docks and one day a huge wooden plank tumbled from a ship and struck him across the lower back, rupturing his kidneys. He was taken to the London Hospital, where he had life-saving surgery. During the operation it was discovered that he had not two but four kidneys. He should have died because two of them had been ruptured in the accident, and yet he lived, only to die on the steps of the hospital as he said farewell to the nurses who had cared for him.

My paternal and maternal grandparents were East Enders and my father was born in Upton Park, before he moved with his parents to the next neighbourhood of Forest Gate and then, as a young married man, out to Harlow new town. We knew these streets around Whitechapel well because we used to visit one of my father's aged aunts who lived nearby in a block of flats in Stepney or travel in at weekends simply to walk and explore. My father had loved the lingering atmosphere of the old East End, loved that it had served as a vessel of migrations over the centuries: first the Huguenots arrived from France, then the Irish when

Ireland was still part of the United Kingdom, before the island of Ireland was partitioned, then Jewish people from the Pale of Settlement escaping Tsarist pogroms, and then, after the Second World War, the peoples from the old empire, especially Muslims from Pakistan and Bangladesh. Many of these arrivals settled in the east because it was the cheapest, most neglected part of the imperial capital and because there was work in the docks and in textiles. As the decades passed, people were leaving as well: working-class whites were moving out to Essex and Kent in search of new opportunities and better housing, especially in the years after the Blitz, and many Jews moved to north London or to southern Africa and the United States. The old Jewish East End now has a kind of spectral quality, a place of shadows and memories, an absent presence.

I loved the East End just as my father did, but for what it is today rather than for what it once was. My London was not the former Scottish First Minister Alex Salmond's London, a 'dark star', as he called it, 'inexorably sucking in resources, people and energy' from the rest of the country. The dominance of financial turbocapitalism unbalanced and distorted the British economy, as Salmond said as he made the case for Scottish independence in 2014. This had resulted in grotesque inequalities, regional imbalances, a dangerously inflated property market in the south-east and rapid demographic change; between 2001 and 2011, the population of white Londoners fell by 600,000 as people moved out in search of more affordable housing, even as the city grew by one million.

The so-called dark star is only one version of London, the city of the City, of financiers, *rentiers* and deracinated plutocrats. There are many other Londons, not least the gritty, intimate, creative city I know well, with its ethnically and culturally diverse polyglot population and thrilling possibilities. It is a city of discrete, interconnecting urban villages, and of resilient people – many of them young, many of them migrants – trying to make their way. It's notable that London also has the highest child poverty rate of any English region and several of the most deprived local authorities. It resists easy categorization and stereotype.

+ + +

As I made my way to the Tube station, bearded Muslim men wearing winter coats over their long tunics and *taqiyah* skullcaps gathered outside their shops selling Islamic books and merchandise; women dressed in black abayas and hijabs strolled by. This was a self-consciously separatist community but settled. What I took from my conversations with Mohammed Mahmoud is that, for a secular generation which has lost faith in established religion and perhaps sought redemption in politics, Islam is a direct challenge because it claims to have the answers to the foundational questions. What's the point of being alive? Who are we and what do we want? How do we live morally fulfilling lives? What does it mean to be part of a religious community, as well as a secular nation? Am I a British Muslim or a Muslim in Britain?

In the Light of What We Know (2014) is a novel by Zia Haider Rahman, a British Bangladeshi. The main protagonist, Zafar, born in a rural village in Bangladesh, as a young boy moves with his family to London. There he experiences poverty and alienation but also rides the escalator of education to reach Balliol College, Oxford, where he studies mathematics and bumps up against the ceiling of the English class system. After graduation, he becomes a successful banker but we first encounter him in 2008, now in disordered middle age, as the financial crisis grips. He is adrift, jobless and homeless, literally and metaphorically, and so moves into a room at an old university friend's grand house in west London. Zafar considers himself to be English but has never felt at home in England. He yearns to belong. 'If an immigration officer at Heathrow had ever said "Welcome home" to me,' Zafar tells his friend, the unnamed narrator, 'I would have given my life for England, for my country, there and then. I could kill for an England like that.'

Embedded in Zafar's remark, the narrator says, 'there was a longing for being part of something', a desire to be at home, and 'take root'.

For the true believer, Islam is both an ethical guide and a complete programme for living. It takes care of the politics and the ethics. It counters doubt with certainty, scepticism with faith. For those Muslims born in England who have embraced Islam with more ardour and determination than their parents ever did, religious commitment has enabled them to take root. Through Islam they have found a home because of the freedoms and greater tolerance they find in England – the freedom to be who they want to be.

People have died in murderous Islamist terror attacks but Britain has largely avoided the 'clash of civilizations' narrative that took hold in the United States and some other European countries. The state has not banned the hijab or religious symbols, as in France. Haunted by the crimes it committed in its former territories in North Africa, France seems, from the outside at least, to be locked in perpetual antagonism with its Muslim Arabs, and with those who would oppose the republican ideal of *laïcité*. The Church of England, by contrast, has been marginalized by successive governments so as to be little more than a shy adjunct of the secular state, as the philosopher Roger Scruton described it. There is no oppositional doctrine to Islam. Alastair Campbell, when he was head of communications for Tony Blair, boasted, 'We don't do God.' David Cameron said of his Christian faith that it was 'like Magic FM in the Chilterns, it comes and goes', a characteristically languid remark. Witty too.

For devout British Muslims faith is not a once-weekly recreation or something that comes and goes; it serves as a complete identity. The francophone Oxford academic philosopher Tariq Ramadan, since disgraced, used to enjoy defining multiculturalism as the 'Islamization of modernity'. This was a theme Michel Houellebecq explored in his novel *Submission* (2015), in which the Muslim Brotherhood, enabled by an alliance with a demoralized political left fearful of the popularity of the National Front, wins power in France and introduces sharia law.

Who speaks for British Muslims? And is England really the world's most Islamic country, as the imam of Finsbury Park said?

He knows it's an audacious claim, but its implications are worth considering seriously if we really want to understand who we are now.

'We are here because you were there,' Sufia Alam had said to me in her cheerful London accent. 'You will have to learn to live with us – because we aren't going anywhere.' I suppose I represented the 'you' of settled white British possession and she the 'we' of the Muslim diaspora. And what she said wasn't strictly true – but she and others I spoke to at the mosque believed it was, including Mohammed.

Sufia said this to me not to provoke but as a statement of fact. 'British Muslims are the grandchildren of the British Empire,' writes Ed Husain in *Among the Mosques* (2021), adding that it is estimated that the Muslim population in Britain will be thirteen million by 2050. Between 2001 and 2016 (the year a majority voted to 'take back control'), the whole population of England grew by nearly 11 per cent compared with 107 per cent for the Muslim population alone in the same period.

Like J. B. Priestley long before him, Ed Husain, an Arabic speaker, has been on a series of English journeys, and he travelled with explicit purpose: to find out what was going on in the mosques and communities of Muslim Britain. 'We are becoming separate tribes with different and opposing identities,' he writes. 'Because we cannot talk openly about Christian or atheist worries about Islam, or Islam's current fears of liberalism, we are all creating a huge void. Who will fill it?'

Husain is disturbed that the 'caliphism and clericalism' he encountered in many mosques are 'sequestering an entire community away from meaningful contact with mainstream Britain' – a version of Mohammed Mahmoud's 'self-ghettoization'. Unless it is confronted, Husain writes, 'white British people will respond to Muslim communalism by developing their own communalism, leading to increased far-right radicalism, which will in turn encourage many Muslims to become more insular and potentially more militant.'

He goes on to ask, what is Britain? 'The Shipping Forecast, while comforting for an island nation, does not tell us of the storms to come in the battle of ideas'.

+ + +

But I wasn't thinking of storms to come as, in the winter darkness, I turned towards the powdery glow of Whitechapel station. I was still thinking about what Sufia Alam had said to me at the Maryam Centre. As I went underground, I heard from not so far away the start of the *adhan*, the Muslim call to evening prayer, being broadcast presumably from the East London Mosque. I was late for my next appointment but nevertheless stopped to listen for a while to a sound that may one day be as familiar throughout England as church bells once were.

PART THREE

5 THE BREXIT MURDER

We tell ourselves stories in order to live.

Joan Didion

The men had been drinking for several hours by the time they arrived at The Stow shopping centre in Harlow. It was approaching midnight on a humid August bank holiday weekend. Arkadiusz Jozwik and his two companions – the men were Polish and lived and worked locally – were hungry and tired. Jozwik bought a pizza from a takeaway and sat on a wall to eat it. It was then that he noticed a group of teenagers nearby, some of them on bikes. The boys, and they were boys, aged fifteen and sixteen, approached and there was a confrontation. The men became loud and antagonistic, and, as each group goaded the other, one of the boys slipped out of the pack and sneaked up behind Jozwik, landing to the back of his head what would later be described in court as his 'Superman punch'.

Jozwik fell – perhaps partly because he was drunk, perhaps partly because he was off balance – and hit his head hard on the pavement, after which the boys panicked and fled. Jozwik was unconscious and blood leaked from his ears as he was taken by ambulance to the town's Princess Alexandra Hospital, from where he was later transferred to Addenbrooke's in Cambridge.

The next day Essex police described the attack on Jozwik as

'brutal' and called it a 'potential hate crime' – the suggestion being that he was assaulted because he was a foreigner and was heard speaking a foreign language, in his case Polish. That alerted the media to the possibility that what had happened on the night of Saturday, 27 August 2016, at The Stow shopping centre was more sinister than a mere routine late-night scrap that had gone seriously wrong. It was a hate crime, a political crime.

This was the febrile summer of the European referendum, when the air was rancid with accusation and counter-accusation and the country had never seemed more divided between those who wanted the United Kingdom to continue as a member of the European Union and those who wanted out; between 'Remainers' and 'Leavers', the identity markers of these strange new times. Like hundreds of thousands of other Poles who had moved to Britain in the years after former communist states from Eastern Europe joined the EU, Jozwik, who was single, believed life in England offered opportunities that his home country could not. In 2012 he followed his mother, a widow, to Essex because he did not want to be alone in Poland. He lived with her and found work in a sausage factory.

The day after the attack in The Stow six youths were arrested on suspicion of attempted murder. Then, on 29 August, Arkadiusz Jozwik – Arek to friends and family – died in hospital in Cambridge, having never regained consciousness. He was forty years old and had suffered a brain injury and a fractured skull.

To this day, no one has established the exact motivation for the attack – a witness reported that Jozwik racially abused one of the boys, who was black or mixed race – but whatever the motive, the impact of the punch that felled Jozwik was felt around the world. The *New York Times* reported that he was 'repeatedly pummelled and kicked by a group of boys and girls'; the BBC called it a 'frenzied racist attack triggered by the Brexit referendum'; the *Guardian* said it 'exposes the reality of post-referendum racism'. And soon it was being called the 'Brexit Murder' as the world's media arrived in the town to report on what had happened.

Every district in Essex voted Leave in the referendum of 23 June 2016 (the pro-Brexit vote in Harlow was 68 per cent compared with the national average of 52 per cent). After Jozwik's death, the Polish president Andrzej Duda wrote to religious leaders in Britain requesting their assistance in preventing further attacks on Polish nationals and the Polish ambassador to Britain was taken on a tour of Harlow. Around the same time, Polish police officers were sent from Warsaw to patrol the area around The Stow, and the Polish community organized a march of solidarity in the town.

'We Europeans can never accept Polish workers being beaten up, harassed or even murdered in the streets of Essex,' Jean-Claude Juncker, then president of the European Commission, said in an annual state of the union address.

The subtext of Juncker's intervention was this: the death of Arkadiusz Jozwik was a manifestation of the xenophobic forces unleashed by the referendum. Harlow and its people were implicated.

+ + +

In the final days of the referendum campaign, Jo Cox, the Labour MP for Batley and Spen, had been murdered by one of her own constituents, Thomas Mair, a fifty-three-year-old who lived alone and worked as a gardener. He shouted 'Britain first' as he attacked the MP in Birstall, and later accused her of being a traitor because she was a Remainer. She was among the brightest of the 2015 parliamentary intake. In London she lived with her husband and their two young children on a houseboat on the River Thames. Before going into politics, she had worked for Oxfam and developed a particular interest in human rights, foreign policy, the Middle East and humanitarian intervention. She was the first sitting member of Parliament to be murdered since Ian Gow in 1990. He was a close associate of Margaret Thatcher's and died after the IRA fitted a bomb on the underside of his car.

Jo Cox's murder seemed even more senseless for being so public: she was shot with a homemade gun and repeatedly stabbed outside a library on a bright summer afternoon as she went about her constituency business. The day before, Nigel Farage had unfurled a billboard poster depicting a long, ragged line of distressed Middle Eastern refugees under the slogan 'Breaking Point'. The meaning was explicit: they are coming here.

Even before the referendum, Jo Cox understood how divided the country was. In her maiden speech to the House of Commons, she shared what she'd discovered while travelling around her constituency, and she wanted to talk about hope. 'We are far more united and have far more in common with each other than things that divide us,' she said. 'Jo Cox might have been the best foreign secretary we never had,' the writer John Bew, a biographer of Clement Attlee, said after her death.

Reading mainstream reports during the referendum, you could have believed the country was besieged – or even at war. We had lost control of our borders! Immigrants were pouring in! Help! Stop! Take back control! Britain first!

The 'Brexit Murder' fitted this narrative of division and despair.

BACK TO THE FUTURE

Sometimes I dream about Harlow. I was born at home, in a rented maisonette in the old village of Potter Street, with just a midwife to keep watch on my mother as my father waited anxiously with my four-year-old sister in another room. I was educated at various state schools in the town and lived there for the first eighteen years of my life.

In these dreams I am who I am – middle-aged, a husband and father – but I'm invariably back in the house in the quiet cul-de-sac on a private estate where we lived as a family of five from 1972 to 1983 and where I spent most of my childhood and adolescence before my parents, unsettled by the decline of the town, moved to Hertfordshire. My father, lucid and calm as he ever was, is alive in these dreams, and I have a sense of having the conversations that his sudden death from a heart attack at the age of fifty-six never allowed us to have.

There was a time, when I first began working in London in my mid-twenties, that I never wanted to be reminded of where I grew up. I could scarcely admit that I was an Essex man, Harlow-born.

There was a blockage. A desire to forget or escape. It was as if I was embarrassed about something I couldn't quite articulate, something to do with the gradations of the English class system and people's perceptions of Harlow as a failed town, as 'Chav Town'.

+ + +

Located at the junction of First Avenue and Howard Way, The Stow opened in the early 1950s as the first of the new town's neighbourhood shopping centres. But, as with so many of the once-fine public and civic spaces, it has been neglected. I know The Stow well. Our family dentist had his surgery there and, when I was in primary school, after each visit to see him, my mother would treat me to a hot sausage roll or sugar-encrusted jam doughnut from Dorringtons, a family bakery which today still occupies the same space in the two-tier shopping centre, close to where Arkadiusz Jozwik was punched, fell and hit his head.

When I returned to The Stow one afternoon, drawn back by interest in the 'Brexit Murder', I was shocked at how shabby and neglected it was. In the pedestrian-only precinct, pound and charity shops – the RSPCA and Salvation Army occupied what were once prime sites – and scrappy fast-food joints proliferated. There was a tattoo and body-piercing shop. A Thai massage parlour was adjacent to an undertaker, a sly juxtaposition of sex and death that would have amused Freud. The Essex Skipper – the original pubs in the town were mostly named after butterflies or moths, just as some of the roads were later renamed after left-wing political heroes, Mandela Avenue, Allende Avenue and so on – was run down and unwelcoming.

It was an unseasonably warm afternoon yet the area seemed desolate. When I returned to my car, three young men were sitting on a wall next to it. One of them introduced himself by saying, 'Good car!' He spoke heavily accented English. He and his friends turned out to be Romanians, recent arrivals, and when I asked what life was like for Eastern Europeans in the town they weren't interested in telling me. I asked if they worked. They said they did not. How long had they been here? Not long. They believed they were coming to a new town. But Harlow wasn't new. It looked old.

NEW TOWN BLUES

My parents arrived in 1959 when there were fewer than 6,000 people in the town (today the population is 86,000 and rising). They had been child wartime evacuees and, because their education was interrupted, they both left school at fifteen, my father (who passed up a scholarship to study engineering) to work as an apprentice shirt cutter and my mother as an assistant in a City of London law firm.

My parents were delighted by how rural Harlow was when they arrived: for the first time in his life my father suffered from hay fever, which mysteriously disappeared whenever he returned for any length of time to the city or travelled overseas. For my parents, moving to Harlow was a form of escape: away from the bomb sites and ruined Victorian buildings and streets of east London and, they were sure, towards a more optimistic future. From the old to the new, always embracing the new.

It was essential to the vision of Frederick Gibberd, the chief architect-planner, that Harlow combined town and country, the urban and rural: he wanted open countryside inside and surrounding the town. He wanted to create 'a fine contrast between the work of man and the work of God'. The valley of the River Stort formed the northern boundary and, as Gibberd wrote, 'small hamlets and fine woods [were] interspersed throughout the area'. Woodcroft, Willowfield, Old Orchard, Lower Meadow, Barley Croft, Hilly Field, Five Acres: the names of the new council or corporation estates were redolent of a pastoral idyll, the lost lands on which the town was built, self-contained district by district. Unlike the surrounding towns – Hemel, Stevenage, Hatfield, Welwyn that were being extended and developed – Harlow in rural west Essex would be completely new, and 60 per cent of the land was compulsorily purchased from one owner, Commander Godfrey Arkwright, the head of an old hunting and landowning family. The first arrivals there considered themselves pioneers, marking out new territory.

Lord Reith, the first director general of the BBC, was chairman of the New Towns Committee. For Reith, the new towns were 'essays in civilization', and he wanted the people in them to have 'a happy and gracious way of life'. Continuing this theme, Sir Ernest Gowers, the first chairman of the Development Corporation and author of a book for civil servants on plain speaking, said of Harlow that it was 'too good to be true'.

In moving the second reading of the New Towns Bill in Parliament in 1946, Labour's Lewis Silkin returned to Thomas More's Utopia. 'My researches on new towns go back to the time of Sir Thomas More,' he said. 'It is a long cry from More's Utopia, to the New Towns Bill, but it is not unreasonable to expect that that "Utopia" of 1515 should be translated into practical reality in 1946.'

In an eloquent speech, Silkin said that 'our new towns must be beautiful'. The ambition was to create a 'new type of citizen' who would have a 'sense of beauty, culture and civic pride'. He continued:

'Cicero said: "A man's dignity is enhanced by the home he lives in". I say, even more by the town he lives in. In the long run, the new towns will be judged by the kind of citizens they produce, by whether they create this spirit of friendship, neighbourliness and comradeship. That will be the real test, and that will be my objective so long as I have any responsibility for these new towns.'

Later, in 1949, the Labour government also created the 1949 National Parks Bill, which Silkin described, in characteristic style, as 'a people's charter for the open air'.

The emphasis in Harlow in those early years was always on novelty – on new hope, new beginnings, new citizens, and on the vitality and promise of youth. Don't look back. Never look back. Yet, in the 1960s, there were reports of a phenomenon that became known as 'new town blues' – the experience of dislocation and isolation felt by those who were struggling to adapt to new ways of living or who simply mourned the loss of the old urban communities.

But I knew nowhere else. By the time I was born, Harlow was known as 'pram town' because of all the young couples starting families there, and the birth rate was three times higher than the national average. Henry Moore, whose house and studio were in the nearby Hertfordshire hamlet of Perry Green, was commissioned to create a stone sculpture for public display that would symbolize the radiant promise of the new town.

Today, Moore's The Harlow Family Group, 2.5 metres high and weighing 1.5 tonnes, is situated in the expansive entrance area to the town's civic centre. A man and woman sit side by side, proud and upright. The man's right arm is wrapped protectively around the woman and she is holding a young child. At its unveiling outside St Mary-at-Latton Church, in Mark Hall Park, in 1956, Sir Kenneth Clark, chairman of the Arts Council of Great Britain, called Moore's sculpture a symbol of the 'new humanitarian civilization' that had emerged from the devastation of the Second World War.

The Harlow Family Group was one of many pieces by notable artists such as Barbara Hepworth, Leon Underwood, Ralph Brown, Elisabeth Frink, Gerda Rubinstein, Auguste Rodin, Karel Vogel bought and commissioned by the Harlow Arts Trust, which was set up in 1953 and supported by philanthropists and the town corporation. It was paternalistic, this desire to create public art for ordinary working people, but the motivation was pure. 'So often sculpture is a sort of cultural concession that has little relevance to the real life of a town but, in [this] case, it has become an integral part of Harlow,' Gibberd said in 1964. He wanted the town to be 'home to the finest works of art, as in Florence and other splendid cities'.

+ + +

This was an era – hard to believe now – when London was depopulating. Before he was married, my father, the only child of a London bus driver, lived in a terraced house in Forest Gate, which, as the name suggests, is where the East End begins to thin out and merges into Epping Forest. My father was a bright boy and a gifted cricketer, and he and his mother were frustrated by the life that was being mapped out for him (his father, Frank, who boxed recreationally in the East End pubs, was a quiet, kindly, unambitious man). He did not want to follow his father onto the buses or work in the docks as some of his family had done. Nor did he want to emigrate to Australia, like one of his uncles – from whom he later inherited the money that enabled him to buy his first house. My father was culturally aspirational. Encouraged by his fiercely protective, austere, red-haired mother (she used to wear a brooch displaying a photograph of her son, whom she called 'everyone's favourite'), he dressed smartly, read poetry, listened to jazz music and bought the *Observer* every Sunday for the books and arts reviews. He liked the theatre and was enchanted by Hollywood. He adored the Marx brothers and W. C. Fields. The East End of his late adolescence was not today's vibrant, polyglot, multi-ethnic realm of hipster bars, boho tech start-ups, barista masterclasses, loft conversions, Balti curry houses, craft-beer festivals, Tinder and Grindr hook-ups, smart clubs and astronomical property prices. He thought he could do better by leaving.

Yet something happened to my father in middle age, a period when his good career in what he always called the 'rag trade' seemed to drift and stall, and he became increasingly nostalgic and introspective. He began to brood on the old world he'd left behind as a young man – the sense of community he'd known as a child, the spirit of friendship, the neighbourliness. Perhaps very belatedly he, too, was suffering from new town blues. He listened repeatedly to music from the 1940s, especially the popular songs of Al Bowlly, the southern African crooner killed by a German parachute bomb that exploded outside his London flat in 1941. 'Oh, no, he's going on about the war years again,' we used to tease. He showed me some of the poems he wrote, always set in the East End during the early 1940s or just at the end of the war. One was called 'Don't Cheer Us Girls We're British', an ironic slogan he'd seen written on a jeep carrying troops along a road close to where he lived.

My father was a war child. The first day of the Blitz, 7 September 1940 – 'Black Saturday' – a day of transcendent blue skies, coincided with his sixth birthday. He was so traumatized by the experience of the assault on the docklands and nearby neighbour-hoods – he recalled burning buildings and an apocalyptic red glow in the sky – that he lost his voice. His father, the bus driver, refused to leave the family home during subsequent intense bombing raids. My father and his mother would hurry to an air-raid shelter when-ever they heard the sirens warning of an imminent Luftwaffe attack; but Frank would stay in the house, even as nearby buildings were being hit and destroyed.

Towards the end of his life, my father spoke often about how the depredations but also the intensity of a child's experience of the home front, and indeed the urgency of wartime more generally, united the people around him: there was a commonality of purpose, a conviction that if they could endure, if they could get through the worst, the future would be better. Which is why Harlow seemed so attractive to him. He believed in Kenneth Clark's vision of a new humanitarian civilization.

War and the wartime command economy (Labour leader Clement Attlee officially became Churchill's deputy prime minister in the coalition government in February 1942, though he was the effective deputy as Lord Privy Seal from May 1940) created the conditions for socialism and a new settlement in Britain. 'The re-volution in England has already begun,' H. G. Wells said on 22 May 1940 when Attlee introduced the Emergency Powers Defence Bill in the House of Commons and sandbags went up across Westminster.

Wells was inspired by the transformation in the structure of the British state. For him, socialism represented modernity, and the socialist state was the only practical means to survive great power competition. In essence, the war required the state to take control of the economy, employment and production. The barri-cades went up, the government assumed Cromwellian powers and the revolution began.

For Orwell, who admired the patriotism of the working class, the 'English revolution' meant something different and it gathered momentum with the epic retreat from Dunkirk. Orwell was interested in a revolution in conception and self-image. That was why he was so taken with the idea of the English officer class adopting what were essentially socialist prescriptions for the country. 'Like all else in England, it happens in a sleepy, unwilling way, but it is happening,' he wrote of the English revolution. 'The war has speeded it up, but it has also increased, and desperately, the necessity for speed.'

Perhaps Wells and Orwell meet over the sheer ambition of the post-war project, which held out the promise of the state transforming not just production and the economy but the people themselves, lifting their eyes upwards. It's useless to imagine, Orwell said, that 'you can defeat Hitler without disturbing the status quo'. The impulse to defend one's country and make it a place worth living in were the same. By enveloping the people, the enabling state would set them free as Gibberd, Gowers and Silkin would have wished.

THE ENGLISH REVOLUTION

To grow up in Harlow, all those years ago, was to be on the front line of the English revolution, to be one of Silkin's new citizens. More than this, you were a cog in a grand social, political and economic experiment. I understand this now, but back then it meant nothing to me. I was just living. My friends and I were children of the welfare state. The social transformations and central planning of the immediate post-war period, as the new Labour government set about building what Attlee called a 'New Jerusalem', had created thrilling possibilities. The National Health Service was established; the National Insurance Act abolished the hated means test for welfare provision; essential industries such as the railways and mining were nationalized; the Town and Country Planning Act was passed, opening the way for mass housebuilding and the redevelopment of huge tracts of land, as well as the creation of the Green Belt; Britain's independent nuclear deterrent was commissioned; the gap between rich and poor narrowed.

This was a very British revolution, and a pragmatic experiment with socialism: the state was powerful but not all-powerful. It was not a vindictive exercise in destruction but one of creation: about a new social contract between the state and the individual to enhance the common good. The monarchy, the landowning families and the ancient public schools (Attlee was a proud Haileyburian) were untouched. Individual freedom and the great British institutions were cherished. The cost of war had impoverished the nation, left it with a ruinous trade deficit and ended Britain's imperial hegemony. But these were new times. Progressive change was not only possible, it was believed to be necessary. As Attlee recognized, the British people 'wanted a new start'. They had suffered and they had endured. Now, he said, they were 'looking towards the future'.

Our lives as children were socially engineered and it seemed everything we needed was provided by the state: housing, education, health care, libraries, recreational and sports facilities. There were play schemes (summer camps) where we gathered to take part in organized games during the long school holidays. Harlow had a network of cycle tracks, among the most extensive in the country, which connected all neighbourhoods to the town centre, the High, and to the two main industrial areas, Temple Fields and the Pinnacles. In 1961, a multipurpose sports centre, the first of its kind in Britain, was opened. It was funded by local people through voluntary contributions via their rates (Connie was an enthusiastic contributor).

One friend has since described the experience of growing up in the town in the sixties and seventies as 'East Germany without the Stasi'. Those of us born and raised there were referred to as 'citizens of the future'. Rural spaces (the so-called green wedges of the master plan, one of which became the town park, with its skating rink, bandstand, nine-hole pitch and putt golf course and animal centre) and planned recreation areas for children were meant to encourage us to lead healthy, active lives and to play in safety. In the words of the 1958 public information film about Harlow, 'If these boys and girls don't grow up to face successfully the problems of their day, it will not be the fault of the architects and planners who helped to give them a start.'

What I didn't realize then was that Harlow was, in effect, a monoculture. The original aspiration was to create a 'classless' society but, growing up there, it felt mostly as if you were living in a one-class town – that was, working class. There was a small middle-class intelligentsia, who participated in Labour Party politics, in the local drama, literary and film societies and who gathered around the Playhouse, which had opened in 1971 for live theatre, films and exhibitions. My father, whose interests were cultural rather than political, was part of this scene.

But nearly everyone I met was white working class. Out of the 250 or so children in my year at secondary school – a huge non-selective, mixed-ability comprehensive, opened in 1959 and enlarged in 1972, one of eight in the town – I remember one boy whose family was Hong Kong Chinese (he ended up running an oriental restaurant in Germany) and two girls whose parents were Indian. Everyone else was white. My classmates' parents had, for the most part, come from the East End or the poorer parts of north London, such as Edmonton or Walthamstow, and many worked in the town's factories and manufacturing plants: the International Telephone and Telegraph Corporation (which by the end of the 1970s employed 8,000 people), the Cossor Group, Revertex Chemicals, Johnson Matthey Metals, Schreiber, Pitney Bowes, United Glass.

These companies had their own social clubs and sports teams, even boys' football teams, which I played against in the recreational league for Newtown Spartak, a name more redolent of the Soviet Union.

Before the introduction of Margaret Thatcher's Right to Buy scheme, which enabled tenants to buy their council houses at a large discount, most of the houses in the town were owned by the council or town corporation. (Even today, a third of the housing stock in Harlow is council-owned.) Yet from 1972 we owned our house and lived on one of the few private developments, or executive estates as they were known. This set us apart somewhat. This and the fact that my father did not work locally in one of the factories but commuted to London, driving there in his Alfa Romeo rather than taking the train. Because he worked in the rag trade – designing, range-building, merchandising – he wore fashionable, often flamboyant clothes, and he travelled widely and often – to India, Bangladesh, Hong Kong, the United States, South Korea.

My father had studied at night school and was unusually articulate – 'posh', my friends called him. But he wasn't posh: he simply did not speak with the local accent, which today we call 'Estuary English', the dialect associated with people living in and around London, especially close to the River Thames and its estuary. My mother called it 'sub-cockney', distinguishing it from the accent of her father, a hard-working and thrifty carpenter who was born, as she liked to remind us, 'within the sound of the Bow Bells' (the bells of St Mary-le-Bow Church, Cheapside), a badge of honour worn by true cockneys.

Daily life at my secondary school was a process of negotiation and adaptation: I could not speak there as freely and candidly as I did at home. At home, if I spoke as I did at school, my mother would chasten me for my glottal stops and h-dropping. At school, if I spoke as I did at home, I would have been mocked as 'posh', a grave insult. If some of my classmates visited our book-cluttered house, I used to hide my father's magazines – the *New Statesman*, the *Listener*, *i-D*, *City Limits* – and newspapers because he did not read the *Sun* or the *Mirror*, like their fathers. I was frustrated that he did not conform to Harlow norms, even though the conformity I wished upon him would have been a betrayal of all that he wanted, who he was, his great expectations. Sometimes when he was out, I'd open his wardrobe and be overwhelmed by the warm, seductive smell of his clothes. I was especially fascinated by his two-colour shoes and exotic shirts and bright ties. Why did he dress so unlike those classmates' fathers who wore donkey jackets and DM boots to work?

There was little sense, in the five years I spent at comprehensive school (I left at sixteen to do A levels at Harlow College), that we were being prepared for university or the professions. I once mentioned, on a whim, that I'd like to study law without knowing what that would have entailed. I was told by a teacher that law was for 'private-school boys', as if that was the end of the matter. *It was useful to get that learnt.* Most weeks it was a case of getting through and getting by. Woodwork, metalwork, motor vehicle studies and home economics were among the subjects. I was hopeless at all of them.

The headmaster – who was falsely rumoured to have fought in the Spanish Civil War – was dictatorial and belligerent. Short, stocky and bald headed, he did not so much walk as strut angrily. He was missing a finger from one of his hands and we fantasized about how he might have lost it. If he'd once had ideals – I discovered decades later that he was a committed communist and was almost blocked from becoming head of the school because of his politics – they didn't seem to inform his style of leadership. The only time I saw him show any emotion other than rage was when, with passionate intensity, he recited in assembly one morning

Wilfred Owen's protest poem 'Dulcet et Decorum Est'. Whenever he strode into the dining hall at lunchtime we looked down at our plates as a chill settled over the room, as if the large windows that overlooked the playground had been thrown open on a winter's day. The ritual was unchanging: the headmaster would shout, rap a coin furiously on one of the tables before shunting several of them across the floor, as if there was some perfect alignment into which he was forever trying to force them. He would then leave the room in a hurry, seemingly embarrassed by what had just happened.

The late 1970s and early 1980s was a period of profound social unrest: football hooliganism, industrial strikes, inner-city race riots, the rise of the skinhead movement and the neo-fascists of the National Front. There seemed to be a psychological connection between the aggression and violence some of us experienced in our daily lives – fights in the playground or in the streets or in pubs or on the terraces – and what was happening in wider society as the post-war political and economic consensus unravelled. With the election of Margaret Thatcher in 1979, Britain was entering another period of revolutionary – or, more accurately, counter-revolutionary – change. A new era had begun.

+ + +

My father liked to remind us that we owed our opportunities as citizens of the future to the idealism of the war generation. But progress isn't inevitable. There's no guarantee that things will keep getting better. Ron Bill, an associate of my mother who worked for the Harlow Development Corporation in its early days, once told me that he and his colleagues had 'reached for Utopia'. 'The town attracted progressives, community-minded people,' he said. 'Frederick Gibberd was an example of such a person. That first wave of people who came to the town in the fifties and sixties

– many of them socialists and communists – they wanted to build something. The trouble is, there wasn't a second wave equal to the first.'

Utopia comes from the Greek and translates as nowhere or no place. Harlow is often called a nowhere zone or left-behind town. *News from Nowhere* was the title of William Morris's futuristic novel about a socialist Utopia. There was only bad news from Harlow following Arkadiusz Jozwik's death in the summer of the referendum.

The suggestion in much of the initial reporting of the so-called Brexit Murder was that in reaching for Utopia the town's pioneers and planners had ended up creating the opposite of what was intended: an anti-utopia. A dystopia.

THE LOST BOY

I went to Chelmsford Crown Court to hear Judge Patricia Lynch deliver her verdict on the Jozwik case. Before proceedings began, I sat in a tatty reception area outside the courtroom directly opposite to where the teenage defendant's family waited. Almost a year had passed since Arkadiusz Jozwik had died, and the defendant, who could not be named for legal reasons, was now sixteen. His family – including his mother and grandmother – were suspicious of my interest and did not want to be interviewed when I approached them. The youth just looked at me blankly. I gave the family my contact details and asked if they would call me, but they never did. I followed up with several phone calls to their solicitor in Old Harlow. But the family had chosen silence.

That afternoon I spoke to the defendant's uncle as he smoked a cigarette in the sunshine outside the court building. He was in his twenties, had a sleeve of tattoos on one arm and expressed bewilderment about what had happened at The Stow. Inside, the youth wore a white shirt several sizes too big, a loosely knotted thick dark tie and plain black trousers. He was short for his age, had a wavy fringe and a wispy moustache. He seemed lost and, at times, even bored as he sat in the box, watched anxiously by his mother. She had a heavy cold, though it was high summer, and I noticed her nails were bitten down to stubs.

The mother looked sadly unsurprised as her son was convicted by a jury of the manslaughter. Jenny Hopkins, chief Crown prosecutor, said she was satisfied that there had been no intent by the youth to kill Arkadiusz Jozwik. It was not a racist attack or hate crime, as had been reported. 'We decided therefore that the correct charge was one of manslaughter,' she said. The court was told the youth had put 'the full force of his body into the punch' and he must have been aware 'when he punched Mr Jozwik in this way that some harm was likely to be caused'.

The chief prosecutor continued, 'This was a senseless assault and with that one punch, which was over in seconds, the youth was responsible for Mr Jozwik losing his life and causing unimaginable anguish to Mr Jozwik's family and friends.'

The judge announced that sentencing would take place on Friday, 8 September. By this time, the media were losing interest in the case. This was no Brexit murder.

+ + +

One rainy morning, I went to see the then head of Harlow Council, an animated Labour councillor called Jon Clempner. He was angry at how, in his view, Essex police had mishandled the Jozwik case, allowing the fires of rumour and allegation to rage out of control. 'The police knew within twenty-four hours that it was not a racist attack or a murder. But they did not close down the speculation until it was too late,' he said. His office was in the civic centre overlooking the Water Gardens, which were originally designed by Frederick Gibberd as a series of parallel terraces and have since been reconfigured and truncated. From the wide, high window, I looked out across the Water Gardens, over a car park, cycle track, some woodland and nearby fields through which I once ran an inter-school cross-country race. Beyond these fields I could see in the far distance the housing estate where my grandfather came to live after he retired, so that he could be closer to his son, who would die before him. He stayed on in Harlow, alone, long after we had left.

Something was missing, however: the high-rise modernist town hall, once considered to be the town's most significant building in its most important space, the civic square. It was demolished in the mid-2000s as part of the first phase of the redevelopment of the semi-derelict town centre. A huge Asda supermarket now occupied the space where the town hall once stood in imposing isolation, like a monumental watchtower.

One afternoon, many years ago, while on a school trip to the High when I still lived in the town, some friends and I detached ourselves from the group and slipped illicitly into the town hall. Local rumour had it that there was a nuclear bunker in the basement and we wanted to find it. But, instead, we took the lift up to the observation tower, where we found ourselves quite alone. We looked out across the surrounding landscape. There, laid out before us, were the cool, clean geometric patterns of the town in which we lived, with its centrally planned network of roads, avenues and cycle tracks, its schools and factories and council estates and green wedges. We remained in the observation tower until it was almost dark, watching in wonder as the lights in the distant houses below were switched on, one by one, their amber shimmer illuminating the grid-like structures on which the town was built. And then the houses seemed to melt away and I tried to imagine what it must have been like here before the new town came, the rural tranquillity and the emptiness, the very absence of people.

CRIME AND PUNISHMENT

On 8 September 2017, the sixteen-year-old boy from Harlow was sentenced to three and a half years in a young offender institution for the manslaughter of Arkadiusz Jozwik. Passing sentence, Judge Patricia Lynch said that Jozwik had been a 'perfectly decent, well-loved man in his prime'. He would be mourned by his family. As the judge spoke, you could hear people in the courtroom sobbing. 'A year has passed since Arek died but every day I miss him as much,' Ewa Jozwik, his mother, said in a statement read out in court. 'There are moments I don't want to live any more.' She was present for the sentencing and wept continuously.

For the defence, Patrick Upward said that the youth, who once again wore a white shirt and black tie as he sat in the defendant box, felt 'remorse' at what had happened – he nodded when he heard this – and made reference to his troubled family background and the serious illness of his father. The court heard that he had two previous convictions, one for threatening behaviour, yet was 'not far removed from being a youngster of good character despite those difficulties'.

In her final address, Judge Lynch said that the defendant had fled the shopping centre after the attack and done 'nothing for the welfare of the deceased'. When the sentence was announced, the youth – who resembled more than ever a lost boy – waved meekly at his family and stumbled slightly as he left the box. His mother, crying now, shouted, 'I love you.' She and other family members hurried out of the courtroom and could be heard crying in the corridor.

It was raining as Ewa Jozwik left the court building in Chelmsford. Asked by waiting reporters outside, several from Polish television stations, if she believed the sentence was fair, she shook her head in a forlorn gesture of frustration or defeat. 'All the time

I can see in my mind the moment I saw him lying motionless in the hospital bed connected to the life-support machine,' she said of her dead son. 'I wanted him to wake up badly.'

Arkadiusz Jozwik is buried in Harlow and the inscription on his gravestone is YOU WERE A DREAM, NOW YOU ARE A MEMORY.

Reflecting on the case, I felt only sorrow – for Jozwik, of course, and those who loved him, but also for the incarcerated youth, 'not far removed from being a youngster of good character', and his family. I felt sorrow, too, for Harlow, which – in the immediate aftermath of Jozwik's death, as the town was flooded with reporters and Polish police patrolled The Stow shopping centre – had come to symbolize all that was perceived to be rotten in England. The vote for Brexit had revealed a fractious and fractured country. Harlow, a once-utopian settlement, was one of the forgotten towns, with a disenchanted and xenophobic population. It had been locked out from prosperity, as if part of another country altogether.

RETURN JOURNEYS

It's taken me a long time to recalibrate the experience of growing up in Harlow. Most of the children I knew, some clever and gifted, never considered for a moment that university was a possibility for them and they contentedly left full-time education as soon as they could. When I first started working in London and spoke to colleagues who'd been to grand schools and lived overseas as children, I thought I didn't have a story to tell and so remained silent about my childhood in Harlow. It seemed far too ordinary. But I now understand just how extraordinarily ambitious the new town experiment was.

Like most of my peers, I very nearly didn't make it to university. I rebelled at Harlow College, missing classes or repeatedly turning up late for them, before eventually dropping out. I used to spend my days talking about doing great things while doing nothing much at all. In my late teens, I found a job as a clerk at the Electricity Council, at Millbank in London. I couldn't afford the train fare so commuted on a coach from my parents' house in a small Hertfordshire town on the River Stort, a journey that took two or three hours on some days because of traffic congestion, and then you had to do it again in reverse in the evening. But it was during those coach journeys that I began reading seriously for the first time. Boredom and inertia became a spur to action.

After six months working as a clerk in a labyrinthine public-sector bureaucracy, I decided to cram-study for A levels. In other words, I gave myself nine months to change my life. This time, I would study politics, in which I had an intensifying interest, and English literature at an evening class. As a result, I came under the influence of a man called David Huband, the kind of inspirational teacher I'd never encountered before, the *one* teacher we all need to meet. He knew people who knew my father and he took particular interest in me. He must have sensed that I was in trouble, existentially alarmed, adrift.

The three hours I spent in his company every Thursday evening, from seven to ten, changed how I thought about the world, and those nine months, from September 1985 to May 1986, working at the Electricity Council, reading and listening to music while on the coach and studying at weekends at Harlow Library or at home, were transformative. At the end of the summer, I left for university: in one bound, I believed I was finally free from Harlow and all its associations, never looking back. Forward, forward, forward.

+ + +

One recent day I went on a bike ride around Harlow: the cycle tracks, though more rutted and uneven than I remember them from my childhood, remain among the lasting achievements of the town. I know few people there nowadays and visit only very occasionally to see my aunt. On one such visit to see Connie, the occasion of her ninety-third birthday, rather than go straight home afterwards, I drove around estates I once knew so well, along roads still familiar, past fields where we used to play. I pulled up outside St Mary Magdalene's Church in Potter Street where long ago I was an altar boy – until playing Sunday-morning football liberated me from the unloved routine.

I'm not sure what I was looking for. I even retraced my morning walk to secondary school, which involved making my way along an alleyway that ran between the gardens of two houses at the end of which teenagers used to cluster intimidatingly while smoking. For amusement or out of boredom they kicked holes in the wooden garden fences and, though they were only one hundred metres or so from the school gates, there were never any teachers around to caution them. On that return visit, as I stood in a car park that had once been our playground, it was as if I could hear the thrilling sound of children's voices all around and, in my chest, I felt tightness, the burning sensation of long-dormant frustrations and regrets.

The school closed several decades ago, and yet there have been days when I have imagined wandering its corridors as if in a dream, entering classrooms that no longer existed, recalling moments that could never be repeated, mistakes that could never be undone. We have appointments to keep in the past . . .

+ + +

Today there are signs of significant renewal in Harlow: 8,500 new homes are being built as part of the Gilston Park Estate development, set out in six 'garden villages' as the town expands north of the train station and the Stort Valley; Public Health England is building a new science and research campus and headquarters which will create thousands of new jobs; an Enterprise Zone is attracting inward investment; a new hospital has been commissioned; the town centre, once so lively on market day, is being redeveloped and will, at last, become fully residential. Harlow is fortuitously situated in the so-called London–Stansted–Cambridge life sciences corridor. It need not be left behind or defined by its past.

In common with most of the other post-war new towns, Harlow declined, especially after the remit of the Development Corporation ended, largely because of a lack of capital investment and the failure to renew its housing estates and infrastructure. Many of the large factories and manufacturing plants closed or relocated, creating unemployment and a loss of collective purpose. As early as 1953, the *New Statesman* warned that, without greater investment, the new towns would bear 'for the rest of their life the marks of early malnutrition'.

From the beginning of the new town, there were obvious flaws in the master plan, most significantly creating a non-residential town centre. Some of the early modish flat-roofed council estates, close to where we lived and known locally as 'the concrete jungle' and 'the Kasbah' because of their oppressively narrow alleyways, were pioneering experiments in modernist design. Less consideration was given to what it was like to live on these brutalist estates, some of which had to be pulled down in later decades because they were built using inadequate materials and failed to meet the government's 'decent homes' standard. Plus, Gibberd did not plan for the preponderance of motor cars, and today many of the small front gardens in the estates have been concreted over to provide space for them.

More recently, former commercial and office blocks in the town centre – notably Terminus House, the tallest building in Harlow since the demolition of the town hall – have been converted, under permitted development rules introduced by the Cameron government, into densely compressed residential units. London councils have dispatched tenants from their areas, many of them unemployed, to live in these residential blocks, now associated with crime and anti-social behaviour. According to the Local Government Association, more than half of all new homes created in Harlow in the year 2019 were from office block conversions. This was not what Frederick Gibberd envisaged for the town; this was never part of the masterplan. 'Our new towns must be beautiful,' as Lewis Silkin said, and former office block conversions were not sites of 'beauty, culture and civic pride'. Nor did they nurture the spirit of friendship, neighbourliness and comradeship – the founding values of the new town.

+ + +

As an energetic, sports-obsessed boy, so much of what I relished when I was growing up – the town swimming pool, the sports centre, the playschemes, the pitch and putt in the park, the imposing and mysterious town hall – was allowed to decay beyond usefulness or was demolished. But perhaps the truth is that the second generation who were born in Harlow and had no experience of wartime or life elsewhere did not believe in the possibilities of the town as their parents had. For them, it just happened to be where they lived, nothing more or less. The children of the idealistic middle class did not stay in the town: they moved on and out – to university, into the world, and often to London, an inversion of their parents' original journey.

There was no second wave of progressives committed to the new town dream.

If I once thought I disliked the town or was embarrassed by my associations with it, I no longer feel that way. I'm grateful the wartime generation reached for Utopia. Was Harlow too good to be true, as Sir Ernest Gowers said? Somewhere along the way it ceased to be special. It ceased to be new. And perhaps towns should grow organically rather than being centrally planned or imposed on people. For me Harlow was always somewhere, not no place or nowhere; it is where I was born and lived for the first eighteen years of life. It is my hometown, for better and for worse, and its story is also the story in microcosm of England since the end of the Second World War – of what the English revolution got right and what it got wrong.

6 STRETCHING THE FLAG

One June morning in the first summer of the pandemic, Patrick Hutchinson, a fifty-year-old personal trainer, security guard and martial arts expert, was playing with his two young grandchildren at home in London when he received a message on his phone from a friend. He opened it and clicked on a link to what turned out to be a propaganda video of Tommy Robinson, formerly of the English Defence League, urging his followers to disrupt a Black Lives Matter (BLM) rally planned for later that afternoon in central London. Hutchinson was 'sickened' by Robinson's provocations just as he had been a few weeks earlier when he'd watched a video of a police officer killing a middle-aged African American named George Floyd in Minneapolis. The assault on Floyd had been captured on a cell phone and shared widely and Hutchinson wept as he watched it. 'It was one of the worst things I'd ever seen, and I've seen some terrible things on the internet,' he said.

The murder of George Floyd was the spark that ignited a conflagration. It led to sustained protests in support of the Black Lives Matter movement in American cities as the campaign for racial justice gathered widespread cultural and political support, but not from Donald Trump in the White House. George Floyd died after a police officer forcefully placed a knee on his throat for at least eight minutes after Floyd had been wrestled to the ground outside a shop. 'I can't breathe!' Floyd pleaded as the officer squeezed the very breath of life out of him. As he died, Floyd called out for his mother and his final, despairing plea was heard round the world during a period when so many people were dying from Covid-19 because they could not breathe. 'We can't breathe' became a rallying cry not only for African Americans but also for black Britons who felt suffocated by racial injustice and who, together with other minority ethnic groups, were being killed or affected in disproportionate numbers by the virus.

The British university-educated left is not alone in being inspired by US social justice politics: the BBC treats American domestic events as if they were directly relevant to Britain, as if the two cultures were more similar than they are, and the murder of Floyd led all news bulletins for several days. The BLM protests spread to British cities and they seemed to unlock something long suppressed: a reckoning with racial justice. In Bristol angry protestors, most of them young and white, pulled from its plinth a Grade-II listed statue of Edward Coulson, a merchant, slave-trader and philanthropist, and dragged it into the nearby harbour; in other cities and towns statues of historical figures associated with imperialism or the slave trade, such as Cecil Rhodes, were targeted. In *The Wretched of the Earth* Franz Fanon wrote about a 'world of statues: the statue of the general who carried out the conquest, the statue of the engineer who built the bridges; a world which is sure of itself, which crushes with its stones the backs flayed by whips'. Now statues were falling and Robinson and other self-styled 'football lads' were mounting a counter-offensive against what they believed was a woke insurgency: an assault on white identity and Britain's proud heritage.

Together with five friends, also martial arts enthusiasts, Hutchinson decided to act. 'When Tommy Robinson invited those guys down, he wanted to create destruction and blame Black Lives Matter for it,' he said. After watching the video and discussing it with friends, Hutchinson abandoned his plans for the day and drove to Vauxhall; from there the men walked to Parliament Square, in Westminster, where protestors had gathered and were being tracked and menaced by white counter-protestors, some of them drunk. Hutchinson and his comrades followed the marchers as they made their way to Trafalgar Square, avoiding the bottles and cans being thrown at them.

At a previous BLM rally there had been violent unrest and Hutchinson thought some of the younger protestors needed protecting not just from the hatred of racist thugs – he euphemistically calls them 'anti-black protestors' – but their own exuberance and excesses. Later that afternoon something remarkable happened to Patrick Hutchinson that changed his life and set him on a new path. During clashes outside Waterloo Station, on the South Bank, he noticed one of the counter-protestors, a shaven-headed white man wearing a T-shirt and denim shorts had become isolated. A multiracial mob was closing in on him at the top of a flight of stairs where he had stumbled. *I can't watch a man being beaten to death*, Hutchinson thought. Without hesitation he made his way through the crowd – there were, he thinks, as many as 300 people gathered around. Employing a fireman's carry, he scooped up the fallen man and, with his comrades creating a protective corridor, he carried him through the crowd to safety and delivered him to a group of nearby police officers. Rather than intervene, they had been using selfie sticks to film the unrest on their phones.

Hutchinson has the physique of a champion athlete and was wearing a black face mask pulled just below his mouth, black beanie and black capped-sleeved T-shirt. A photograph of him was taken by Dylan Martinez, a professional photographer. The symbolism was unmistakable. Here was a black man carrying a white bloodied anti-BLM protestor to safety: it circulated on Twitter and became one of the defining images of the pandemic summer.

Later that evening, Hutchinson's phone started ringing and it scarcely stopped for the next six months. Everyone wanted to speak to him and soon he needed his own professional PR support team. He was featured in a special 'Heroes' edition of *GQ* magazine and was interviewed by Prince Harry, and he later published a book, *Everyone Versus Racism*, co-written with a young poet called Sophie Thakur. Structured as an open letter to his children and grandchildren – Ta-Nehisi Coates's *Between the World and Me* is an apparent influence – the book reflects on the effect of Hutchinson's intervention that afternoon and his desire for reconciliation. He writes about his experience of coming to maturity in London during an era of racial conflict and about his desire to reach out across racial and culture difference. 'What has shocked me the most is how one transformative image can have the power to break and recast a narrative,' he said.

When I spoke to Hutchinson, he returned repeatedly to the death of George Floyd. 'There have been so many police killings of black men in America, and each one is as harrowing as the next,' he said. 'But for me the George Floyd murder – it was: "Enough is enough". It was the nonchalance of that police officer, just looking in the camera, no expression. It's like he was saying: "What are you going to do about it?" And he was killing the guy, with his knee in his neck. The guy was crying out for his mum and the officer just didn't care. And the other officers around him were just standing there doing crowd control. They were all complicit.'

+ + +

The man carried to safety by Hutchinson has the name of a character from a Martin Amis novel, Bryn Male. He turned out to be a few years older than Hutchinson, a retired police officer and he claimed to have been defending statues from the protestors. One of his friends described Male, a Millwall supporter, as a 'patriotic Brit, England through and through'. Note the conflation of Britain and England, as if the two were interchangeable. Britain is England, and England is Britain. And Bryn Male is a patriot, 'England through and through'.

Hutchinson pities rather than despises Male. 'He's my age, right. He's fifty-plus, still trying to get into a tear-up. You think he'd be trying to chill with the grandchildren,' he said. 'When it came out he was a former policeman – that was a mic drop moment. We've been trying to tell you for many a year that the police are institutionally racist and you won't believe us. Well, here you are. What more do you need to believe us that there's an issue with some serving police officers.'

Patrick Hutchinson grew up without a father in Battersea, south London, and was raised by his mother, Maureen. He recalls gangs of 'headhunters', the Chelsea hooligan firm, marching through the estate on which he grew up on match days during the late 1970s and early 1980s, when the racial abuse of black players at football matches was routine and routinely tolerated. He liked football but didn't attend many professional matches because he found the racism on the terraces so upsetting; he admired the young pioneering black Crystal Palace player Vince Hilaire. In childhood he watched Bruce Lee films and read martial arts magazines and so he took up taekwondo and Thai boxing. Martial arts taught him self-discipline and humility, and gave him confidence. Hutchinson did not seek confrontation on the streets because he fought in controlled environments inside gyms.

His book is an intimate letter to his family, as well as a manifesto for far-reaching change. He challenges what he calls the 'micro-aggression' of 'embedded racism' – an unbalanced school curriculum, unconscious bias, subtle or coded discrimination in the workplace – he values education and explains why participation in sports can create team spirit and good character. He's hopeful that from this era of fragmentation we can emerge with greater shared commitment to racial justice. As he wrote on Instagram on the day he rescued the man from the mob, 'It's not black v white. It's everyone v the racists.'

The nationalist far right think England is white. Or should be, as they believe it once was. This matters to them because one of the more popular claims on national identity is being the vast majority. You might say it's their only real claim. It isn't, but it underpins the other claims, and partly explains the antagonism and their desperation. The old Millwall terrace chant is relevant in this context: 'No one likes us/We don't care.'

'They think they're defending Englishness,' Hutchinson said of the old EDL crowd. 'They think they're the last line of defence. If they don't defend what it means to be English, no one will.'

But which England and whose idea of England are they defending? And which is more representative of who we are now?

+ + +

The self-styled football lads are a throwback to the hardcore terrace culture I grew up with and experienced as a child at matches in London: belligerent, resentful.

The 1980s were mostly a desolate era for English football. Our clubs were banned from European competitions following a rampage by Liverpool supporters at the Heysel Stadium in Brussels before 1985 European Cup final. A wall collapsed and thirty-nine people died, mostly rival Juventus fans. It's hard to believe now that the match was played, with dead bodies piled up inside the crumbling stadium. Scottish, Welsh and Northern Irish clubs were excluded from the UEFA ban; they were independent of England and in Europe, a sporting foreshadowing of the later Brexit divisions.

The image of England football supporters softened in the years after Italia 90 – the World Cup of Gazza's tears, Pavarotti's 'Nessun Dorma' and a spirited semi-final defeat to West Germany in Turin – after which English clubs were readmitted to European competitions. With the creation of the Premier League in 1992, marketed as a 'whole new ball game', the embourgeoisement of the people's game had begun. A more family-friendly fan culture emerged as English football opened up to outside influences. In this new era, as Mark Perryman has written, football stands became an 'important space for defining the symbols of Englishness: the St George cross, an England shirt, a terrace anthem . . .'.

By the time of the 1996 UEFA European Championship, Euro 96, the first major football tournament to be held in England since the 1966 World Cup, the national culture was changing again. We were less than a year away from New Labour's landslide victory – sensing the mood Blair announced that 'Labour's coming home' – and the devolution settlement for Scotland and Wales (but not for England) and the Good Friday Agreement that followed from it. Even before the creation of the Scottish Parliament and the Welsh Assembly in 1999, the cracks in the unity of the United Kingdom were widening: a renewed sense of national consciousness was growing among both the English and the Scots, and it found release through sport, especially football.

I almost never watch reruns of old matches; the thrill of live football for me lies in uncertainty, in not knowing what happens next. But as we emerged from the first nationwide lockdown, the BBC started broadcasting notable matches from Euro 96.

The repeats were a form of displacement activity: that summer the Euros should have returned to England as part of a trans-European tournament played in eleven cities across different countries; Wembley would host the semi-finals and final. The Covid pandemic ended that plan and, with the Tokyo Olympics also postponed, we initially had no live sport to watch. What interested me about the BBC repeats of Euro 96 was less the football itself than the opportunity offered to experience again something of the atmospheric pressure of those times.

'I have measured out my life in Arsenal fixtures, and any event of any significance has a footballing shadow,' wrote Nick Hornby in his memoir *Fever Pitch* (1992). It can sometimes feel a bit like that for me as I recall World Cup and Euros summers of the past. One match particularly fascinated me: England v. Scotland, originally played on Saturday, 15 June 1996, but repeated as live by the BBC on Saturday, 6 June 2020. I was at the original match and, as I watched it again, looking out for myself in the crowd, I was carried on a wave of emotion back to that warm, sunny day in London. What did we want back then?

THE RETURNING GHOST

What was most striking to me inside Wembley that afternoon of the Scotland match was the ubiquity of the English flag. When did fans of England embrace the St George's Cross? When I was growing up, the English flag was mostly associated with eccentrics or nasty nationalists, and some of my acquaintances at school were caught up in hooliganism; several of them were imprisoned for rioting on a cross-Channel ferry on the way back from a match on the continent.

Look at photographs or film footage of England's 1966 World Cup final against West Germany at Wembley and you'll see there's something obviously missing: the English flag. The flags being carried and waved are Union Jacks. Even the official World Cup mascot, an anthropomorphic lion called World Cup Willie, wore a Union flag jersey. This was an era when Englishness and Britishness were still pretty much considered to be coterminous or interchangeable; when Englishness was invariably associated with native-born whiteness, and the United Kingdom could be rationalized as a mini-English empire.

From the Act of Union of 1707, what Jeremy Black in *English Nationalism* calls the 'political tone and agenda' of the new British state were set in London and southern England. 'This was the basis of British consciousness, a development that did not so much alter the views of the English political elite, for whom Britain was essentially an extension of England, but, rather, that reflected the determination of the Scottish, and, to a lesser extent, Welsh and Irish Protestant elites to link their fate to the British state.'

Fabio Capello, the Italian coach of the England team from 2008 to 2012, described the 1966 World Cup victory as the 'returning ghost' of the national game. It was an astute observation because English football does seem haunted by the events of that imperishable July afternoon, when Alf Ramsey's side, captained by the young blond-haired gentleman East Ender Bobby Moore, defeated West Germany after extra time to win the World Cup at Wembley. My father, a West Ham fan who revered Moore, watched the game at home in our maisonette in Potter Street. He cherished it as one of the most memorable afternoons of his life.

What followed that World Cup triumph were 'thirty years of hurt', in the words of the David Baddiel, Frank Skinner and Lighting Seeds song 'Three Lions (Football's Coming Home)', which reached number one in the charts during Euro 96. Leaving Wembley that afternoon of the England–Scotland match, I recall looking up at the stand above me, and there were Baddiel and Skinner, the two television comedians, dancing and singing along to their own song as it blared out. That image of their uncomplicated, laddish happiness remains frozen in time.

'Three Lions' is an ironic celebration of English defeat and English yearning. It returned to the top of the charts twenty-two years later during England's run to the World Cup semi-finals in

Russia and was a hit again during the Euros in the summer of 2021. It has a catchy, anthemic chorus but that's not enough to explain its enduring appeal. Deeper forces are at play and they have something to do with the theme of belonging. Home, homecoming, homeland: football's coming home – to England, where it all began and belongs. Yet somehow, somewhere, something meaningful has been lost along the way, hence the hurt and the idle dreaming. England's dreaming. Dreaming of England.

In *The Football Man* (1968) Arthur Hopcraft wrote that the game of association football in England was 'inherent in the people'. It was the people's game, played by the people for the people. Football 'had not been "only a game" for 80 years', he wrote, 'not since the working classes saw in it an escape route out of drudgery and claimed it as their own'.

Football has changed so much since the publication of Hopcraft's book, especially at the highest level of the Premier League, and to those who pay to watch them, the best players can seem as remote as Hollywood stars. But English football clubs remain much more than businesses, franchises or brands. Football was invented and codified in England. The clubs grew out of their local communities, and even today, when most of the owners, the coaches and two-thirds of the players in the Premier League are from countries other than Britain, they serve as vessels of continuity across the generations. 'When you start supporting a football club,' Dennis Bergkamp, the former Arsenal player, once said, 'you don't support it because of the trophies, or a player, or history. You support it because you found somewhere you belong.'

Fandom can be irrational, enraging, and even absurd. But football allegiance matters deeply to many millions of people, as was revealed by the passionate and angry response to the putative European Super League, which collapsed under the pressure of the opposition to it in 2021. Fandom is a marker of identity and belonging – to a cause and institution over which you have no control but to which you feel a deep sense of loyalty and attachment. It is a covenantal commitment. For all its calculated commercial cynicism, football can push us apart but it can also bring us together as little else can. We witnessed this remarkable capacity to unify during the summer of 2021 when Gareth Southgate's team reached the final of Euro 2020, delayed by a year because of the pandemic. For the historian Robert Colls, football is one of the great civil cultures of these islands, and sport more generally is inseparable from Englishness – because it is 'something that has seeped into every part of who we are without us hardly knowing it'.

+ + +

There's nothing self-congratulatory about 'Three Lions' but it can be misinterpreted as being so. The truth about 'Three Lions' is that it is a popular song about a popular sport – our national game – and it is also a happy-sounding song about sadness and loss, not ownership and entitlement. A persistent sense that something is missing – or has been lost or taken away from the English – flows like a underground stream through the centuries. Talking about his film *Chimes at Midnight*, a reimagining of Shakespeare's *Henry IV*, the American director Orson Welles said, 'There has always been an England, an older England, which was sweeter, purer . . . You feel a nostalgia for it in Chaucer, and you feel it all through Shakespeare.' For the critic Peter Parker, a biographer of the poet A. E. Housman, 'melancholy and nostalgia are present from the very beginnings of English literature'.

English history is an optional subject at GCSE, but the national past, as Helen Thompson of Cambridge University reminded me, has been absorbed 'in local traditions, place names and memorials, its continuities are represented by a still popular monarchy, and they are writ across the island's landscape'.

England's historical place names and memorials are constant reminders, if you only care to notice them, of what has gone before, of what has been lost and gained. In contemporary Northumberland, for instance, you can sense the deeper past pressing in all around you; churches and schools are named after Cuthbert, an Anglo-Saxon saint of the early Northumbrian Church, and St Cuthbert's Day is celebrated on 20 March. Many of our pub names are also historical signifiers: the Royal Oak, the Priest Hole, the White Hart, the Rose and Crown, the Red Lion . . . From ruined castles and dissolved monasteries to the enclosures of common land, the English landscape is haunted by the presence of what is absent. Nostalgia and loss are the themes of 'Three Lions (Football's Coming Home)'.

GERMAN LESSONS

In the summer of 2006, I was sent by the *Observer* newspaper to write about the World Cup in Germany. I wasn't a sports reporter and the requirement was for me to write only one long piece a week in an era before online journalism became all-consuming: blogs, podcasts, tweets, on-the-whistle quick takes. I had a spacious rented two-floor, three-bedroom apartment. It was opposite the Adlon Hotel, from a high window of which the pop singer Michael Jackson once idiotically dangled one of his children, and a short walk from the Brandenburg Gate. I should have shared the apartment with other reporters but they never arrived in the city until the day before the final, which was played at the Berlin Olympiastadion. On those mornings when I wasn't travelling, I'd stroll to the nearby Hauptbahnhof, buy a selection of newspapers and magazines and then sit outside at a pavement cafe. I'd look on in the sunshine as different groups of fans from all over the world arrived in town, often dressed in national colours or replica team shirts.

Until they were knocked out in the quarter-finals (after a botched penalty shoot-out, naturally), England were based in Baden-Baden – 'so good they named it twice' was the running gag. Victoria Beckham, Cheryl Cole and the other so-called WAGs were present in the Black Forest spa town for the duration and their public moves were tracked by the media. I was elsewhere, enjoying a kind of lonely freedom. I had a generous expense account from the paper and time enough to explore and be a *flâneur*: the rhythm of my weeks was measured out in England matches. All accredited journalists received a complimentary first-class rail pass and I used it to travel widely. I even spent a few days in Dresden, away from the football, because I was curious to see how the city had been restored.

It was a hot, dry summer and the mood in Berlin was often euphoric: the country experienced, bashfully at first and then with a kind of thrilling abandon, a patriotic reawakening during those six World Cup weeks. Something similar had happened in England during Euro 96 but the events in Germany seemed deeper, more explicitly political. Arriving there at the start of the tournament, I saw few German flags on open display, but by its end, Deutschland-Flaggen were ubiquitous and hundreds of thousands of people were gathering at city centre Fan Fests to drink beer and watch the games on big screens.

Jurgen Klinsmann's energetic team ended up reaching the semi-finals; they lost 2–0 to Italy, the eventual winners, in an outstanding match in Dortmund, which I attended. But that defeat mattered less overall than the changed mood in the country: it was as if hosting the World Cup had liberated Germans into feeling much better about their country. It was my good luck to be in

Germany during those weeks because you saw a country changing around you as a revitalized civic patriotism was embraced.

A similar spirit of openness led Germany, in an entirely different geopolitical context, to open its borders in 2015 to perhaps a million refugees from the Middle East and South Asia, many of them in flight from perpetual civil war in Syria. Angela Merkel's unilateral intervention was not universally welcomed, of course: it emboldened national populists across Europe, not least inside Germany where the far-right Alternative for Germany rose fast, and Nigel Farage is convinced that it was decisive in tipping the vote for Leave in Britain. Merkel and the EU were eventually forced into a cynical deal with Recep Tayyip Erdogan's Turkey – a multi-billion-euro aid package – to reduce the flow of refugees into Europe. The past is never past, as Germany knows more than any other European country, but Merkel's decision to open Germany's borders showed just how much her country had changed: words matter in politics but actions can matter more.

+ + +

There is a subtle distinction to be made between history and collective or cultural memory. Removing statues or changing the names of buildings and institutions – in the town where I live the Rhodes Centre, named after Cecil Rhodes, was promptly renamed during the BLM protests – does not erase history or alter the historical record. But such acts are signifiers of change, markers of identity – *that was then, but this is now, and this is who we think we are today and these are our values*. Toppling statues and renaming buildings will only carry us so far: we need to create a common life in the country which is shared by all ethnic groups rather than allow ourselves to be divided by reactionaries on the one hand and identity activists on the other who take their lead from the fierce, hyper-partisan campus politics of the United States.

Tony Blair addressed some of these issues in a *New Statesman* essay in the week after the 2021 English, Scottish and Welsh elections. In what was widely considered to be his most significant intervention in Labour politics since he stepped down as leader, he wrote about what he thought the left was getting wrong:

> People do not like their country, their flag or their history being disrespected. The left always gets confused by this sentiment and assume this means people support everything their country has done or think all their history is sacrosanct. They don't. But they query imposing the thinking of today on the practices of yesterday; they're suspicious that behind the agenda of many of the culture warriors on the left lies an ideology they find alien and extreme; and they're instinctively brilliant at distinguishing between the sentiment and movement. They will support strongly campaigns against racism; but they recoil from some of the language and actions of the fringes of the Black Lives Matter movement . . . People like common sense, proportion and reason. They dislike prejudice; but they dislike extremism in combating prejudice.

During my childhood, racism, unconscious or otherwise, was embedded in the culture, from the 'golliwog' figure appearing on the Robinson's marmalade jars we had on our breakfast table to 'light entertainment' primetime TV shows such as *The Black and White Minstrel Show* and *It Ain't Half Hot, Mum*, which was set in Burma towards the end of the Second World War and featured a white British actor in blackface and turban speaking in a hammy Indian accent. It's a mark of progress that such programmes are now considered to be unwatchable.

The Victor comic to which I had a subscription was full of orientalist tropes and *Boys' Own* adventure stories about wartime acts of heroism. One improbable strip, 'Three on the Terror Trail', featured three menacing turbaned Sikh men, the so-called Dacoits, as well as giant rats, in a bucolic England. My sense of the past in childhood was framed by empire and animated by stories of wartime. Today, as the historian Richard J. Evans has written, 'there is no agreement on how the memory of empire should be incorporated into the national identity . . . What we remember as a society derives in the end from the kind of society we are, and reflects the kind of society we want to be.'

Who do we want to be? Should we remember the imperial past with shame and outrage, as some activists motivated by a belief in cultural and individual liberation demand, or with scepticism and a sense of proportion? It should be the latter – because although an accommodation with the imperial past is necessary for the harmony of our multi-ethnic future, if we are ever to scale those empathy walls, we must learn from context and work out what's best in the context. To love your country is to tell the full truth about it and to grapple with its complicated legacies. But we must also be alert to prejudice without becoming extreme or morally censorious in combating prejudice. We must be intolerant of the haters but also of intolerance itself, especially if liberalism hardens into a kind of self-righteous illiberalism.

THE SUMMER OF SOUTHGATE

The England football team is an ideal prism through which to view the changing face of the nation. The first black footballer to represent England was Viv Anderson, the former Nottingham Forest and Arsenal defender who made his debut in an international friendly at Wembley in November 1978. In 1984, when John Barnes scored a wondrous solo goal to inspire England to a 2–0 victory over Brazil in Rio de Janeiro, a racist faction of England's travelling support refused to accept the result. England had only won 1–0 because one of the goals had been scored by a black man, they said.

Tolerance of racism was commonplace in European football throughout the 1980s, the 1990s and into the 2000s. In 2004, England's black players were racially abused during an international match in Madrid. Gary Neville was playing that night and, at the start of the BLM protests, he publicly expressed regret that he'd remained silent and had failed to comfort his black teammates after the game.

A few months after that match in Spain, I commissioned the writer Martin Jacques to report on racism in Spanish football. Jacques understood something fundamental: that football is the fault line of racism in Europe because it mirrors and gives expression to society's passions and prejudices. 'No other activity, be it cultural or political, commands the emotion, passion and allegiance, certainly of men, in the same way,' he wrote. 'Football is the cultural lingua franca of European men . . . Indeed, it is about the only activity in which men collectively and publicly express their own emotions.'

He concluded that racism was endemic in the game but that modern football also had a subversive, rebellious quality. 'Football is the game of the masses, which is why it is increasingly a game of colour . . . Football offers a level playing field for the poor . . . and it is difficult to think of another walk of life where those not only of African descent but also largely from poor countries are so admired and acclaimed.'

But it was a game of colour only on the pitch. That is why it has taken so long for racism in sport, and indeed wider society, to become such an urgent national priority and why Neville belatedly expressed regret for his previous silence. As recently as 2016, Colin

Kaepernick, a San Francisco 49ers quarterback and civil rights campaigner, was ostracized by the National Football League, and condemned by Trump, because he 'took the knee' during the national anthem to protest at police brutality and racial inequality in America. In the aftermath of the murder of George Floyd, Premier League players also started taking the knee, in synchronized solidarity, at the start of games, and so did the England team. As the team took the knee in two friendlies before Euro 2020, they were booed by a small section of the crowd, and their collective action was dismissed by Priti Patel, the Conservative home secretary, as mere 'gesture politics'. At the end of the tournament Patel was criticized by Tyrone Mings, the England and Aston Villa defender, who tweeted: 'You don't get to stoke the fire at the beginning of the tournament by labelling our anti-racism message as "Gesture Politics" & then pretend to be disgusted when the very thing we're campaigning against happens.'

England have been fortunate through these years of division and political polarization to have had Gareth Southgate as their coach and manager. He began his playing career at Crystal Palace in a team including several black players, notably Ian Wright, the striker who found greater fame at Arsenal. Wright remembers the young Southgate as a geeky, atypical footballer; he had O levels, after all. He was intelligent, contemplative and articulate but others underestimated him at their peril: by the age of twenty-three, he was Crystal Palace captain and would lead every club for which he played.

Gary Neville once said of his England career that certain key players were associated with specific clubs. He, David Beckham, Rio Ferdinand and Paul Scholes were Manchester United players. Steven Gerrard, Steve McManaman, Michael Owen and Robbie Fowler were Liverpool. Frank Lampard and John Terry were Chelsea. But Gareth Southgate was first and foremost an England player. For him, country came before club.

When you hear Southgate speak about the responsibility of his role and the deep attachment he has to his country, it's as if you are listening to the understated voice of the ordinary, decent England fan. In many ways, with his hesitant speech patterns, clipped beard and modest waistcoats and suits, Southgate can come across as a rather old-fashioned figure in the hyper-modern, aggressively competitive, image-conscious world of top-flight football. But he knows who he is and what he represents and knows the difference between patriotism and nationalism, and cherishes the former. More than this, he understands the need for a patriotism that is both generous and enhances national cohesion rather than undermines it.

England was represented at Euro 2020 by a harmonious, likeable multiracial squad of players who seemed relaxed in their patriotism and comfortable about wrapping themselves in the St George's Cross. The squad was drawn mainly from the working-class communities of the south-east, the Midlands and the northern towns and cities, which don't often feature in stereotypes about Englishness. Many of the players had emerged not from elite academies but the lower leagues.

'We have the chance to affect something bigger than ourselves,' Gareth Southgate had said of his squad in 2018. 'We're a team with our diversity and our youth that represent modern England. In England we have spent a bit of time being a bit lost as to what our modern identity is. I think as a team we represent that modern identity and hopefully people can connect with us.'

He was right: his team did affect something bigger. The Russia World Cup coincided with an extraordinary heatwave at home, the hottest and most enduring since 1976. For a few weeks, as England played their way to the semi-finals, millions of us were united by an interest in the football. The writer Alex Niven coined a neologism to describe the mood in the country during those weeks: 'Southgate-ism'.

I asked him what he meant by it. 'For me Southgate-ism refers to that brief, heady moment in the summer of 2018 when the turmoil of the 2010s seemed to give way to a more positive atmosphere in England – obviously the narrative was slightly different in Wales, Scotland and Ireland,' he replied in an email.

> With hindsight the 2017–19 interlude already seems like a strange hiatus, but in the middle of it there was this weirdly hot summer after a brutal winter, and an unusually exciting, good-natured World Cup in Russia. The strong showing of the England team under Gareth Southgate genuinely united a broad swathe of people living in England who otherwise wouldn't have felt anything in common.
>
> But while some have said this offers a model for 'progressive patriotism', I'm sceptical that Southgate-ism can ever become a political reality. It seems more like the exception that proves the rule as far as Englishness goes: a haunting glimpse of what might have been in a country without our burden of traditionalism and lack of republican and modernist credentials.

It turned out to be more than a glimpse, since we experienced the enduring power of Southgate-ism in the summer of 2021, and this time even more of the nation seemed unified behind the team. Before the tournament, responding to the anguished debate about his team taking the knee, Southgate published an essay on the Players' Tribune website, entitled 'Dear England'. Instead of avoiding questions about national identity, patriotism, the culture wars and racism, Southgate leaned into them because, as he acknowledged, he should not 'just stick to football' but rather use his position of influence to 'interact with the public on matters such as equality, inclusivity and racial injustice'.

In the essay he recalled his early experiences as a fan of the England team. 'You remember where you were watching England games. And who you were watching with. And who you were at the time.' Beautifully said, and so true. He described what it means for his players, 'a special group', to represent their country and commended how some of them had effected lasting change in society through their activism – an implicit reference to the campaigns of Marcus Rashford, Raheem Sterling and others in the squad.

Southgate understands that love of country should be something deeply felt but not ostentatiously stated and that football is one of the primary means through which many millions of people express their national identity. Deep skeins of national pride run through and are reflected in the national team. 'The imagined community of millions seems more real as a team of eleven named people,' as the historian Eric Hobsbawm wrote. Southgate knows too that football and politics are not separate but endlessly intertwined, especially the politics of race, nation and identity. His England team have begun to reclaim the flag of St George from its old toxic associations with whiteness and the far right – a process that began spontaneously at Euro 96 when a new, more hopeful expression of English identity was showcased, and other multiracial England teams in other sports – rugby, athletics – have also embraced it.

Southgate was rebuked by some commentators for being 'woke' and an apologist for the more extreme factions of the BLM movement after the publication of 'Dear England'. This was absurd. His own politics are complex and he is extraordinarily politically literate. His political interventions are so interesting because they are at once progressive and conservative. He is respectful of tradition and institutional wisdom – the repeated references he makes to the Queen, the military, his grandfather's wartime service – while understanding how society never stops changing, while retaining an essence that underpins all change. One is reminded of Orwell's remark in 'England Your England' that the country has 'the power to change out of recognition and yet remain the same'. A changing changelessness.

+ + +

The key to understanding Southgate's vision of England is to accept that he rejects binaries and false oppositions. For him it is never a question of either/or. You can be both a progressive and a conservative. You can take the knee and love your country. You don't have to choose between diversity and tradition; between the Englishness of his grandfather and the Englishness of Marcus Rashford. His mode of leadership is informed by social virtues: courage, compassion, humility, modesty, restraint, pragmatism, the fulfilment of our obligations to others. 'This team is playing for all of us,' wrote the anti-racism campaigner Shaista Aziz.

Under Southgate the England national team has become a symbol of multiracial unity but it also embodies some of the contradictions of the English nation within a disunited United Kingdom. England has no official anthem, for instance, and during pre-match formalities the players sing 'God Save the Queen'. (The England cricket team has chosen 'Jerusalem' as its unofficial anthem.) Scotland, by contrast, has its own anthem, 'Flower of Scotland', and the Welsh 'Land of My Fathers'. When England play Scotland, 'God Save the Queen' is greeted with derision by Scottish fans, though it is their 'national' anthem too. 'Flower of Scotland' is booed in return, as it was at Wembley in 2021, when England and Scotland were drawn against each other in the group stage as they had been at Euro 96 – the match in which Gazza, his cropped hair peroxide white, scored *that* goal. I was present at Wembley for both games, twenty-five years apart. So much had changed and yet it hadn't: we were still trying to determine what England *is* before guessing what part England *can play* in the huge events that were happening.

+ + +

Westminster politicians have been reluctant to promote Englishness (rather than Britishness, as Gordon Brown did) for fear of what may be unleashed. There is no such reluctance among Scottish politicians to promote Scottishness. 'The other parts of the union enjoy their own political identity and space, their own democratic institutions and their own democratic powers, England has none of these,' the academic and former Labour MP John Denham said in a Speaker's Lecture delivered at Parliament during the 2018 World Cup. 'England, as England, is absent from our national political debate and conversation.'

During the build-up to England's World Cup quarter-final against Sweden in Samara, south-west Russia, Theresa May succumbed to pressure from campaigners and agreed to fly the St George's Cross over 10 Downing Street on match days. But May did not do so with confidence or because it revealed what was in her heart; she much prefers cricket, in any event. From the outside it looked to me as if this complex, shy and introverted politician, an instinctive 'Briton' who often referred in speeches to 'our beloved Union', had been coerced into making a symbolic gesture to appease a certain restiveness. She did what she thought she ought to do rather than what she wanted to do. Boris Johnson displayed no such reticence during Euro 2020 and attended matches at Wembley wearing an England replica team shirt.

THIS IS ENGLAND

Early in the pandemic, the health secretary, Matt Hancock, who later resigned because of a violation of rules on social distancing he'd introduced, demanded that, in the spirit of greater social solidarity, Premier League footballers should take a pay cut. Before the crisis, the elite clubs' business model was founded upon the expectation of ever-rising television rights deals from home and overseas markets and exploiting the blind loyalty of supporters. Premier League footballers, because of their wealth and celebrity, are a convenient target for politicians.

Football's global popularity and considerable soft power attract the covetous desires of acquisitive plutocrats, Russian and American oligarchs, and Gulf autocrats. It lavishly rewards the best players and their agents, and in recent years has become largely colour-blind: if a player is good enough, no matter where he is from in the world, he will play and be paid what the market rate commands. The women's game is much less well remunerated.

Some elite professional footballers are poor role models, but many are not. It's true that the most gifted, from a very young age, live privileged, cloistered and pampered lives. Most players leave school at the age of sixteen, but this doesn't mean that they lack intelligence or are ignorant or uninterested in what is happening in the world around them. Marcus Rashford and Raheem Sterling are notable examples of socially engaged footballers. Like their England teammates Jordan Henderson, Tyrone Mings, Bukayo Saka and the captain Harry Kane, who wore a rainbow-coloured armband in solidarity with the LGBT+ community during Euro 2020, they do not conform to stereotype.

Rashford grew up in Wythenshawe, Manchester, the youngest of five children of a single mother who worked as a cashier in a betting shop, and early in the pandemic he embarked on a campaign to nudge the government into extending its free school meals scheme to the most underprivileged children in the summer holidays. Under pressure from Rashford's spirited campaign – he was interviewed on the main BBC News, published an article in *The Times*, published an open letter to the government and tweeted frequently and forcefully – Boris Johnson eventually announced the creation of a £120 million 'Covid summer food fund' for disadvantaged children. Rashford had won a notable political victory but though he was delighted he was not satisfied. 'I don't want this to be the end of it because there are more steps that need to be taken and we just need to analyse the response,' he told the BBC. 'People are struggling all year around, so we still need to learn more about the situation people are in and how we can help them best.'

He has been true to his word and continues to make well-timed political interventions. 'Who runs Marcus Rashford?' it was asked. The answer, some claimed, was Roc Nation Sports International, an agency founded by the American rapper JAY-Z whose business mission is to fuse social justice and sport: in its own grandiose self-description it is less an agency than a 'movement'.

Rashford is no phoney or stooge of woke capitalism. He is one of the country's leading anti-poverty campaigners and people listen to him because they know he is authentic. His actions are rooted in experience of childhood poverty and struggle; he was the recipient of free school meals. During one debate in the Commons, Boris Johnson even referred to him as 'the real leader of the opposition'.

'The barriers have been well and truly broken,' wrote Simon Oliveira, a long-time adviser to David Beckham, of Rashford's campaigns. 'Top athletes, and the organisations they represent, can collectively reach more people than almost any politician and connect.'

This power of connection and their mastery of social media

have given the new generation of activist super-players extra-ordinary influence. They understand the power they have and are no longer prepared to tolerate personal abuse or to be misrepresented. In the run-up to the Russia World Cup, Raheem Sterling, the Manchester City winger, was traduced in the tabloid press for having an image of an assault rifle tattooed on his leg. Was he glorifying violence or gangster culture?

This moment served as Sterling's public awakening – and repositioning. It was time to tell his own story. First, he published an article on the Players' Tribune website in which he described his impoverished early years in Jamaica and the murder of his father; the tattoo of the gun served as a permanent reminder of his father's violent death, he claimed. Sterling's mother uprooted the family to London when he was five, and he described how he helped her clean lavatories so that she could earn enough to continue her own studies; she now runs a care home. Sterling was restless and disruptive at school and one teacher said to him that he would either end up in prison or play football for England. He grew up in the shadow of Wembley Stadium and dreamed of one day playing there. Many years later, he arranged for 550 children from his old school to have tickets for an FA Cup match at Wembley.

'All I have to tell you is that fifteen years ago, we were cleaning toilets in Stonebridge and getting breakfast out of the vending machine,' he wrote in his Players' Tribune piece. 'If anybody deserves to be happy, it's my mum. She came to this country with nothing and put herself through school cleaning bathrooms and changing bed sheets, and now she's the director of a nursing home. And her son plays for England.'

Sterling is now a prominent activist-player and anti-racism campaigner: he helped galvanize support for Black Lives Matter. In one campaigning video – featuring present and former players

– released on the eve of the resumption of the Premier League after the first lockdown, Sterling declared: 'I will never tire of being black.'

'There's only so much people can take,' he told the BBC. 'There's only so much communities and other backgrounds can take – especially black people. It's been going on for hundreds of years and people are tired and people are ready for change.'

+ + +

Rashford and Sterling personify a new rising multiracial English national self-consciousness, informed by a more active sense of citizenship and the desire to engage in social and political causes that transcend the old divisions. They do not preach an abstract, atomized diversity; what they share is a vision of England and of the future that is different and better than what they knew as children. Rashford, Sterling – and indeed Patrick Hutchinson, whose story began this chapter – share something else besides: inspirational mothers. And they love England, as it is but also most importantly for what it could become.

As Rashford wrote on Twitter, when he discovered the first stage of his free school meals campaign had prompted a government U-turn, 'I don't even know what to say. Just look at what we can do when we come together, THIS is England in 2020.'

Or recall how Sterling concluded his Players' Tribune piece, which ends on a note of jubilation: 'I'm telling you right now . . . England is still a place where a naughty boy who comes from nothing can live his dream.'

Raheem Sterling and Marcus Rashford might, as England footballers, be living their dream – or something close to it – but their activism shows they have not forgotten most of the people who are not, and they are using their wealth and celebrity to do something about it. Their public interventions are never divisive, partisan, condemnatory or absolutist. They respond with dignity to the unconscionable racist abuse and random threats of violence directed at them and their families on the unregulated social media platforms, invariably from anonymous user accounts, tolerated by the tech giants.

Where they lead, others will follow. Because of its popularity and capacity to create moments of mass public togetherness as we experienced during the summer of 2021, football in England is a mirror in which we see reflected something of who we are now and where we belong. Is football still inherent in the people, as Arthur Hopcraft wrote all those years ago? The top-flight professional game is far too globalized and ruthlessly commercial for anyone to make so romantic a claim about it today. The Premier League is a hyper-meritocracy: one of the purest manifestations we have of let-it-rip, free-market, winner-takes-all globalization.

Yet under the leadership of Southgate, the England team has become a symbol of national unity. That was the dominant narrative of the summer of 2021. In an email sent to FA staff after the Euros, Southgate wrote, 'Football won't and cannot resolve all those issues on its own, but we have seen the power and influence it can have at its best.' He wanted to create not only a 'world champion team', he wrote, but a 'more tolerant and respectful society'.

The old exclusivist England is a country of the past. As the historian David Olusoga has written, England, by some projections, will by the middle of the century be around one-third black and minority ethnic. Today, not only through its footballers but through its writers, its artists and its musicians, England stands as one of the most diverse, socially liberal and tolerant countries in Europe. Establishment liberals have an understandable tendency to bemoan what is wrong with their country, but Southgate's England signifies a lot about what is right. He and his players have shown us how to stretch the flag so that it may be wrapped around not just some but all the people all the time. *This* is England. An England in which you don't have to choose between diversity and tradition. An England for all.

7 A VISITOR FROM THE FUTURE

One winter afternoon during the 2019 general election campaign, as Boris Johnson toured the country promising to 'get Brexit done', Gillian Duffy visited the Regal Moon pub in the Lancashire town of Rochdale. 'She's here now!' someone gently chided as she bought herself a drink at the bar. And then he added: 'You've been on the telly again!'

Mrs Duffy is an unlikely public figure. A long-time widow and retired former children's care worker, she lives alone in a terraced house in Rochdale, a short drive from the historic centre of what was once one of Lancashire's most productive mill towns during the Industrial Revolution. She owes her minor celebrity to an unexpected encounter she had with the then prime minister Gordon Brown during the 2010 election campaign as the New Labour era was coming to an end.

That brisk, dry April afternoon Mrs Duffy put on a dark red-collared coat and left her house to buy some bread and milk. She didn't know Labour's travelling circus was in town, and as she made her way up the hill towards a local supermarket she saw police motorcycle outriders and assumed there'd been an accident. It was then that she noticed a Labour Party campaign bus, as well as TV camera crews and a cluster of men in dark suits. 'Who's here?' she asked a cameraman. Mrs Duffy's curiosity was noticed by Sue Nye, the director of government relations and a close aide to Gordon Brown: his 'gatekeeper'.

'Are you Labour?' Sue Nye asked Mrs Duffy.

'Of course, I'm Labour.'

'Would you like to speak to the prime minister?'

'Yes please.'

Mrs Duffy was escorted across Bentley Street to meet Gordon Brown, who was flanked by Simon Danczuk, the Labour candidate for Rochdale who would later become a national embarrassment to the party, and surrounded by advisers, security protection officers and representatives from the media. Brown had none of Tony Blair's emotional intelligence or communication skills, and in the TV footage you can see from the outset that he's awkward and fretful. A persistent criticism of Brown during the campaign was that – like most politicians – he avoided challenge or direct confrontation and liked to speak only to the converted, hence Sue Nye's initial question about Mrs Duff's political allegiance: 'Are you Labour?'

Mrs Duffy wears spectacles and has a florid complexion and grey, curled, helmet-like hair brushed back from a high forehead. She begins by telling Brown that her family are lifelong Labour voters. Her father was a window-cleaner and her mother worked as a weaver in the mills. 'My father, even, when he was in his teens, went to Free Trade Hall to sing "The Red Flag". And now I'm absolutely ashamed of saying I'm Labour,' she says to Brown.

Brown is not expecting that. 'Now, you mustn't be, because, what have we done?'

The question is rhetorical, and so he begins to answer it.

'We've improved the health service, we're financing more police, neighbourhood policing, we are getting better schools, and we are coming through a very, very difficult world recession. You know what my views are. I'm for fairness, for hard-working families . . .'

Mrs Duffy interjects, her sharp, alert eyes focused intently on Brown. 'I don't think it's happening in Rochdale.'

Politicians can too easily forget that for most people politics is local, experienced in the decline of the high street, the closure of a library or children's play centre, inadequate transport and civic infrastructure, poor schools, a hospital in special measures or a health centre where no one answers the phone.

Brown responds by attempting to flatter Mrs Duffy. He tells her she's a 'very good woman: you've served your community all your life'.

'I have,' she says, resisting his charm. 'I've worked for the Rochdale Council for thirty years, and I worked with children and handicapped children.'

'Working with children is so important, so important,' Brown says, lowering his voice, straining for sincerity.

Mrs Duffy immediately changes tack and asks why, at the age of sixty-six, she is still being taxed on her dead husband's pension.

Brown tilts his head, sways a little from side to side, and looks quizzically at the woman, as if he's trying to work out who she really is and what she wants. Beside him Danczuk, the jacket of his dark suit open over a white shirt and tie, looks as if he's holding his breath. He senses where this conversation is going and he doesn't like it.

'Well, we are raising the threshold at which people start paying tax as pensioners,' Brown says, tapping his fingers in the palm of his left hand. 'But yes, if you've got an occupational pension you may have to pay some tax but you may be eligible for the pension credit as well, you should check.'

Mrs Duffy shakes her head and says that she's not eligible.

Brown and Danczuk are uneasy. And Brown starts addressing Mrs Duffy as he might the House of Commons, listing New Labour achievements, as if he's reciting tractor production figures. 'You know we're linking the pension to earnings in two years' time, we've got the winter allowance, as you know, which I hope is a benefit. We have done the bus passes, we have done the free eye tests, free prescriptions.'

The repeated use of 'you know' is ostensibly deferential but is in fact an act of condescension, a familiar trope the very powerful or very clever use in conversation. *Of course, you know!*

But, like an adept political interrogator, Mrs Duffy cuts him off and changes direction again.

'How are you going to get us out of all this debt, Gordon?'

It's a tough question, and the personal touch – 'Gordon' – carries with it a direct challenge. Britain remains mired in what is being called the Great Recession and the national conversation is dominated by questions about the national debt and the annual budget deficit. The Conservative charge against Brown's government is that it has lost control of public finances. Brown is a Keynesian and a champion of fiscal stimulus (tax cuts and emergency public spending) and active monetary policy (ultra-low interest rates and quantitative easing). He believes he knows the way out of the crisis. As a former chancellor of the Exchequer, he is much more comfortable on fiscal matters, and it shows.

'Because we have got a deficit reduction plan to cut the debt in half over the next four years,' he says calmly. 'We've got the plans, they've been set out today. Look, I was a person who came in . . .'

Mrs Duffy, who left school aged fifteen, is unconvinced, and comes back at Brown, expressing frustration at what she considers to be an unfair benefits system. Brown nods to indicate he's listening and wraps his left arm across his body as if he's holding his right arm in place, as if he fears the arm making quick, involuntary movements, like something out of *Dr Strangelove*.

'The three main things what I had drummed in when I was a child was education, health service and looking after people who are vulnerable,' Mrs Duffy says. 'But there's too many people now who aren't vulnerable but they can claim, and people who are vulnerable can't claim, can't get it.'

Brown promises that there is 'no life on the dole for people any more. If you are unemployed you've got to go back to work. It's six months.'

Mrs Duffy is in control and moves on to immigration, a subject about which Labour is uncomfortable, not least because of the disconnect between the party's leadership, which welcomes free movement and open borders, and many of its long-time voters who are unsettled by the rapid inflow of migrants.

'You can't say anything about the immigrants,' Mrs Duffy says, echoing a refrain heard often by Labour MPs when they talk to their constituents. 'All these Eastern Europeans what are coming in, where are they flocking from?'

The verb 'flocking' alarms Brown, who produces a pained smile: this is not what he expected at all. His eyes narrow and his voice quickens.

'A million people have come from Europe but a million British people have gone into Europe,' he explains. 'You do know that there's a lot of British people staying in Europe as well.'

He leans in much closer to Mrs Duffy, as if he wishes to confide in her. 'Look, come back to what were your initial principles: helping people – that's what we're in the business of doing. A decent health service, that's really important, and education. Now these are the things that we have tried to do. We're going to maintain the schools so that we can make sure that people have that chance to get on. We're going to maintain the health service so that—'

Mrs Duffy interrupts him again. She will not allow Brown to settle into a rhythm. She raises student debt.

'And what are you going to do about students who are coming in then, all this that you have to pay, you've scrapped that, Gordon.'

Brown is confused. Is the phrase 'coming in' a reference to

overseas students, and thus code for uncontrolled migration? He does not know what exactly he is supposed to have scrapped.

'Which one?' he replies.

'To help people who go to university.'

'Tuition fees?'

'Yes.'

'Yeah, but look, we've got—'

'I'm thinking about my grandchildren here,' Mrs Duffy cuts in. 'What will they have to pay to get into university?'

Brown offers a utilitarian explanation – it's all about the number of new graduates and about measurable targets, as Blair pledged it would be all those years before.

'You've got 40 per cent of young people now going to university—'

Danczuk loyally interjects: 'More than ever.'

Brown accepts the prompt. 'More than ever, so you've got to have some balance. If you get a degree and you earn twice as much after you get the degree then you've got to pay something back as a contribution. But there are grants for your grandchildren, there are grants, more grants than ever before. You know, more young people are going to university than ever before, and for the first year the majority of people going to university are women – so there's big opportunities for women. So, education, health and helping people, that's what I'm about. That's what I'm about.'

Brown finally moves to end the conversation and, shaking hands with Mrs Duffy, tells her she is wearing the right colour today – the red of her coat collar. They both laugh.

Brown returns to his car but does not realize a Sky News microphone is still attached to the lapel of his jacket – a microphone the Labour media team requested he wear – and he is wired for sound. As the door of the car closes, he is heard saying: 'That was a disaster . . . You should never have put me with that woman. Whose idea was that?'

'I don't know, I didn't see her,' a male aide replies anxiously.

'It was Sue's, I think. Just *ridiculous*.'

Brown spits out the last word, his anger palpable.

The aide attempts to reassure him that the media will not broadcast his exchanges with Mrs Duffy. 'Not sure that they'll go with that one.'

The prime minister understands what has happened. 'They will go with that one.'

'What did she say?'

'Oh, everything,' Brown says, despairingly. 'She was just a sort of bigoted woman who said she used to be Labour, I mean, it's just ridiculous.'

The car pulls away, with Brown inside it: he is moving on to his next media engagement, an interview with BBC Radio 2's *Jeremy Vine Show*, and he initially has no idea about what is unfolding in Rochdale, as Sky News start replaying, on a continuous loop, his remarks about Mrs Duffy being a bigot. In Brown's own idiom, they have gone with that one, and the rest of the media go with it as well.

Mrs Duffy is played a recording of Brown's comments and her response is broadcast live on national television. Her eyes aflame, she expresses disgust and claims Brown 'shut her down completely'. Asked by a journalist how she feels, she says: 'Very upsetting that. What did I say to be bigoted there? What was bigoted? I just asked about the national debt?'

Soon afterwards, Brown arrives at the studio for the BBC interview, which is to be recorded remotely. It is a radio interview but it is also filmed and so we can see how Brown reacts when for the first time he hears his comments about Mrs Duffy played back to him: he recoils and crumples, as if he believes this could be an

election-defining blow, confirmation, if any were needed, that politicians are hypocrites because they never mean what they say. No
one wishes to have their private views exposed, least of all a Labour
prime minister who has dismissed a long-time Labour voter as a
'bigoted woman', and live on air Brown apologizes to Mrs Duffy.
He concedes the question about immigration was 'really annoying'
but regrets his response to it.

Then something remarkable happens: Brown decides to, or is
advised to, return to Rochdale, where he visits Mrs Duffy at home.
She welcomes him in but does not have any milk in the house to
make a cup of tea – she never made it to the shops, after all – so
offers the prime minister a glass of whisky. Brown emerges from
the house forty-five minutes later, his dark, grey-flecked hair neatly
brushed and parted. With broadcasters and photographers gathered
outside the house, he smiles warmly, assumes the air of a congenial
chat-show host, and says, as if he is discussing an old friend:

'I have just been talking to Gillian. I'm mortified by what's
happened. I've given her my sincere apologies. I misunderstood
what she said and she has accepted that there was a misunderstanding and has accepted my apology. I'm a penitent sinner!
Sometimes you say things you don't mean to say.'

Or mean things you don't say, he might have added.

The television cameras track Brown's car as it is driven slowly,
funereally, away from the estate, away from Mrs Duffy and from
Rochdale, the once-noble Lancashire town where the cooperative
movement was founded in the high Victorian period. But what is
gone and what is to come cast their shadows, and as Brown peers
out of the car window his face seems frozen in misery.

Meanwhile, in a car park across town, Simon Danczuk is sitting
alone in his car smoking cigarettes as he listens to multiple voice
messages. He has been visiting a local prison and has only now
switched on his phone. He gave up smoking before the campaign

began but the stresses of the day have broken his resolve, and he lights another cigarette as he discovers what has happened to the prime minister in his absence. Danczuk stares out into the early evening gloom and feels a sense of foreboding just as he did when he first saw Mrs Duffy approaching earlier that afternoon. *Are you Labour?*

WHAT DID MRS DUFFY KNOW?

The story of the 2010 election did not end as Gordon Brown would have wished. Labour lost (though Danczuk won) and the Conservatives were returned to power for the first time since 1997, in a right-centre coalition with the Liberal Democrats, the defining mission of which was fiscal retrenchment, budget deficit reduction and the rolling back of the expansive, protective Labour state. 'There is such a thing as society,' the new prime minister David Cameron said early on, adapting a famous remark from Margaret Thatcher. 'It's just not the same as the state.'

I travelled with Brown by train to Newcastle just before polling day; I shadowed him as he campaigned in Sunderland and, on the return journey to London, when my tape recorder was switched off and he could relax over a beer, we talked about the early years of New Labour and his ambition not only to remake the party but the country as progressive, liberal, forward-looking, open and globalized. Brown knew he was losing the 2010 election and our conversation became reflective, even elegiac, especially when we were joined for a drink by Peter Mandelson, who was also on the Newcastle trip.

The campaign had been personally painful for Brown; he was haunted by the encounter with Mrs Duffy and frustrated he'd lost the support of the Murdoch press, once assiduously courted by New Labour. He kept telling me he could not get his 'message out through the papers'. We spoke about the MPs' expenses scandal

– it had broken a bond of trust between politicians and the public, he said – but he was encouraged that Cameron's socially liberal, 'modernized' Conservatives had not renounced the New Labour era. 'The point about the Conservatives is that they believe that they cannot win an election by running against New Labour,' he said. 'They are for the political landscape we have created.'

In retrospect, Mrs Duffy knew something Gordon Brown did not: unlike the Conservatives, she rejected the political landscape created by New Labour. She was troubled by uncontrolled migration, student debt and the national debt, by welfare fraud and the neglect of and underinvestment in the north, as well as weakening social cohesion. She knew that many other long-time Labour voters shared her unease and sense of loss. 'He tried to shut me down,' Mrs Duffy had said when she discovered the prime minister had called her bigoted, and a lot of long-time Labour voters felt just as she did: shut down, shut out.

+ + +

In an essay on the 1988 US presidential campaign, Joan Didion described how the political process was excluding the people for whom it professed to speak. It was becoming limited 'to its own professionals, to those who manage policy and those who report on it, to those who run the polls and those who quote them, to those who ask and those who answer the questions on the Sunday shows, to the media consultants, to the columnists, to the issues advisers, to those who give off-the-record breakfasts and to those who attend them; to that handful of insiders who invent, year in and year out, the narrative of public life'.

Something similar was happening in Britain, and that afternoon Mrs Duffy interrupted the smooth flow of Labour's narrative of public life. The gatekeeper opened the gate for Mrs Duffy and she walked straight through it. *Are you Labour?*

By the end of the decade, Labour had lost Scotland, and the Scottish National Party (SNP) had consolidated their hold on power. For the SNP, as Andrew Marr wrote, 'love of country and its own interests are the same thing'. Which is what one party states say.

In December 2019 Labour suffered its worst national general election defeat since 1935, as the 'Red Wall' enclosing its traditional strongholds in the English north and Midlands was broken apart as voters abandoned the party of the British Left as they had done in Scotland before them. Labour lost once-safe seats in former mining constituencies such as Workington, Rother Valley and Bolsover, where memories of the bitter miners' strike of 1984–85 cut deep. In Hartlepool, at a by-election in May 2021, another brick from the crumbling Red Wall was removed when the Conservatives won the seat for the first time since its creation in 1974. Brexit was realigning our politics; a reckoning on this scale was inconceivable to Gordon Brown on that day when I travelled with him from Newcastle.

Ed Miliband once said to me that he thought Nigel Farage's UKIP posed a greater threat to the Tories than to Labour. That was not how Farage saw it. 'I'm coming after Labour voters,' he told me in November 2014. 'Everybody thought that people's tribal allegiance to Labour was as strong, if not stronger, than the tribal allegiance to the Conservative Party. What we're actually finding is, they don't even recognize the tribe. They just don't . . . The middle-class person who doesn't think about politics very much, but is concerned about where school fees are coming from or whatever it may be – that middle-class person still thinks of the political spectrum that the Conservatives are more on their side than the other one. Increasingly what we're finding is the people that come from the Labour side of the equation don't think anyone's on their side.'

Farage had a better understanding of how to use to his advantage the disruptions of the present moment than Miliband and Labour, as it turned out.

+ + +

After her encounter with Brown, Labour stayed close to Mrs Duffy: she served as both a totem and a warning. Simon Danczuk would call her several times a week to chat about politics and she officially opened his new constituency office. He encouraged her to endorse David Miliband for the party leadership in 2010, which she did. 'We need to win the confidence of many more voters like Mrs Duffy if we are to be serious about winning the next election,' David Miliband said after being photographed with her on a visit to her house in Rochdale. 'This new government is not on the side of people like Gillian Duffy. I am determined that the Labour Party will be.'

After David Miliband was defeated by his younger brother in a leadership contest from which their relationship never recovered, Mrs Duffy was invited to London to meet Ed Miliband, who had succeeded Brown. 'This is the person we have to convince,' the new Labour leader breezily announced to aides as Mrs Duffy was ushered into his office.

Her lasting impression of the Palace of Westminster was unfavourable. 'Go into the bars in Parliament, as I did. I said to Simon Danczuk: "Is this real?" These people are running our country. They're in a bubble. They don't know how we're suffering in the north.'

I asked her to reflect on her encounter with Brown and subsequent celebrity. 'I'm a pub quiz question now, you know: "Who was that bigoted woman from Rochdale!?" But really everyone just centred on that one last question. But I went with the economy first. Then I went with education. Then benefits. And then finally I went with immigration. Everyone who called me afterwards only wanted to talk about immigration. I didn't object to immigration. If people want to come here, learn or work, and then go back: you can't object to that. But I was worried about control. Students were coming in – but not to learn, they stayed here. Then he called me a bigot. All I wanted to know was about the economy. We're still paying for the Second World War.'

She was grateful Brown had returned to see her that afternoon. 'My nephew was in the house and asked if I was going to make him a cup of tea. I didn't have any milk! He said, "Give him a glass of Scotch then." He stayed for well over half an hour and said he was profoundly sorry – that's a big word.'

Mrs Duffy mentioned a programme she'd been watching about the abuse of underage girls by grooming gangs and she was disturbed by it. The Rochdale case and others like it have caused lasting resentment in the north. 'I talked to them [the police],' says Holly, one of the victims in *Three Girls*, the BBC drama about the case. 'And I talked to them. And I talked to them. And then they turned round and called me a liar.'

'There was a fifteen-year-old girl from Rochdale,' Mrs Duffy said. 'She was pumped full of drugs by the gang. She was crying out for help but no one listened to her.'

She repeated the sentence. 'No one listened to her. At that time, in our period of life, if you said anything about an Asian man – from Pakistan or Bangladesh – it's just race discrimination. They said this girl was silly – that she was talking nonsense. But this girl was repeatedly being raped.'

THE STRANGE DEATH OF LABOUR BRITAIN

Mrs Duffy voted for Brexit but, despite her disenchantment with the Johnson administration, she did not vote in the 2019 general election. She believes working-class voters in Labour's former fortresses in the north did not leave Labour: Labour left them behind long ago in its embrace of globalization and cosmopolitanism. From its beginnings Labour was an uneasy coalition of the organized working class and the Fabian or Hampstead intellectual. But today the coalition is fragile. What unites a Brexit-supporting, early school-leaving, working-class voter in, say, Burnley or Darlington and a graduate liberal bourgeois voter in Islington or Brighton? One wants tight controls on immigration while the other favours open borders and free movement. One wanted to leave the European Union and the other passionately wanted to remain. One yearns for social cohesion while the other embraces greater racial, sexual and gender diversity. A class culture gap has opened up.

Doing politics well is about getting the balance right and adapting to and learning from context – call it pragmatism. Labour believes it can still find the right balance, that it can unite the working-class or aspirational lower-middle class voter in Hartlepool and the middle-class graduate voter in Hampstead in a new cross-class, cross-cultural coalition. But something is missing. The invisible chain linking the nation together is broken.

'One cannot see the modern world as it is unless one recognises the overwhelming strength of patriotism, national loyalty,' Orwell wrote in *The Lion and the Unicorn*. 'In certain circumstances it can break down, at certain levels of civilisation it does not exist, but as a positive force there is nothing to set beside it. Christianity and international socialism are as weak as straw in comparison with it.'

Orwell could be romantic about the good sense of the ordinary man and woman. 'At any normal time, the ruling class will rob, mismanage, sabotage, lead us into the muck; but let popular opinion really make itself heard, let them get a tug from below that they cannot avoid feeling, and it is difficult for them not to respond.'

In Labour's Brexit-supporting heartlands, many of the party's former voters had an emphatic message for Corbyn and the London leadership in 2019, and it was repeated loud and clear eighteen months later in Hartlepool: 'Enough! No more!' This was more than a tug from below: we were witnessing a complete rejection of a party that once purported to represent the labour interest but which, in the view of some of its former supporters, had been captured by sectarians, bourgeois bohemians and university-educated Europhiles. Unfairly or otherwise, Corbyn and his closest allies were accused of hating their own country.

The decline of Labour – once hegemonic in the industrial north and Scotland – is both a warning of what can go wrong when pragmatism and compromise are rejected and a tragedy. It's a tragedy because what happened was not inevitable: the warning lights were flashing red all the way along the road from Blair to Corbyn, from the Iraq War to the Brexit referendum. By contrast, the Conservative Party has an instinct for power and a genius for survival: it shape-shifts, it adapts, it bends with the wind. It keeps winning – in England, at least.

+ + +

When Brown met Mrs Duffy, she must have seemed like a figure from the past, an unwelcome reminder of what Labour used to be before it was 'modernized'. 'I hear people say we have to stop and debate globalisation,' Tony Blair said in a 2005 conference speech, two years after the invasion of Iraq and four years after China had joined the World Trade Organization, which inaugurated the era of modern globalization. 'You might as well debate whether autumn follows summer.'

But one way of understanding Mrs Duffy is to see her not as a figure from the past but as a visitor from the future. She accepted the natural rhythm of the seasons but wanted to stop and debate globalization, and it was as if her role that afternoon in Rochdale was to warn Labour of what awaited it in the world to come. For a period, she became one of the emblems of the party's struggles – wooed by the Miliband brothers, interviewed by the newspapers – before being forgotten by Corbyn and Starmer.

'I couldn't do it,' Mrs Duffy said of the 2019 general election when we spoke nearly a decade after she was stopped in the street by Sue Nye and asked if she was Labour. 'I just couldn't vote for Corbyn. I didn't want him to be Labour leader. He's a Londoner who just serves his own community and his own group. He had no idea how fed-up people were in the north. We have old mining towns now voting for a Tory government. Unbelievable! My father – he was very left-wing – would have been turning in his grave. Why were they cheering Boris Johnson and his girlfriend in the north? That they were prepared to vote for Boris shows how bad things were.'

Mrs Duffy recalled seeing the young Tony Blair speak at a school in Rochdale not long after he became Labour leader. 'He just swept in. He had this energy and optimism. A young fellow, he wanted to get rid of the Tories – I believed in him then and what he said. "Let's hope he gets in," I said to my husband afterwards. "He's going to get in," he said. Blair was wrong about Brexit but he was right about Corbyn, who never said sorry.'

And then, repeating the phrase she'd used while discussing the young girl who was drugged and repeatedly raped by a grooming gang in Rochdale, but whose pleas for help from the police were ignored, Mrs Duffy said: 'No one listened to us. They didn't listen in Scotland either, did they?'

THE FABRIC OF PLACE

The Scottish experience – particularly the sudden and dramatic collapse of support for the Labour Party there – is relevant to the north of England, which also suffers from a long-standing democratic deficit. The 'North' is often spoken of as if it were homogenous but it obviously has its own historical, geographical, cultural and economic differences and rivalries. There is no coherent northern nationalist movement – as there is in Cornwall – and there is no bottom-up agitation for the creation of a Northern Assembly. The 'North' is not the fifth 'nation' of the UK. But there is frustration beyond the Red Wall about rule from and by Westminster. With each passing year, the pressure increases for more effective devolution in England as metro mayors in cities such as Manchester, Liverpool and Newcastle demand more decentralization of power and greater control over executive decision-making. Community begins with locality.

The Conservatives were re-elected with a big majority in 2019 not only 'to get Brexit done' but because they promised 'to level up' – another example of the party's pragmatism and flexibility, its shape-shifting and willingness to learn from context and work out what is necessary in the context. The idea of levelling up is incoherent but it presumably means boosting prosperity and opportunity beyond the south-east. England has a greater level of inter-regional inequality than any other large country in Europe. Andy Haldane, formerly chief economist at the Bank of England and now at the Royal Society of Arts, pointed out to me that the gap between the richest and poorest regions in the UK is almost twice as large as in France and three-quarters larger than in Germany. 'These income disparities across the UK are broadly mirrored in wider metrics of well-being, such as wealth, medical health and subjective measures of happiness,' he said in a 2019 speech delivered at St James Park, Newcastle.

Born on a council estate in Sunderland before his family moved to Leeds when he was a young child, Haldane has been thinking creatively about spatial inequalities, as well as other economic and social disparities. In September 2021, Haldane was announced as head of the government's levelling up taskforce, on secondment from the RSA. He went to a state comprehensive school and studied economics at Sheffield University and Warwick University before joining the Bank of England in 1989, where he stayed until 2021. He described himself as an 'imposter down here in London' but he moved with serious intent and ambition through the hushed, burnished corridors of the Bank.

After the vote for Brexit, Haldane began visiting different parts of the UK, sometimes staying overnight in towns in northern and coastal England. 'I wanted to experience first hand what's going on because the data only gets you so far.' He described his approach as anthropological, as an exercise in what Clifford Geertz calls 'deep hanging out'.

'I don't want to confine my window on the world to companies, much less CEOs of companies,' he said. 'I've been wandering around and chatting to people I might not otherwise chat to. As it turns out, the kind of people that I grew up with anyway. This is as deeply countercultural for the policy community as it's possible to imagine. This stuff is bleedin' obvious, if you're a sociologist, an anthropologist or a journalist, but it's less bleedin' obvious if you're a nerdy economist like me.'

Haldane addresses community groups, schools, faith groups, trade unions, charities, businesses – the institutions of civil society. He's interested not only in economics but in social capital, who has and doesn't have it and why. He pointed out that around 15 per cent of the population in Britain leave school 'functionally illiterate' while 50 per cent are 'functionally innumerate'.

I visited Haldane while he was still at the Bank – in atmosphere and design part cathedral, part Oxbridge college and part temple to Mammon – and in his office we discussed 'agglomeration effects', the social benefits of connection and how the most skilled, creative and ambitious among us cluster together in dynamic, thriving and culturally diverse locations: London, Oxford, Cambridge and Manchester. But what happens to those who, through circumstance or choice, are left behind in areas of poor infrastructure, reduced opportunity and neglected public spaces?

'Stories have always been the way humans make sense of a complex world and the way knowledge is spread,' Haldane said in his Newcastle speech. 'Stories also shape people's sentiment and decision-making, every bit as much as hard cash.'

He recalled visiting nearby Ashington, the old mining town where the World Cup-winning Charlton brothers were born. Since the last pit closed in 1988, many people in the town had lost the dignity and camaraderie that derives from meaningful, productive work, and this had 'led to permanent damage to the supporting eco-system – infrastructure, skills, jobs, social spaces'.

Haldane arrived by taxi in Ashington late one evening because there was no other way in. There were no buses and, as he said, 'I had narrowly missed the last passenger train from Newcastle by around fifty-five years, courtesy of Dr Beeching.'

Richard Beeching was a former chairman of British Railways whose report in the early 1960s into the future of the railways resulted in the closure of nearly 4,000 stations and 8,000 miles of track. Many towns were left without any passenger rail links. 'The costs of these closures for the towns concerned have been only too clear,' Haldane said. Inferior transport infrastructure remains an enduring challenge for the north:

One of the most important has been a loss of population, especially among younger, skilled workers. The 1 in 5 places most exposed to rail cuts have seen 24 percentage points less growth in population than the 1 in 5 least exposed. Disconnection from the mains has, for these towns, meant large-scale loss of people and skills . . . Ashington may well be less well served today than it was seventy years ago. The same is probably true of a great many other towns, large and small, right across the UK.

+ + +

Boris Johnson addressed some of these themes in a speech he gave in Manchester three days after becoming prime minister in July 2019. He lamented the decline of the old mill towns of the north-west – Oldham, Preston, Burnley, Bury, Bolton, Rochdale, Blackburn – and, despite speaking as the leader of a party that had been in power for a decade, he described how they faced 'endemic health problems, generational unemployment, down-at-heel high streets. The story has been, for young people growing up there, one of hopelessness, or the hope that one day they'll get out and never come back.'

Johnson's speech piqued my interest because I've been deeply hanging out in the north-west for several decades. I have friends and family living across the region and I was married in Bury Parish Church, a stately garrison church of medieval origin but rebuilt in the nineteenth century. The fine civic and ecclesiastical buildings in Bury, and other former textile towns – the town halls, the great churches, libraries, former post offices and Victorian arcades, sometimes empty or neglected, as they are in the centre of Oldham, for instance – stand today as a rebuke to the diminished ambitions of successive governments.

Who now seeks to build the beautiful buildings and conservation areas of the future in these towns, and others like them, and why not?

When I first began visiting these former mill towns I was struck by how religiously and racially divided they were. Bury, where my wife grew up, is home to one of the country's leading Deobandi seminaries. Founded in the city of Deoband in Uttar Pradesh, Deobandism, as rigidly interpreted by the Taliban and teachers of the madrasas of north-west Pakistan, preaches a puritanical, literalist, unforgiving iteration of Sunni Islam.

One understands why migrant communities cleave to one another but, over the years, I watched in Bury, and other nearby towns, as many local Muslims abandoned Western-style clothes: you saw more women in burqas and niqabs and men grew long beards and wore ankle-length white tunics in the Salafist style. Investment was flowing into the mosques from Saudi Arabia and other Gulf states and with it came the Wahhabi preachers, and their zealous fundamentalism. We were witnessing what the academic Mona Siddiqui calls the 'Arabization of Islam in Britain'.

It was obvious that, though they'd experienced racism and discrimination, these communities were becoming not less but more confident in their cultural and religious identity, in their sense of settled possession, which contrasted with many poor working-class whites' sense of unsettled dispossession.

The separation of Muslims in the former mill towns of the English north deepened during the New Labour years, creating mutual distrust and suspicion. 'In such a climate, there has been little attempt to develop clear values which focus on what it means to be a citizen of a modern multiracial Britain and many still look backwards to some supposedly halcyon days of a mono-cultural society, or alternatively look to their country of origin for some form of identity,' concluded a 2001 Home Office report into community cohesion, commissioned by New Labour following racial conflict between local Asians and whites in Oldham, Burnley, Bradford and Leeds.

Migrants from Pakistan and Bangladesh started arriving in Oldham and other northern towns in large numbers in the 1950s and early 1960s. They worked in the mills, established their own discrete communities and were bonded by religion and ethnicity. A form of unofficial apartheid operated and there were areas the recent arrivals understood were closed to them. Certain schools became Muslim-majority, or Muslim-dominated, and white families tried to keep their children out of them.

By the early 1980s – the cotton industry had gone, leaving behind empty factories and boarded-up mills – 30 per cent of the workforce in Oldham was unskilled or had no qualifications; many local Muslim women could not read or speak English and this contributed to their self-ghettoization. The far-right British National Party were organizing in the town.

In 2000, Darcus Howe, a black British writer and political activist, visited the town to make a Channel 4 documentary, *White Tribe*. He returned to London 'with a feeling of dread' and predicted that there would be violence in the racially divided town, which eventually erupted in 2001, when there were running street battles between whites and British Pakistanis. 'Oldham illustrates much that is wrong with race relations in this country,' Howe wrote in May 2001. 'Those who are in charge of communities in the inner cities know little about the people whose lives they are responsible for: who we are, where we come from, what we aim at. Even some black leaders have no idea.'

While making *White Tribe*, Howe encountered, for the first time, people whom he unkindly said 'fitted the American description white trash':

Their homes had a stench of decay: of damp, sweat and stale food cooked days before. The little picket fences were collapsing. The roofs were leaking. I interviewed a young man, tall and emaciated, and he described the constant fear of physical harassment by Asians. His sister was a heroin addict, a prostitute with a Pakistani pimp. His elder brother, he said, remembers a time when most whites engaged in Paki-bashing; they were hostile to their 'funny religion' . . . In those days, the elders of the Asian community had considerable influence. A young Asian in Blackburn was once beaten almost to death for challenging them and their dodgy leadership.

Howe accused municipal leaders of using housing funds to separate the communities:

The Labour mafia presided over this process. The quality of the housing they built is a disgrace . . . Most white workers in Oldham have supported the Labour Party for generations. New Labour has abandoned them while it parades its goods before Middle England. To accuse them now of harbouring fascist ideas is shameful. The economic base of Oldham and the political institutions it created have gone, leaving the white working classes stripped naked of all they had built for themselves. Speak to them and you will find that they complain that they are neglected, while the Asians are looked after by the government. Our political leaders have been strutting on the electoral stage, completely oblivious to the social degeneration that is taking place under their noses. It is a terrible indictment of modern politics.

Howe was writing nine years before Gillian Duffy met Gordon Brown. As the then prime minister discovered – and our unpredictable politics repeatedly shows – we seldom know what we think we know. *Are you Labour?*

In 2016, the Casey Review, another independent review into community cohesion, this time commissioned by the Cameron government, criticized the failures of state integration policies and expressed concern about rising Islamist extremism. The report concluded that Britain was becoming ever more diverse and that its different racial groups were increasingly integrated, but some communities were at the same time becoming more segregated.

'In some council wards, as many as 85 per cent of the population come from a single minority background, and most of these high minority concentrations are deprived Pakistani or Bangladeshi heritage communities,' wrote Louise Casey, who led the review. 'But there's more to it than that. I have also seen and heard that this sense of retreat and retrenchment can sometimes go hand in hand with deeply regressive religious and cultural practices, especially when it comes to women. These practices are preventing women from playing a full part in society, contrary to our common British values, institutions and indeed, in some cases, our laws.'

+ + +

Jim McMahon is Labour MP for Oldham West and Royton and understands the social and economic challenges in the old mill towns of the north perhaps as well as anyone I've spoken to. One wet winter morning, when I visited McMahon at his constituency office on Union Street, we discussed the legacy of the Oldham race riots and the crumbling of Labour's Red Wall. Labour's defeats had disturbed him. In May 2021 he would lead the doomed Labour campaign to defend Hartlepool from Conservative capture, a by-election defeat in the north-east which led Keir Starmer to conclude the party had 'lost the trust of working people'.

'The undercurrent was there. For me it wasn't a 2019, 2017 or even 2015 problem – this goes back decades,' McMahon said. 'This is about power: economic, social and political power. You can't get to the third until you sort out the first. There are too many people in Oldham who lack economic power. For a long time, they've put their trust in Labour to fix that, and for whatever reason we've not been able to.'

We'd previously met at several dinners in London – he always ordered off-menu, a burger and chips – and we'd kept in touch. The son of a lorry driver, McMahon left school at sixteen to work in a cash-and-carry warehouse, 'doing the trolleys'. 'There was a conversation about college at home. But, to be honest, you just get a job,' he recalled. He did a day-release course at Oldham College and later became an audio-visual technician at Manchester University. When his partner became pregnant – his son Jack is now an adult – they moved to Failsworth, Oldham. He was persuaded to get involved in local politics and eventually became leader of the council and then an MP in 2015. 'I recognized that to achieve change – and I wanted a lot of change: a new park, a new play area, a new school, new house centre, new district centre; and we did it all, by the way – the levers of power are important. The challenge is to rebuild the fabric of place.'

Oldham in effect comprises seven small towns and because of its hilly topography you can, from certain vantage points, see in the distance the dynamic, sprawling city that is today's Manchester, growing and expanding as if before your eyes. Originally a hilltop wool town on the cross-Pennine route between Manchester and York, Oldham grew extensively with the expansion of the cotton industry and coal-mining. It has many areas of entrenched deprivation and the town centre has a high density of listed former civic buildings but, dismayingly, some of the most distinguished stand empty.

Relations with the Muslim Asian community have improved since the riots; the community leaders are committed to the town,

McMahon said. 'But generationally that will probably change. How do you convince somebody – you go to university, to Manchester and you rent or buy a flat – to choose Oldham as a place to come back to?'

He understands how it feels to live precariously, without secure work or networks of support. Or to grow up believing that, if you have ambition, you must leave. He's not a sectarian and aspires to moderate the language of politics. He wants people to have more social capital and greater control over their lives. 'As a society, we have been drifting apart and politics is a reflection of society.'

There are some days when, from one of Oldham's windy hill-tops, McMahon looks at the bright lights of Manchester, only five miles away, and knows something is missing. 'You see the red lights of the cranes that are building in Manchester, all the activity there,' he said. 'You don't see the same in Oldham. Town centres and high streets are really struggling. They become a symbol about where the town is going. When people see shutters rolled down or the boards on the windows, they're disheartened.'

He paused and looked across the table, as if issuing a direct challenge. 'If Oldham was a town built on key industries and those industries aren't here any more, what are the new industries?'

A RIVER RUNS THROUGH IT

I pondered this question as I drove into Rochdale town centre and was reminded of something Andy Haldane had said when I visited him at the Bank of England. Reflecting on his period of deep hanging out in some of the Brexit-supporting towns of the north, Haldane said, 'You go to these places, and in a spatial sense, they are but a stone's throw away from a thriving, bustling city, but it feels like outer space! And the notion you might commute there to get a job is la-la land for people who live there.'

It was mid-afternoon, six weeks before the country would be locked down, and it was as if night was already falling. I parked my car in Town Hall Square, behind the neo-Gothic building which Nikolaus Pevsner said possessed a 'rare picturesque beauty' and was 'one of the most ambitious High Victorian town halls of England'. The cafes I approached were closed, or in the process of closing, and I could not find anywhere to buy a hot drink: it was midweek yet the atmosphere was somnambulant.

I ended up buying a pot of Earl Grey tea in a near-deserted Regal Moon pub – the former site of the art deco Regal Cinema – and idly flicked at my phone, looking at emails. Later I wandered alone through some of the majestic rooms of the Grade-I listed town hall which now seemed like a memorial to an age of greater certainty, my footsteps reverberating in the silence. It was completely dark when I left the town hall. In the near distance, as I stood by the clock tower, I could see the lights shining in the high residential tower blocks known locally as the Seven Sisters. They were completed in the 1960s and officially opened by Labour's Richard Crossman in more optimistic times. The constant roar of passing traffic distracted me. Our mission, Jim McMahon had said, must be to 'rebuild the fabric of place'. Politics is about place: where we live, work, meet, gather, interact. But what happens when a place loses its purpose?

When the cooperative movement began in Rochdale the Victorian boomtown knew what its purpose was, and the Rochdale Society of Equitable Pioneers, many of them weavers, were motivated by shared belonging and a common ethic which amounted to a powerful desire to push back against exploitation – Blake's dark satanic mills – and create a more equitable society. Somewhere along the way we lost that greater commitment to the common good.

It was raining, the pavements had a sombre shine and I walked over to the River Roch, streaming silverly through the town centre, the same river that had once powered some of the cotton spinning wheels in the great mills of northern England. I closed my eyes and for a while just listened to the turbulent rush of the water.

PART FOUR

PART FOUR

8 LOCKDOWN

In the summer before the first lockdown, an old friend who lives with his family in Brighton called to say that he and his mother Margaret were planning a return visit to Harlow and would my mother and I like to meet them in the town for dinner. It turned out to be a nostalgic homecoming for Margaret, who sadly died only a few months later.

During what turned out to be her final farewell to Harlow, Margaret visited three friends and former neighbours at Tye Green Lodge, a care home in the old village of Tye Green. One was blind and two had dementia. It was poignant to hear what had become of people I'd once known and in whose gardens I used to play during the long school holidays.

In his original masterplan, Frederick Gibberd preserved long-established villages and hamlets like Tye Green because he understood their presence would enhance the environment of the west Essex new town. Whenever by chance I heard mention of Tye Green over the years, I pictured the big gardens of the old houses we believed were haunted, the small, cramped, musty shop where we bought crisps and comics (long since closed) and the working farm where my parents bought eggs and cream (also gone).

One evening in the early weeks of the pandemic, my interest was piqued when, on the BBC regional news, it was reported that Tye Green Lodge, which has sixty-one beds and is operated by Quantum Care, a self-described 'not-for-profit care provider', had been quarantined after a coronavirus outbreak. The Lodge was built on scrubland we used to call the Orchard. Over a four-week period, before the first national lockdown, seventeen residents and one member of staff died. Seven residents died in hospital after they'd tested positive for Covid; the others died with or from the disease but were never tested. I wondered if Margaret's friends were among the lost.

The tragedy of Tye Green Lodge was a parable of the vulnerability of our care homes. As the government floundered, patients were prematurely discharged from hospitals to care homes without being tested for the virus, with inevitable consequences. No testing was available in the homes and staff were not provided with adequate personal protective equipment (PPE); some of them were moving from home to home as itinerant freelance workers.

Why did this small story matter beyond my own personal interest in it? It mattered because it revealed in microcosm something much bigger: that the country was not logistically or morally prepared for the pandemic shock. First, it re-emphasized how slow the British government had been to respond effectively to the emergency, especially in care homes. On 25 February, the government stated: 'It remains very unlikely that people receiving care in a care home . . . will become infected.' In mid-March, in a panicked intervention, 25,000 patients were discharged from hospital to create extra bed capacity, many to care homes, and some of them inevitably carried the virus with them.

Second, it demonstrated that what had happened at Tye Green Lodge (and many other similar homes) was not an aberration but part of a pattern of neglect several decades in the making. Successive governments have evaded responsibility for the crisis in social care, believing it could be fixed by private business. This told us something about their preference for short-term fixes over the difficult choices that are required to grapple with one of the most challenging issues of our times: an ageing population that is living longer but not necessarily healthier lives. Britain was a market society that had privileged quick resolutions and just-in-time supply chains over long-term strategic planning and national resilience. The fundamental question now was this: what do we owe each other as citizens and what are we prepared to do about it?

MADE IN CHINA

We all have our pandemic stories. Mine began when I called my friend Michael Barrett, an infection biologist at the University of Glasgow, because I wanted to know what he thought about the new coronavirus that was circulating in Wuhan, the capital of Hubei Province. Would it stay in China or spread around the world? How worried should we be? Where had it come from?

One theory was the virus may have originated in bats and transited to humans, through an intermediary host such as an infected farm animal sold at a Wuhan wet market, or perhaps even a pangolin, the most trafficked animal in the world. At first, the Chinese Communist Party (CCP) responded to the extreme infectivity of the virus by trying to cover it up and then, when this was no longer sustainable, by putting Wuhan into quarantine, an intervention described as 'unprecedented in public health history' by the World Health Organization (WHO). Another theory was that the virus had escaped from the Wuhan Institute of Virology after it was altered by 'gain of function' experiments making it more virulent and transmissible.

Mike and I have known each other since our primary school days and, together with another old friend, we were all set to visit Sri Lanka to follow an England cricket tour. Even then Mike was doubtful the trip would be possible. As a research scientist, he allows evidence to inform his judgements. He's not easily alarmed but during our conversation he sounded *alarmed* about the new highly contagious pathogen, not least, he said, because the Chinese authorities were so 'comprehensively alarmed'. The CCP had the experience of the severe acute respiratory syndrome (SARS) epidemic of 2003–4 to guide its response: the new coronavirus appeared to be less lethal than SARS, but more contagious, it had a longer incubation period and it was spreading asymptomatically. We would soon have to lock down and close schools, here, too, Mike predicted.

Ever since the 1970s scientists had been warning about the emergence of new zoonotic diseases as humans irrevocably overstepped ecological limits. In the era of the climate emergency and as so many natural habitats were being destroyed, was the new future already here?

The people featured in those early news reports from China were wearing protective clothing and face coverings, and they moved through this blanched world like aliens from another planet. How many of us, then, thought that shutting down a modern city would be possible in the open societies of the West? We had our answer soon enough.

The first confirmed cases of the new coronavirus in Britain were on 29 January and concerned two Chinese nationals who became ill while on a trip to York. The government had made no attempt to close the borders or stop potentially infected people entering the country. The next day the WHO belatedly declared Covid-19 a 'Public Health Emergency of International Concern'. On 6 February, a British businessman named Steve Walsh, from Hove in Sussex, was diagnosed with the virus and began a two-week period of isolation at St Thomas' Hospital in London. He'd recently returned from a conference in Singapore and had then travelled to the French Alps for a skiing holiday. He was later linked to eleven other cases and was the first British 'super spreader'.

On 28 February, a man from Surrey became the first person

to have caught coronavirus without having left Britain, which proved the virus was spreading within the country; in March a woman in her seventies died from Covid-19 in hospital, the first official death in Britain (though we now know that others had died from Covid-19 before that date).

By this time, the respiratory virus was circulating freely among the population, and the British government was floundering because its pandemic preparation plan had been devised for some new strain of influenza, not a new coronavirus that spread through human-to-human transmission. In northern Italy intensive care units were now crashing under the strain of Covid infections. On 3 March, Boris Johnson joked that he'd shaken hands with coronavirus patients during a hospital visit and would 'continue to shake hands'. That same day, the Scientific Advisory Group for Emergencies (SAGE), whose members support government decision-making during emergencies, cautioned the public 'against greetings such as shaking hands and hugging, given existing evidence about the importance of hand hygiene'. On 11 March, the WHO finally declared coronavirus an exponentially increasing pandemic, and yet the four-day Cheltenham horse racing festival, which attracts huge crowds to the racecourse at Prestbury Park in Gloucestershire, went ahead even as mass gatherings were cancelled across mainland Europe.

I had tickets for the Cheltenham Festival but chose not to attend after another conversation with Professor Barrett. 'We will all soon know someone who has had the virus and then someone who has died from it,' he said gloomily. 'The Covid surge has begun.' This assessment turned out to be bleakly true and illness and loss soon touched everything. By this time, the surviving residents of Tye Green Lodge were quarantined in their rooms and no outsiders could enter the care home.

On 12 March, the government inexplicably abandoned

community testing – which meant infected people could not be identified and isolated until they were in hospital – and seemed prepared to let it spread exponentially through the population in an attempt to create 'herd immunity'. Mitigation had been chosen over prevention and containment. But then everything changed.

THE COVID MODELLER

On 16 March Neil Ferguson, an epidemiologist at Imperial College London and a member of SAGE, published what has since become a notorious (and much-disputed) report. Its findings so disturbed the government that it made an abrupt change to its Covid strategy and hastened the UK into lockdown and the economy into recession.

From the middle of January onwards, Ferguson's infectious disease modelling team at Imperial College had warned about the risks SARS-COV-2 posed to public health. Ferguson's initial modelling of the disease was based on flu transmission but he refined it as more precise data became available, notably to take account of the catastrophe unfolding in Lombardy. By mid-March his co-authored report stated that, if unchecked, the virus could kill more than 500,000 people in the United Kingdom and more than two million in the United States. Even with mitigation, the Imperial College report said, 250,000 could die in the UK and up to 1.2 million in the US. 'Suppression is the only viable strategy at the current time,' the report concluded. The media seized on it and the headlines were lurid.

'The figure of 500,000 deaths was never really going to happen,' Ferguson told me. 'But the number that really did influence things was that if we did everything short of a lockdown, we would end up with 250,000 deaths in the UK, and with a level of NHS demand which would be unsustainable. Those are the numbers which really changed policy.'

Spooked by the Imperial College report, the British government did more than simply change policy: it panicked. On the evening of Monday, 23 March, in a televised address, Boris Johnson, an instinctive libertarian who as a frivolous newspaper columnist had specialized in ridiculing the nanny state and Brussels bureaucrats, declared a national emergency. We were entering what turned out to be the first of several lockdowns – Johnson told us which behaviours were and were not permitted under the law – and in the days that followed, a surreal silence fell upon the land as we braced ourselves for what seemed like the horror of mass death and illness. Covid was a disease against which we appeared then to have no medical solutions other than to lockdown and isolate. 'We talk about lockdown now as if it's something standard that governments do,' Jeremy Farrar, director of the Wellcome Trust, said. 'It's not. It's bizarre. It's a horrific thing to do. Societies haven't been locked down since the Middle Ages. But if you lose control of an epidemic, then it is your last resort.'

Neil Ferguson regrets not having been more emphatic in his recommendations at SAGE meetings earlier in the crisis. 'I should have been more forthright in making the case for lockdown. Pandemics are not like hurricanes,' he told me. 'You don't hunker down, weather the storm, and then everything goes back to normal. It's a dynamical system, it's a virus spreading in the human population: what happens to it depends on how we behave, how we interact. What we've learned of this virus is that health systems cannot cope with a surge.'

Born in 1968, Ferguson grew up in Wales – his father was an educational psychologist and his mother an Anglican priest – and he studied physics at Oxford before he switched to mathematical biology after completing a PhD. He'd been entangled in public controversies before. His modelling work on both the swine flu epidemic in 2009 and the foot-and-mouth outbreak in Britain in 2001 was described as 'overzealous'. One of his models predicted that in the worst-case scenario 65,000 people in the UK could die of swine flu; the actual figure was no greater than 500. One Devon vet called the contiguous cull of cattle and sheep in 2001, in which as many as six million were killed, 'carnage by computer'.

Nothing prepared Ferguson for becoming one of the public faces of the pandemic: 'Professor Lockdown'. He was traduced and ridiculed in the newspapers and on social media by lockdown sceptics who casually dismissed the menace and lethality of the virus. Imperial College had to put in place very specific cybersecurity around Ferguson's email accounts, and its own servers, because there were days when his account was being spammed with over ten million hostile emails.

Less than two months after the publication of the Imperial College report, Ferguson – by this time he'd caught and recovered from Covid after self-isolating for two weeks – resigned from his advisory role on SAGE after a newspaper revealed that his girlfriend (who was in a polyamorous marriage) had visited him at least twice at his London flat, thus breaking the spirit of lockdown. This was a period when partners could not be present at the birth of their children; when weddings were being cancelled and fewer than ten people could attend funerals; when elderly grandparents could only glimpse their families through closed windows, and people living alone endured months of isolation.

Ferguson was denounced for hypocrisy and, on the evening of his resignation, was shamed on social media. The American multi-billionaire businessman Elon Musk tweeted: 'This guy [Ferguson] has caused massive strife to the world with his absurdly fake "science".'

It was a profoundly painful and chastening experience. 'I look back and think, "How could I have been so naive?"' Ferguson said.

He loathes the sobriquet Professor Lockdown. 'Absolutely hate it! I also got bizarrely categorized as almost a semi-official government spokesman. If you go back to the SAGE meetings, I was never sceptical about lockdown, but I was always very, very conscious of the economic and social impact it would have. I suppose I felt a need to explain it to people, communicate why it was necessary.'

Despite his many appearances in the media, Ferguson never saw himself as a public figure, least of all a Covid celebrity. 'You have a professional side, and it didn't really impinge on my personal life in that strange cognitive disconnect between yourself as a personal individual with relationships – a complicated personal life – and my professional life. And the two came crashing together. I was stupid and naive, and I regret it. It was very traumatic for my wife and son.'

+ + +

For my friend Phil Whitaker, an experienced medical doctor working on the front line against the virus, lockdown was the correct policy decision but imposed too late. He remains sceptical of Ferguson's original modelling, however, because he believes it either overestimated the size of the surge of coronavirus cases in Britain or underestimated the efficacy of lockdown measures, or both. This mattered because the models created the chilling prospect among public health experts that innumerable sick patients would not receive the life support they needed – decisions would have to be made about who lived or died – as had happened in northern Italy.

'That fear led to the sheer panic we witnessed,' Whitaker recalled. 'The panic led to the policy of evacuating medically fit inpatients from hospital at top speed, with no regard to Covid-19 positivity, into nursing homes. As the reality unfolded, the modelling had vastly over-predicted numbers and the policy looked increasingly negligent.'

What had happened at Tye Green Lodge was an early warning of policy error and system failure.

BE NEAR ME

The first lockdown coincided with unprecedentedly radiant spring weather; April and May 2020 were officially the sunniest on record. The roads fell silent, schools closed and the skies seemed empty. Freed from our old routines – the daily commute, the school run, the office meeting – some of us sought comfort and solace in nature, marvelling at what could be seen, and how it made us feel, now that we had time enough to see, notice, hear, appreciate.

Some people took up bird-spotting or simply listened to birdsong; the daily walk became a source of consolation, we shared memes on social media of elusive wild animals appearing in previously densely populated, car-cluttered urban settings; we delighted that white stork chicks had hatched in the wild in Britain for the first time in several centuries and that mountain goats had invaded the streets of Llandudno in north Wales. Some of us took up running or cycling or gardening. Children drew and painted pictures of rainbows and put them in the windows of their homes, humble expressions of shared solidarity and resilience. Some people reconnected via Zoom with old friends and lovers. Or binge-watched movies and drama series on Netflix. Or exercised while watching Joe Wicks online fitness work-outs. My early lockdown obsession was trees after I failed to identify a majestic white poplar at the bottom of the garden of the house we'd recently bought. After this, I tried (and mostly succeeded with the help of a downloaded app) to identify nearly every new tree I encountered. Why had I never done this before?

Through the warm days of early summer, between Zoom and Teams calls and online staff meetings, I worked at a weathered wooden table beneath the silvery shadows cast by the white poplar, the sea-like sound of the wind among its shining leaves. I spent evenings, when I wasn't watching the news or television with our son, reading books I'd read before, or had never finished, or had merely glanced at. That led me to the poems of Tennyson and to the long, interconnecting series we know as 'In Memoriam', seventeen years in the making. It is dedicated to, and a long lament for, Arthur Hallam, a charismatic friend Tennyson had met at Cambridge – Hallam had been engaged to the poet's sister Emily Tennyson.

Hallam died suddenly, aged twenty-two, from an aneurism while travelling with his father in Vienna, and reading Tennyson's elegy for his friend seemed somehow appropriate as the Covid mortality and infection rates were gravely announced on the nightly BBC News. We were being forced into a greater consideration of mortality's salience: an all-consuming awareness by individuals that their death is inevitable.

Every Third Thought by Robert McCrum is a book about coming to terms with mortality. When he was forty-two, McCrum suffered a severe stroke which left him disabled. He's not a religious believer and, in this book, having just turned sixty, McCrum is feeling more physically vulnerable than usual after one day he falls in the street and ends up in hospital. And he is unsettled by regrets: the failure of a marriage, career frustrations, missed opportunities.

'To me, the mystery of death and dying is only equalled by the mystery of life and living,' he writes:

Consoling narratives must be patched together from
transient fragments of experience. So why not celebrate

'nowness' and live in the present? Discover the joy of wisdom and experience. Cherish your family. Celebrate the human drama in all its magical variety. In truth, there is no other sensible narrative available. Unless you believe in an afterlife – which I don't – this must be the only way forward.

Suffering can be redemptive: in McCrum's case it was. 'Until we are sick, we understand not,' as John Keats wrote.

We should all wish that the pandemic had not happened, and no one would surely willingly suffer in order to grow spiritually. But the fundamental question for me back then was this: what had we lost but also gained during the crisis? Would individuals and societies experience a form of post-traumatic growth or revert to the careless and destructive ways of old?

+ + +

One spring afternoon, in the pre-pandemic world, I'd visited the philosopher and writer Bryan Magee at the nursing home where he was living in Headington, Oxford. Magee had been seriously ill and could no longer walk, but he remained extraordinarily lucid. We talked about his long career as a public educator, broadcaster, politician and writer. We'd met once before at his London flat, two decades earlier, and as an undergraduate I'd valued his work.

Magee was a self-described agnostic yet remained open to the possibility that death was not the absolute end. 'I do genuinely believe the possibility that death might be total extinction,' he said. 'We may be obliterated, annihilated, but it's only a possibility; something else might be the case, and I generally believe that too.'

Even in early childhood Magee felt the presence of death and as an adult he was sometimes driven, as he told me at our first encounter, 'to the edge of despair' by unanswerable existential questions. A future in which he would not exist seemed unthinkable to Magee, and yet he could not stop thinking about it. 'He'll be remembered for many things but, for me, nobody wrote more hauntingly about mortality,' Matthew Syed wrote of Magee.

The closing paragraph of Magee's book *Ultimate Questions*, what he considered to be his final philosophical statement, is among the most haunting he wrote because in it he contemplates his own death. 'I can only hope that when it is my turn, my curiosity will overcome my fear – though I may then be in the position of a man whose candle goes out and plunges him into pitch darkness at the very instant when he thought he was about to find what he was looking for.'

Sigmund Freud said during the First World War that 'no one believes in his own death'. That's not quite right: we believe in the finality of death itself but most of the time try to avoid thinking about it because such thoughts can lead to feelings of hopelessness and terror. But death – of loved ones, of friends, of strangers – seemed omnipresent during the first peak, and I struggled to escape from the pressure of it as some of my own friends' parents died from Covid and every day the suffering of so many others was revealed.

What I liked most about 'In Memoriam' was its refusal to submit to despair: as a reader you're taken on a long journey from darkness to light, from mourning to reconciliation. It ends with the marriage of Tennyson's sister and, with his religious faith revitalized, the poet's acceptance of death's inescapability. Most strikingly, even as the poet reaches out for happiness, Arthur Hallam remains close to him, in his memories, in his prayers, an always-absent present. 'Be near me,' the poet says, and the dead man is.

THE HUMBLING

By the late summer of 2020, Rishi Sunak, the chancellor of the Exchequer, who was sceptical of lockdowns and wanted to prioritize economic recovery, prepared to unwind the government scheme that offered generous financial support to furloughed workers: people were in effect paid by the state not to work. And we were being urged to 'Eat Out to Help Out' to stimulate consumer demand, as well as return to work. But as autumn arrived, the government changed course again and announced a second wave of infection was sweeping across these islands. The fragile unity of the early spring had long since dissipated. Unemployment was rising along with the national debt. Lockdown sceptics were marching against state restrictions. As many as six million people were reported to be taking anti-depressant medication. Support for Scottish independence was surging. The misnamed United Kingdom was becoming a land of fissures as what should have been a unified nationwide effort in response to the pandemic exposed deepening divides.

On the evening of Saturday, 31 October 2020, a wet, windy Halloween, a media conference was called in haste at 10 Downing Street. Boris Johnson, flanked in what was a familiar ritual by his medical and scientific advisers Chris Whitty and Patrick Vallance, announced England would be locked down for a second time because the virus was spreading dangerously again (there was no mention then of the potential threat posed by new variants such as B.1.167 that later emerged in India).

This lockdown was different from the first because it was not truly nationwide: Scotland, Wales and Northern Ireland – the devolved administrations, as Johnson called them when discussing a 'four nation approach', a new phrase in the political lexicon – would decide their own response. This was England's lockdown, and England's alone. The 'four nations' of the kingdom were pulling against one another rather than together: the devolution of health, and many other responsibilities, meant lockdown was not co-ordinated across Britain, for better and worse. It seemed as if the Johnson administration spoke for England alone, though divisions within England remained significant, with northern mayors such as Labour's Andy Burnham in open revolt against central command from Westminster.

By this time, officially more than 45,000 people had died in the UK from Covid-19 and that stormy weekend we reached a harrowing milestone as the number of confirmed coronavirus cases surpassed one million. Within a few weeks the official death figure had passed 50,000, and it continued to rise remorselessly so that by the end of the year more than 70,000 had died. Against this backdrop, a no-deal Brexit would have been not only irresponsible but calamitous. It did not happen. A free trade deal between the UK and EU was eventually signed, without celebration or fanfare, on Christmas Eve 2020.

The New Year did not bring a change of fortune because of the spread of a new, more infectious variant of the virus, B117, which was first identified in the south-east. It became known as the Kent variant and, inevitably, overseas as the British variant.

On 4 January 2021, the day after many children returned to school in England after the Christmas holiday, the United Kingdom entered another lockdown; this replaced the unconvincing tiered system of local restrictions in England. Daily recorded infection rates were now exceeding 50,000 and children sent back to school on the first Monday of the first school week of the New Year were told to stay at home the next day because schools were 'vectors of transmission'. By the end of January, the number of people who had died from Covid passed 100,000. Only a mass nationwide vaccination programme of a kind never undertaken before could unlock the country.

The hastily arranged Halloween media conference provided an opportunity for the prime minister to find a tone and an idiom appropriate for what was a moment not only of national mourning but of cognitive shock. Johnson is a writer. He speaks Latin and Ancient Greek and admires the great classical leaders, notably Pericles. Earlier in the year Johnson had nearly died from Covid-19, and when he came out of hospital, he'd given an impassioned, breathless speech about his gratitude to the NHS for saving his life. I'd never heard him speak as he did that day – so authentically from the heart, with such power and emotional truth.

For whatever reason – a reluctance to deliver bad news, a fear of the wrath of the libertarian right in his party, a fundamental unseriousness – he could not, as David Brooks wrote of Donald Trump's response to the pandemic, step outside of his political role and reveal 'himself uncloaked and humbled, as someone who can draw on his own pains and simply be present with others as one sufferer among a common sea of sufferers'.

The one sentence of Johnson's from the Halloween media conference that truly resonated was when he said, 'We've got to be humble in the face of nature.'

+ + +

Humility in the face of nature: much of what my old friend Michael Barrett, the infection biologist, had predicted at the start of the crisis had come to pass – the spread of the virus outside China; its lethal threat to older people and those with comorbidities; the introduction of Wuhan-style lockdowns and quarantines across Europe; home working and the closure of schools. During the first lockdown, according to the International Labour Organization, 80 per cent of the global workforce had been disrupted in some way, and 1.4 billion young people were furloughed from education. 'The new coronavirus achieved in days what both progressives and nationalists had long been fighting for,' wrote Bruno Maçães. 'Powerful economic interests were sidelined, whole industries had to temporarily close down, oil consumption plummeted, national borders were closed and export bans imposed.' This, said the economic historian Adam Tooze, was 'flat out the most extraordinary thing to have happened in modern economic history'. What had been once unimaginable was more than simply imaginable: it had happened.

In his book *Feline Philosophy: Cats and the Meaning of Life*, John Gray mocks the vanities of the secular faith in continuous progress. 'Our lives are shaped by chance and our emotions by the body. Much of human life – and much of philosophy – is an attempt to divert ourselves from this fact.'

Like Gray, I do not believe in the inevitability of progress, and yet through this darkest phase of the Covid crisis I retained a belief in the possibility of progress – by which I mean, I retained, as many of us did, a stubborn belief in the genius of science to carry us through.

Pandemics and infectious diseases pitilessly reveal the arbitrariness of fate and the frailty of the human condition. The interconnectedness of our world merely enhances its fragility. The virus may have emerged in and spread from China but Chinese scientists had sequenced the genome of SARS-COV-2 and shared it with the world, firing the starting gun on the race for a vaccine. By the end of 2020, the world had a plurality of vaccines against coronavirus – one of the first was developed by a team led by Sarah Gilbert at Oxford University's Jenner Institute in association with AstraZeneca, an Anglo-Swedish pharmaceutical firm – and inoculations had already begun in Britain.

The production of vaccines was collaborative and multinational – batches of the British state-backed Oxford-AstraZeneca vaccine were manufactured at the Serum Institute in India – but placing pre-orders for them was a high risk in the early phase of development. There was no guarantee which ones would be effective. The wealthier states were able to mitigate that risk by placing orders for multiple vaccines, which left poorer countries scrambling to catch up or without any supplies. The age of vaccine nationalism was upon us.

+ + +

My mother had her first jab on 30 December 2020 as part of the national vaccine programme organized through the NHS; I had mine a few months later in the reassuringly modest setting of the hall of a local primary school. My appointment was at 6 p.m. and I arrived five minutes early. I was checked in and shown straight to a table where I was greeted by a friendly nurse and a nursing assistant. Nearby uniformed service personnel from the 4 Armoured Medical Regiment guided and assisted. I chatted briefly to the nurses, I was asked to read a medical questionnaire and then I was jabbed, one of more than 900 at the school that day and of nearly one million across the country. I left the building at exactly 6.02 p.m., the whole experience being both moving and extraordinary efficient. It reminded me of the humble ritual of voting on election days – the low-key setting, the volunteers, the purposeful bustle as people come and go, the trust and decency of it all.

Walking home that evening, I recalled the early outbreak of the virus at Tye Green Lodge and reflected on how much had changed in the world since then. In the West we lived in the most technologically advanced and globally interconnected societies in human history. Yet we knew now we could be overwhelmed by plagues and disease just as our ancestors were, and that our way of life could be abruptly curtailed, stopped, halted. We could be locked down. The whole experience was a turning point in the flow of history, as John Gray put it. From here we would be on a permanent state of pandemic alert.

History does not have a *telos*, a fixed direction of travel and end point. History is discontinuous and contingent, perhaps even circular, as the ancients believed. In these times, we better understood how life is shaped by chance and randomness and what it means to live in a world of finite resources and vulnerable ecosystems. What would come next?

TWILIGHT OF THE UNION

When I wasn't working, during that first pandemic winter, I watched a lot of football on television, as distraction and entertainment: games without crowds. During one FA Cup match, Manchester United v. West Ham at Old Trafford, played on an icy February night and shown live on BBC television, my friend the novelist Ed Docx pressed send on a sombre tweet: 'Something so haunting about watching two great clubs playing without a crowd in the snow. As if it's already the future and we're looking back at a documentary about these bleak years.'

Not for the first time recently, I thought of the closing lines of Tennyson's 'Ulysses'. Until the experience of lockdown forced me to seek out unread or half-read books from my shelves, I'd never really considered its theme of loss before, and it was curious that I turned to it now, this poem from the high Victorian period:

> We are not now that strength which in old days
> Moved earth and heaven, that which we are, we are;
> One equal temper of heroic hearts,
> Made weak by time and fate, but strong in will
> To strive, to seek, to find, and not to yield.

We had not yielded. And we had been gifted a second chance to look again at what both the Brexit process and the Covid crisis had revealed about what wasn't working within and between the nations and regions of the United Kingdom. If we spurned the opportunity for national renewal, if we returned to the old pre-pandemic ways, the Union would not survive.

9 UNTIED KINGDOM

The wheel is come full circle: we are here.

This is a book about Englishness, English identity and how England has changed over the last twenty years or so, in which I ask questions rather than attempt to provide definitive answers because I want readers to reach their own conlusions. When he swept to power in 1997, Tony Blair believed we were at the beginning of a new, more optimistic era in British politics and society. When you rebrand something – a company, a political party, even a country – you try to tell convincing stories about it. Narratives shape politics. In the nineties, Blair sensed that people were open to being told a new national story – about England, about Britain, about the future. He wanted to give an optimistic account of the country Britain would become under his leadership. He wanted to tell a story people could believe in. Who were we? Blair thought he knew. He told a story about a 'new' party and a 'new' country that was modern, progressive, meritocratic, dynamic, open to the world and above all youthful. He wanted to lead a young country – the country of Cool Britannia and Britpop and of the new globalization. He did not want to look back, in anger or regret, because he was rushing towards the future. For Blair, anticipation of the future makes the new times 'faster, more exciting'. It was as if he wanted to be unchained from history, to bring about a shift in national consciousness.

'I want us to be a young country again,' he said defiantly in that 1995 Labour conference speech, as if this could be willed into being. Then, more emphatically: 'We *will* be a young country, equipped for the future with a just society, a new politics and a clear understanding of its role in the world.'

As Labour leader, Blair won three general election victories and was a principal advocate of the new double liberalism – social and economic – and so were the 'modernizing' Tory Cameroons who took power after New Labour in 2010. Blair favoured greater European integration, open borders, free markets, outsourcing, the deregulation of finance, and the free movement of goods, capital, services and people. He led military interventions in Sierra Leone and Kosovo. Emboldened by their outcome, in a speech in Chicago in April 1999, in the aftermath of the NATO intervention in the southern Balkans, he defended Western values and made the 'moral' case for becoming 'actively involved in other people's conflicts'. He later proselytized for the wars in Iraq and Afghanistan, and seemed to believe that history was on his side – or at least that he was on the right side of history. But as the historian Robert Tombs wrote, 'Those who claim that history is on their side are abusing it: and the abuse of history is one of mankind's oldest cultural endeavours.'

The story didn't end as Blair – or indeed David Cameron – would have wished. It continued with Brexit and a disunited kingdom. What didn't they understand about their own country? What didn't they know?

What they didn't know – or perhaps chose to ignore – was that during the New Labour years, and after them, other powerful forces were in play, in deep or peripheral England, far from the great cities, the 'New Citadels' of globalized wealth as the French geographer and author Christophe Guilluy calls them. Something was stirring in the old industrial towns, the conservative shires and the faraway run-down coastal regions: an inchoate English revolt. It took many forms – the vote for Brexit, a provincial rebellion against metropolitan power, was perhaps its ultimate expression – but it was a revolt all the same.

Since the 2008 financial crisis, and the Great Recession that followed, British politics has seemed confused and disordered, and so have the politics of many other Western liberal democracies, not least the United States. When I started thinking about this book, the British Parliament was deadlocked over Brexit, and I wanted to know then whether we as Britons still shared some underlying common experience, something that could bring us together in all our difference, in spite of our differences. Was it even appropriate to speak of Britain as a single united country at a time of rising English and Scottish nationalism? The pandemic made that question seem even more relevant.

WE THE BRITISH

Among our closest neighbours, when I was growing up, were three Sicilian families from a poor rural community. Two Sicilian brothers had married two sisters and, after they settled in Harlow, they lived next door to each other on our quiet cul-de-sac; the sisters' younger brother lived just across the road, with his wife and family, in a corner plot. The Sicilian families came to England in search of greater opportunity and established what became a successful business, a commercial nursery in the Lee Valley where they farmed cucumbers and supplied them to supermarkets. It was always a thrill to be invited to the nurseries, and sometimes when we were there and weren't playing in the local woods, or in the huge, echoing barns and warehouses, or relishing the defamiliarizing humidity inside the futuristic greenhouses, we helped assemble the cardboard boxes in which the cucumbers were stacked. This work was a source of valuable pocket money. The children of the Sicilian families were my close friends. They were born in Essex and spoke Estuary English but never called themselves English. For some reason this used to bother me while also offering early insight into the complexities of identity questions in the multinational British state in which I was growing up and trying to understand. 'Why isn't there a British football team?' I used to ask my father. 'We'd win the World Cup.'

My friends had Italian names and spoke an Italian dialect at home. They supported the Italian national football team and celebrated noisily outside our house when Italy won the 1982 World Cup in Spain. They were also unapologetically British. I once tried to convince one of my friends that he was English and for some reason it mattered to me greatly that he agreed. He almost did; I say almost because in the end, despite my prompting, he just couldn't describe himself as English. 'I'm British,' he said. 'And Sicilian. And Italian.' But not English. Never English. 'I support Arsenal but I'd never support England,' he laughed, and this hurt me. It should not have. It was entirely natural for him to retain an emotional loyalty to his ancestral homeland and family heritage. It took me a long time to understand that his rejection of the English football team was not a rejection of England, and certainly not of Britain, the country he called Great Britain. It was just that my friend had deeper loyalties to a country in which he'd never lived but whose culture ran through him.

I encountered similar attitudes among my black friends at university – this was in the late 1980s – who called themselves British, or more accurately Black British, but never English. They were born in England and especially relished London street culture – the football, music, fashion, nightclubs – but Englishness remained a problematic concept and identity. For them, it was associated with whiteness and the legacy of colonialism and empire, with feelings of exclusion and memories of the casual racism of the mainstream culture of their childhoods. British, not English. Never English.

+ + +

Britishness was an institutionally constructed, officially imposed identity, shaped by a sense of imperial mission. As a unifying identity it was perhaps at its most coherent during the two world wars and their immediate aftermath, and the Royal Family, the BBC and NHS were once the supreme embodiments of the idea of Britain. As a binding sense of British nationhood fades away, and with it a shared vocabulary and common purpose, we can ask: what is England?

England emerged out of the ancient kingdoms of Wessex, Mercia and Northumbria and, in the tenth century, Athelstan, King of the West Saxons, used the new title of 'Rex Anglorum' – 'King of the English'. Under the rule of Athelstan, England became one nation for the first time in 929. It has had strong central government since Anglo-Saxon times, though there have been periods of prolonged dynastic and civil war, and it has entrenched class and regional divisions, especially between north and south. Even today much of the land of the British Isles is owned by the aristocracy, the 6,000 families and their relatives, the so-called cousinhood, whose influence and control were historically exerted through inter-marriage and through the Conservative Party, the House of Lords, Oxford and Cambridge, the great public schools, the Inns of Court, the armed forces and the Crown. Her Majesty's Land Registry has not carried out a cadastral survey of Britain and as much as 30 per cent of the land in England and Wales remains unregistered though privately owned.

The explicit connection between feudalism, land ownership and political power was not severed finally until 1999, when all but ninety-two of the hereditary peers were removed from the House of Lords. In total the United Kingdom occupies sixty million acres, of which forty-one million are designated 'agricultural' land, fifteen million are considered 'natural wastage' (forests, rivers, national parks and mountains) and owned by institutions such as the Forestry Commission, the National Trust and the Ministry of Defence, and four million are the 'urban plot', the densely congested land on which most of the people of these islands live. As it stands, 69 per cent of the acreage of Britain is calculated to be owned by 0.6 per cent of the population.

Following the Act of Union of 1707, the Protestant succession was adopted and the English became British. The transition was consensual not coercive. British national identity and an island mentality were constructed in opposition to an 'Other' – Catholicism, hostile and rivalrous European states, especially France. The island nation had settled boundaries, 'marked out by the sea, clear, incontrovertible, apparently pre-ordained. "Fenced in with a wall which knows no master but God only"', as Linda Colley wrote. Scotland within the Union retained autonomous legal, religious and educational institutions, but Britishness was seen as an extension of or merged with Englishness. 'As a political and cultural force, Englishness had to be kept elitist, while in its popular form it had to be effaced,' wrote Robert Colls in *Identity of England*. After the Act of Union, Britain was never an unqualified nation-state – it was half empire and half nation broken into four.

Britain never completely acquired the crucial marks of modern statehood, such as having a written constitution and a formal separation of powers. Since the Second World War, Britain (specifically England) has absorbed waves of migrants perhaps more successfully than any other European country and without the emergence of a significant neo-fascist party or movement, as in France. The notion of post-imperial Britishness – as a legal, civic, inclusive, non-racial identity – has eased this absorption of millions of people of different backgrounds, religions and ethnicities. Modern British identity is much less prescriptive than its French equivalent, with its commitment to secularism, liberty, equality and fraternity. Or the American ideal of pledging allegiance to the flag. 'We don't do flags on the lawn,' as David Cameron once put it.

England is the largest country in Europe not to have its own political institutions, however. The English do not have a parliament or official national forum in which to debate Englishness, and so England has not fully reimagined itself in the way Scotland has done since the creation of the Holyrood parliament. 'The idea that England does not, or should not, have its own history is interesting rather than strange: it is unimaginable that the same argument could be made about Ireland, Scotland or France,' writes Robert Tombs in *The English and Their History*. 'A history of England seems to unsettle people: the past, it seems, is not dead; it is not even past.'

The original devolution reforms of 1999 were introduced to provide a workable solution to the asymmetric power and dominance of England within the United Kingdom (84 per cent of the UK's population of 66 million live in England). But with the rise of Scottish nationalism, the English have been 'forced to ask themselves the kinds of questions that other nations' have long engaged in, writes Krishnan Kumar in *The Making of English National Identity*. The resulting tension between English and Scottish nationalism may yet lead to the break-up of the UK.

+ + +

In the summer of 2019, Stormzy, the rap superstar from south London, became the first black British solo artist to headline at the Glastonbury Festival. He made his entrance on the Pyramid Stage, at a time of rising fatalities from knife crime on the streets, wearing a stab-proof vest. Designed by the street artist Banksy, it was emblazoned with a Union Jack, a subversive reinterpretation of the traditional 'John Bull' Union flag gentleman's waistcoat. Jonathan Jones, a *Guardian* art critic, called it 'the banner of a divided and frightened nation'.

Stormzy's Glastonbury performance, wrote the journalist Gary Younge in a *GQ* profile of the rapper, had political purpose: to 'widen the public imagination of the breadth, depth, scale and range of Black British culture'. Younge likened Stormzy to one of 'Gramsci's organic intellectuals', one who: 'emerges from their social class without formal, bookish training but an ability to articulate the interests and influence the consciousness of that class. They have lived its experiences, are embedded in its culture and speak in its vernacular. Stormzy's is the voice of a generation raised through war, austerity, capitalist collapse, left realignment and racist revival: socially libertarian and economically statist; idealistic about what is possible, resigned to what is likely, contemptuous of what is happening; the tone of defiance and disdain in his work cuts through.'

In his own defiant self-description Stormzy is 'Black British'.

'It's super deliberate,' he said, 'in my pronunciation, in my diction, in my stance, in my dressing, in my attitude. This is Black British. I wear it with pride and honour . . . Black British is part of British culture . . . We're a part of it, but we've been getting left out of the conversation. I make a point of it. There are so many people who came before me that had to go through whatever for me to be there, for me to be the first black British male to headline [at Glastonbury].'

For many black men and women, as for Stormzy, as for my old university friends, Black British is an identity distinct from being black and English. In the words of Jonathan Jones, the

Banksy-designed stab vest 'helped Stormzy speak for England' at Glastonbury. If so, why was the vest not emblazoned with the cross of St George? Perhaps it should have been – because Stormzy knew his headline presence on the Pyramid Stage was both a victory and a challenge, and not only to the racists who would reject him. *Black British is part of British culture.*

Modern British identity serves as a big, broad umbrella under which citizens from diverse cultural and ethnic backgrounds can gather and shelter. The bond between patriotism and unionism, cherished by my mother's generation, has weakened considerably over recent decades and British nationalism has lost much of its salience. Labour built its political powerbase in the twentieth century on being a party of British nationalism and today it struggles to know for whom it speaks, which explains Keir Starmer's despairing comment about losing the 'trust of working people'.

The notion of Britishness as a binding, cohesive multinational identity still matters greatly. Even more so when 14 per cent of the population, 9.5 million people, were born outside the UK (5.9 million from non-EU countries), and one in four children have a foreign-born mother. Fundamental to what it means to be British today is to have plural or multiple and overlapping identities. Emma Raducanu, a US Open tennis champion at the age of eighteen, is an inspirational model new Briton. Her mother is Chinese and her father Romanian. She was born in Toronto and came to live in England as a very young child. She went to state schools in Bromley, south London, and her talent was nurtured by the Lawn Tennis Association, the governing body of British tennis: she did not go to the United States or warm climate continental European countries to develop her game.

But a plural society needs more than plural politics and plural identities; it needs a shared commitment to a common good that unites different groups and classes through civic engagement and democratic politics, and this remains elusive because the Anglo British elite finds it increasingly difficult to appeal to a unifying British identity, to a unifying sense of who we are. Perhaps we only truly discover who we are or long to be, at the deepest level, in those fleeting moments when we come together to celebrate Emma Raducanu's astounding tennis triumph in New York, or venture out to clap for the carers, or delight in the success of Team GB at the Olympics. 'As a card-carrying Scottish nationalist, the only time I ever feel remotely British is following the Olympics, often cheering on random British athletes in random Olympic sports,' wrote Mark Redmond, from Edinburgh, in a letter to the *New Statesman*. 'And watching re-runs of Mo Farah and Jessica Ennis being roared home in London 2012 still brings tears to even my bitter separatist eyes.' What moves Mark Redmond to tears is surely what moves many other people as well – the desire to belong and commune, to feel part of something which is greater than yourself and more than an imagined community.

SCOTLAND RISING

Since the Second World War, Scottish immigration levels have been relatively low compared to those in England, and it can be hard for some Scottish nationalists I've spoken to over the years to understand why Britishness matters to so many from minority ethnic backgrounds in England and why they fear it being ripped away from them. One seldom hears the SNP speak about what could be lost, as well as gained, from the break-up of Britain and how it might affect all the peoples of these islands, not just those living and working in Scotland. In 2014, for instance, 88 per cent of the 632,000 immigrants who arrived in the UK settled in England and only 6 per cent in Scotland.

The SNP rejects ethnic nativism and promotes non-racial, civic nationalism: it sincerely welcomes immigration and freedom of movement. But there is no Scottish Stormzy.

+ + +

In the years before the 2014 independence referendum campaign, I watched from London but also closer at hand the growing political awakening of Scottish national consciousness. Back then First Minister Alex Salmond's aspiration for independence was not one of stark separation or rupture: he emphasized continuity or what has been called unionist-nationalism (though the SNP rejected the term). The SNP favoured a social union, a currency union, a monarchical union, a defence union within NATO, as well as membership of the EU. This proposition was dismissed by his opponents as 'independence lite' or 'post-nationalism'. In the immediate aftermath of defeat, Salmond called it the dream that shall never die.

In the final days before the vote, I spent some time in Glasgow and Edinburgh, where the intellectual atmosphere was inspiring: Scotland was not an independent state but I discovered it was increasingly exhibiting what the pro-independence commentator Gerry Hassan called an 'independence of the mind'.

By contrast, at Westminster, there was insufficiently rigorous engagement with the long-term trends that had weakened the Union and powered the rise of nationalism: devolution, deindustrialization, the decline of cross-border working-class solidarity, the weakening of Protestantism and the decline of the trade unions and the labour movement. Defining issues such as the currency, pensions, debt, fishing rights and North Sea oil revenues were fundamental to the debate but nationalism is ultimately about much more than economic self-interest. It is about national sentiment and structures of feeling. It is about identity, self-determination and, at its most romantic, something approaching an imagined sense of enraptured communion. The Scottish novelist Irvine Welsh described the aspiration for independence as the 'metaphysical hope that the world could be made into a better place'. But belonging and identity are not just about expressions of hope: they are forged, as British identity was, in war and difference and violence, as well as solidarity. And no nationalism is entirely benign, as the rifts within the SNP and independence movement which led to the creation of Alex Salmond's breakaway Alba Party have shown.

+ + +

Long after the polls had closed on 18 September 2014, after a late dinner, I walked back to my hotel through the silent, near-deserted streets of Edinburgh's Georgian New Town. I ambled slowly, savouring the experience of being in the Scottish capital at such a historic juncture. The immediate destiny of the United Kingdom was unknown. I took note of which flags were being draped from which high windows – the Saltire or the Union Jack – and I experienced to my surprise a surge of sentimental attachment to my own British identity. I feel something similar when watching the wonderfully spirited Laura Muir, the Scottish middle-distance runner, competing for Team GB.

In the event, the city of Edinburgh voted overwhelmingly to remain in the UK and that night, as I wandered through the spacious, ordered streets of the New Town, I realized I'd never seen so many Union flags on display in Scotland other than at an Old Firm Glasgow football derby; most of them had gone by the next afternoon. Could this be the moment to remake Britain and British identity? I'd asked the historian Tom Holland over lunch in an Italian restaurant on George Street the previous day. Holland, a romantic unionist, said, 'I think we're going to be all right.'

By 'we' he meant Britain and the unity of the United Kingdom.

Would it be all right?

The next morning, at 7 a.m., David Cameron emerged from 10 Downing Street to welcome the vote by Scots to remain part of the United Kingdom. He'd just been speaking to Alex Salmond, who would resign as first minister later that day. Salmond and his advisers were dejected by defeat and exhausted by the gruelling campaign, and as they watched Cameron's address on television in Edinburgh, they sensed he was making a serious political mistake.

'I have long believed that a crucial part missing from this national discussion is England,' Cameron said as he stood outside 10 Downing Street. 'We have heard the voice of Scotland – and now the millions of voices of England must be heard.'

Why speak of England at such a moment? Cameron would have been well served by reading Abraham Lincoln's second inaugural address, in which the great Civil War president eschewed triumphalism as he sought to unite North and South and heal the ravaged nation. But Cameron was reacting to the logic of the political situation in England, not Scotland. By raising the English Question – the question of English votes in the House of Commons for English laws – Cameron was attempting to address England's relationship with the rest of the Union, appease his restive backbenchers and head off Nigel Farage and his people's army. Farage was the first politician interviewed live on BBC television at the end of Cameron's short address.

'Cameron was signalling his belief that a distinctive English sense of grievance about how England is governed was not only politically salient, but also (potentially) mobilizable,' wrote Alisa Henderson and Richard Wyn Jones in *Englishness: The Political Force Transforming Britain* (2020).

English nationalism was being pitted against Scottish nationalism: the Conservatives would profit from the resulting tension at the 2015 general election as the SNP – and by implication the Scots themselves – were cast as the enemy within, plotting darkly with Ed Miliband's Labour.

+ + +

The 2014 independence referendum campaign transformed Scotland; the turnout was a remarkable 83 per cent. It created one of the most motivated and politically sophisticated electorates in Europe and left Scotland, and more widely the independence movement, on a permanent election footing: no sooner had the referendum been lost than the campaign for the next one began.

Nine months after the referendum, Labour was routed, losing forty of its forty-one seats to the SNP; Nicola Sturgeon's party won fifty-six of the fifty-nine Westminster seats. There would be no coming back for Labour in Scotland, where it had been hegemonic for so long.

The Conservatives won the general election in 2015 with a small overall majority, but it was notable that four different parties topped the polls in the four constituent territories of the United Kingdom – the SNP in Scotland, the Tories in England, Labour in Wales and the DUP in Northern Ireland. The kingdom had become untied. The voting pattern was repeated at the 2021 Scottish Parliament and Welsh Assembly and the English local and mayoral election. The incumbent parties – the SNP, Welsh Labour and the Conservatives in much of England outside London and Manchester – were victorious. Labour are strong in Wales, which has its own regional and linguistic divisions, as well as a long-standing but subdued independence movement.

Visit Scotland today and you know independence remains a defining cause as well as an ideal – one cannot say the same for Wales. There's a restlessness for alternatives in Scotland, for a transformative political settlement; it has only become stronger since Nicola Sturgeon became first minister in November 2014. One senses a palpable desire to build a new country: an independent Scotland within the European Union.

Most Scots under the age of fifty put their European identity before their British identity and support independence. The younger they are the more ardent is their support. I seldom encounter a prominent Scottish artist, musician or novelist who is prepared openly to make the case for the Union. Their example matters because artists create a culture and climate of opinion.

In his 2010 novel *And the Land Lay Still*, James Robertson tells the story of modern Scotland from the Second World War to the post-devolution settlement and the SNP's rise to power. The central character is a photographer called Michael Pendreich, whose late father was also a photographer but much more successful than his son. Pendreich is curating a retrospective exhibition of his father's photographs which capture some of the 'decisive moments' of post-war Scottish history. As we learn more about the father, we also learn more about the history of modern Scotland – about its gradual recovery from world war, the decline of the shipyards and heavy industry, the oil boom, the poll tax rebellions and the creation of the Scottish Parliament. It is a state-of-the-nation novel about a nation struggling to become a state. It's also a novel about the land: the landscape, the topography, the sea, the weather. Robertson understands that nations are defined by the stories we tell about them or the stories they tell about themselves. Tony Blair understood this as well. The story Robertson tells in *And the Land Lay Still* is one of rising national consciousness. Scotland today does not lie still; it is divided between unionists and nationalists and restlessly on the move.

THE CONDITION-OF-ENGLAND QUESTION

As Scotland moves towards independence or at least a second make-or-break referendum, England is struggling for self-definition and self-understanding. Yet, even as the United Kingdom fragments, or perhaps because it fragments, we are also experiencing a reawakening of English national consciousness.

What is this new, emerging, inchoate England?

We could call it Gareth Southgate's England as we experienced it during the heatwave of 2018 and then again more intensely during the summer of 2021. Or Mohammed Mahmoud's England, the imam of Finsbury Park who said 'Stop!' during a month of murderous terror attacks. Or Marcus Rashford's England, the footballer who became the unofficial leader of the opposition as schools closed and children lost access to vital networks of support. Or Patrick Hutchinson's England, the martial arts expert who carried a stricken belligerent in the culture wars to safety as the mob closed in. Or Li Hua's England, the lone survivor of the tragedy in Morecambe Bay who found he belonged in a country far from China. Or Connie Scott's England, my nonagenarian aunt who 'fought against giants' to try to save her local doctors' surgery. Or the England of Royal Wootton Bassett, the town that wept for the returning dead from the wars in Iraq and Afghanistan. Or the England of Lewis Silkin, who thought he'd glimpsed Utopia amidst the council estates and green wedges of an Essex new town.

What matters about these lives and predicaments is that, in the end, they are all our predicaments. A nation is more than a collage of identities. And these Englands have their own dark shadows. The final of the Euros was marred by thuggery and rampages by supporters at the gates of Wembley, and some of England's black players were grotesquely abused on social media at the end of the match after their defeat to Italy in a penalty shoot-out. My aunt's campaign was futile: Osler House Surgery was closed on schedule. Lewis Silkin's utopian new town is today disparaged as a dystopia. These are the very contradictions and unstable realities the nation is going to have to live with.

'For too long, one version of Englishness has dominated British politics,' writes Andy Beckett, a historian of the early Thatcher years. 'Proud, white, both confident and defensive, often xenophobic, always anti-Europe, this Englishness has changed as little as the tabloid front pages that have bellowed it out for decades. Brexit is one of its greatest victories. The continuing Conservative ascendancy is another.'

There is no one dominant 'version' of Englishness. The culture of England is always changing, always absorbing new influences while being simultaneously shaped by its history, landscape, language and institutions. Mrs Duffy, Stormzy and the rest of us must make of it what we will. For nothing is certain and nothing is ever settled.

In *The Condition of England* (1909), Charles Masterman, the Liberal MP, social historian and friend of Winston Churchill, attempted to anatomize Edwardian Britain, on the cusp of era-defining change – the Victorian age had gone and the First World War was but five years away. At the age of thirty-six, Masterman despaired at the class divisions and inequalities in society, and he was caught between two worlds, between something that was dead and something that was powerless to be born. 'It is an age in passing. What is coming to replace it? No one knows.'

He was living in an era of 'acceleration' and 'amazing advance' – as we are – of extreme technological innovation and disruption, of 'telegraphs, telephones, electricity, bombs and aeroplanes'. The rapidity of social and political change made him anxious and he would die in 1924, the year of the first minority Labour government, an alcoholic. For Masterman, inspired by the example of the moralists of the high Victorian era, the condition-of-England question was not economic or political: it was moral and spiritual. 'Optimism and pessimism, in face of any civilisation in a changing world, are equally untrue, equally futile,' he wrote in a postscript to the book. 'Progress is always impossible and always proceeding. Preservation is always hazardous and always attained. Every class is unfit to govern; and the government of the world continues.'

As a Liberal and social reformer, he believed in progress but accepted it was not inevitable. What was gained could be easily lost. 'To accept all and to reject all are in this case equally desperate courses. To turn aside in despair, to hold aloof in disdain, to proclaim from the heart of comfort an easy approval, are policies traitorous to the public good.'

Though largely forgotten, Masterman's book has contemporary relevance because it thrillingly captures how it feels to live in an age in passing. We feel something similar today as we try to make sense of what it is we have lived through, where we might be heading next and what it all means for the condition-of-England question, as well as the unity of the United Kingdom. 'We know little of the forces fermenting in that strange laboratory which is the birthplace of the coming time,' Masterman wrote. He felt the weight and pressure of that coming time – just as we do.

For this much we know: England is not a young country, as Blair wished it to be. England is old – the Venerable Bede wrote of an English people in the eighth century – and there are fewer older nation-states, as opposed to civilizational states such as China. Today English nationalism is the most disruptive force in British politics. 'It's also the most perplexing,' wrote the *Economist*'s Adrian Wooldridge. 'The distinction between "English" and "British" has always been hazy, and now the very meaning of "Englishness" is changing before our eyes. Its current transformation makes the nationalism on display in England perhaps the newest in the world, as well as the oldest.'

The English, as they are today, rather than as they used to be, or wish to be, are locked in a cycle of convulsive change, whether the United Kingdom endures or not. But every new beginning comes from some beginning's end. The break-up of Britain would also mean new beginnings for England and Scotland. And so the cycle starts anew.

EPILOGUE

The long, final paragraph of *Homage to Catalonia* (1938) is one of the finest written by George Orwell. Recently returned from the Spanish Civil War, where he fought as a volunteer for the POUM militia and was shot in the throat by a sniper on the Aragon front, Orwell finds the mood in southern England to be beguilingly calm. The people seem oblivious to the gathering storm in Europe.

And then England – southern England, probably the sleekest landscape in the world. It is difficult when you pass that way, especially when you are peacefully recovering from sea-sickness with the plush cushions of a boat-train carriage under your bum, to believe that anything is really happening anywhere. Earthquakes in Japan, famines in China, revolutions in Mexico? Don't worry, the milk will be on the doorstep tomorrow morning, the *New Statesman* will come out on Friday. The industrial towns were far away, a smudge of smoke and misery hidden by the curve of the earth's surface. Down here it was still the England I had known in my childhood: the railway-cuttings smothered in wild flowers, the deep meadows where the great shining horses browse and meditate, the slow-moving streams bordered by willows, the green bosoms of the elms, the larkspurs in

the cottage gardens; and then the huge peaceful wilderness
of outer London, the barges on the miry river, the familiar
streets, the posters telling of cricket matches and Royal
weddings, the men in bowler hats, the pigeons in Trafalgar
Square, the red buses, the blue policemen – all sleeping
the deep, deep sleep of England, from which I sometimes
fear that we shall never wake till we are jerked out of it by
the roar of bombs.

The Great Recession, the Scottish independence referendum and
the surge in support for the nationalists, Brexit, the crumbling of
Labour's Red Wall and Covid were not enemy bombs so much as
political depth charges that jerked us out of our own deep sleep
of England. Plagues change history and the history of human
behaviour. Now we have reached another inflection point, the
moment at which the collective mind opens and new ways of
thinking become possible.

The pandemic has revealed uncomfortable, sometimes hidden
truths, and exposed both the British state's strengths and its weak-
nesses. The UK led the world in vaccine research and more than
750,000 people responded to the government's appeal for help by
volunteering to assist the NHS in the early days of the crisis in an
expression of national unity; but it also recorded one of the world's
highest death rates as the virus interacted with pre-existing medical
and social ills to lethal effect.

Most of us tolerated lockdowns and our freedoms being radically
curtailed because we were not prepared to abandon the elderly, the
vulnerable or the already sick to their fate. Young adults and particularly schoolchildren suffered greatly. Robert Halfon, chair of the
educational select committee and Harlow's MP, warned of 'an
epidemic of educational poverty'. As one of my millennial colleagues
said of young people's experience of the pandemic: 'We took one

for the team.' She was right – they did, without significant protest or unrest; 88 per cent of job losses during that first year affected those aged thirty-five or under.

+ + +

England remains as chronically, if not complacently, divided as it was, but it is not asleep. We now know what's at stake. And we know that, unless we can forge a greater sense of common purpose within and across these islands, the British umbrella under which we have sheltered for so long will be torn asunder. During the first wave of coronavirus, friends of my mine, competitive businessmen and women, started asking fundamental questions about the purpose of what they did, beyond making money. 'Never waste a good crisis in dealing with chronic problems' was a phrase I heard spoken often – meaning that we could use the upheaval caused by the pandemic to take new approaches to problems such as the climate emergency, or the way we travel and farm, by using technology to work and communicate, or creating more resilient supply chains.

Lockdowns created a long, forced pause, a time to reflect. Perhaps we did not fully answer the question 'Who are we?' before the pause button was released, but the answer to this question will come out of what we do and what we want and how we respond to the new world.

A nation, wrote Benedict Anderson, is an 'imagined political community'. It is imagined because we can never know most of our fellow countrymen and women, 'yet in the minds of each lives the image of their communion'. For Anderson, nationhood 'is always conceived as a deep, horizontal comradeship'. But a nation is more than an imagined community because people are embodied and embedded in relationships and networks which inform and shape their everyday experiences. A nation has a history, cultural inheritance and traditions. It also has a material reality that is about people and practices and the places where we live, work, commune and interact – the high street, school, park, sports club, pub, parish, as well as the countryside and places of worship. If we neglect these places, if the communities beyond the great cities are deprived of investment and opportunity, if individualism becomes too rampant, our collective aspirations are dimmed.

The anthropologist Ruth Benedict defines culture as 'the raw material of which the individual makes his life'. The key word here is 'raw': questions of national identity are often visceral and seldom benign, which is why if elites break from the common culture, or people believe the culture is threatened, there is a powerful reaction.

The loss of one's culture is, writes Benedict, a 'loss of something that had value equal to that of life itself, the whole fabric of a people's standards and beliefs'. For Orwell, culture was not the best that has been thought and said in the world, as it was for Matthew Arnold, but the ordinary life most people lead, what was and what was chosen to be 'inherent'.

For numerous different reasons, as I explore in the stories in this book – some of them, I see now, about small, heroic interventions at moments of heightened public stress – many people came to feel their culture had been disrespected. The political class were not listening, and worse still, they kept making impossible promises – about the Iraq War, about bogus migration targets, about the effects of austerity of which it was said 'we were all in it together', about a new settlement with the European Union. These false or foolish promises undermined the authority of the multinational state and its social contract with citizens, and it undermined people's trust in elite and institutional wisdom. The fabric which holds us together, no matter how loose the weave, was torn. There were mutinies. And yet there was nothing comparable to the gilets jaunes insurrection in France.

Can we reweave the social fabric? Can we discover a more generous and harmonious English identity which is not inward-looking or defined by resentful nationalism? Or preoccupied by loss and nostalgia? Or even by banal optimism? More than this, can we achieve a state of balance which reflects the best of who we are?

Throughout the pandemic our fellow citizens put common purpose before individual interests, society before self, the 'We' before the 'I'. This was exemplified supremely by the national vaccine roll-out, a mission-driven project showcasing the best of the entrepreneurial state, university research and business expertise and development. It was organized through the NHS, with efficiency and moral unity, and with notable contributions from legions of volunteers. Above all else, it was fair. You couldn't buy your way to the front of the queue. The elderly and most vulnerable were prioritized. The politicians and the powerful had to wait their turn like everyone else. There was civil peace. Here writ large was an expression of common decency, something to savour and hold on to.

+ + +

As all legal restrictions on social gatherings were lifted in the summer before the winter in which the Omicron variant began to spread so rapidly, one of my cousins hosted a party on his Suffolk farm to celebrate his mother Iris's ninetieth birthday. Iris was told she was going to the farm for an intimate lunch not a larger family party and it was lovely to witness her delighted surprise as we emerged from behind some barns and stables to greet her. Here we all were, the Essex diaspora, the extended clan reunited after a long, enforced separation. Only Connie and her eldest daughter, who'd returned to the town, still lived in Harlow. It was a warm afternoon and we spent much of the party outside as hares and muntjac deer bounded through the nearby dry, gold-turning fields.

That afternoon I asked my mother and her two sisters about their experience of the pandemic and how it compared with the austerities and limitations of wartime, and they spoke about the England of their childhoods and the England of today. 'Everything has changed and yet something has endured through all change,' my mother said. Her comment reminded me of something, though I couldn't quite recall what it was. Later, I remembered – it was Orwell's remark in *The Lion and the Unicorn*: 'What can the England of 1840 have in common with the England of 1940? But then, what have you in common with the child of five whose photograph your mother keeps on the mantelpiece? Nothing, except that you happen to be the same person.'

Those of us fortunate enough never to have experienced world war were tested during the pandemic in ways few of us could have ever expected. When peace arrived, the wartime generation aspired to build the New Jerusalem. What do we want?

A theme of this book is the crossing of borders, internal or external, and some of my characters are border stalkers: their journeys take them in and out of England, and their sense of identity, of who they are and believe themselves to be, is contested or challenged. It's a book about arrivals, departures and returns – or thwarted and non-returns. I contrast the ceaseless movement which defines globalization with the experience of those who speak for the settled, the ordinary, the familiar, the unexceptional, for what goes on enduring with little public recognition. They are the unnoticed – and it was the unnoticed who voted in large numbers to leave the European Union, which was why Brexit was such a psychological shock for the cognitive elite. The unnoticed were noticed. They were tugging at the political class from below. Which defines us in the long run? The exceptional or the ordinary? Here we return to Orwell's theme of changing changelessness or to Masterman's idea of a progress that is always impossible and always proceeding. The meaning of who we are lies in these paradoxes, an English identity always changing, always contested, never settled.

'It's time to go home,' my mother said, as the long summer day in Suffolk faded into dusk.

ACKNOWLEDGEMENTS

I should like to thank everyone whom I interviewed during my research. Many thanks in particular to the following who are quoted in this book: Tasnime Akunjee, Michael Barrett, Jeremy Black, Tony Blair, David Brooks, Jon Clempner, Paul Collier, Lilian Cowley, Gillian Duffy, Nigel Farage, Neil Ferguson, Paul Francis, Andy Haldane, Li Hua, Jeremy Hunt, Patrick Hutchinson, Jim McMahon, Fraser Marlton-Thomas, Theresa May, Mohammed Mahmoud, Alex Niven, Helen Thompson, Robert Tombs, Connie Scott, Phil Whitaker, Graeme Wood and Reverend Canon Thomas Woodhouse.

I am also grateful to the writers quoted in these pages and to the police officers who spoke to me about their investigations into the Morecambe Bay tragedy.

Andrew Gordon, my agent, has provided consistently wise guidance, and so have my editors Georgina Morley and Marissa Constantinou. I am grateful for their commitment to this project and for their patience, care and encouragement throughout. I am grateful, too, to the wider Picador team, especially Chloe May and Jessica Cuthbert-Smith for steering the book through the copy-editing and production process and to Stuart Wilson for the cover design. Emily Bootle, Peter Hall, Alex Lawrence and Anoosh Chakelian provided invaluable research support. Sarah Cowley, Andrew Gordon, Adrian Pabst and Jonathan Rutherford read drafts, or draft chapters of this book, and made excellent editorial suggestions. Conversations with Michael Aminian, Robert Colls, Alison

Hibberd, Katy Shaw, Mike Kenny and Ed Smith were helpful. Sigrid Rausing commissioned the article for *Granta* that inspired this book and I have explored some of the ideas for it in my Editor's Note columns. Mike Danson has never wavered in his support for the *New Statesman* since I became editor and I am grateful to him. Special thanks to my editorial colleagues who, through the pandemic, worked with such tireless dedication and enthusiasm on the magazine and website.

My constant companions in lockdown were Sarah and our son Edward, and I thank them for their love, kindness, good humour and companionship.

NOTES

PREFACE

Office of National Statistics. Data and analysis on coronavirus (COVID-19), https://www.ons.gov.uk/peoplepopulationandcommunity/healthandsocialcare/conditionsanddiseases.

CHAPTER 1: THE ENGLISH QUESTION

Anne Applebaum. *Twilight of Democracy* (Allen Lane, 2020).

John Bew. *Citizen Clem: A Biography of Attlee* (Quercus Publishing, 2016).

Linda Colley. *Britons: Forging the Nation 1707–1837* (rev. edn, Yale University Press, 2009).

Paul Collier. *The Future of Capitalism* (Allen Lane, 2018); conversation with the author (Jason Cowley).

Robert Colls. *Identity of England* (Oxford University Press, 2002).

Robert Colls. *George Orwell: English Rebel* (Oxford University Press, 2013).

Jason Cowley. Interview with Theresa May: 'The May Doctrine', *New Statesman*, February 2017, https://www.jasoncowley.net/profiles/theresa-may-the-may-doctrine.

Nigel Farage – quoted in Alwyn Turner. *All In It Together: England in the Early 21st Century* (Profile Books, 2021); conversation with the author.

Mark Fisher. *Capitalist Realism: Is There No Alternative* (Zero Books, 2009).

Mark Fisher. *Ghosts of My Life: Writings on Depression, Hauntology and Lost Futures* (Zero Books, 2014).

Mark Fisher. *K-Punk: The Collected and Unpublished Writings of Mark Fisher* (Repeater, 2019).

Three essential essays on Mark Fisher and his legacy, from which I have used comments about or by Fisher:

> Simon Hammond. 'K-Punk at Large', *New Left Review*, July/August 2019, https://newleftreview.org/issues/ii118/articles/k-punk-at-large.

> Lola Seaton. 'The Ghosts of Mark Fisher', *New Statesman*, January 2021, https://www.newstatesman.com/mark-fisher-postcapitalist-desire-review.

> Jenny Turner. 'Not No Longer but Not Yet', *London Review of Books*, May 2019, https://www.lrb.co.uk/the-paper/v41/n09/jenny-turner/not-no-longer-but-not-yet.

Michael Marmot. 'Health Equity in England: The Marmot Review 10 Years On', Health Foundation, February 2020, https://www.health.org.uk/publications/reports/the-marmot-review-10-years-on.

Andrew Marr. 'The New Right Revolution', *New Statesman*, December 2019, https://www.newstatesman.com/politics/uk/2019/12/new-right-revolution.

Ferdinand Mount. *English Voices: Lives, Landscapes, Laments* (Simon & Schuster, 2016).

Alex Niven. *New Model Island: How to Build a Radical Culture beyond the Idea of England* (Repeater, 2019); conversation with the author. Niven is a lecturer in English literature at Newcastle University, was friends with Mark Fisher and worked as an editor at Zero Books.

George Orwell. *The Lion and the Unicorn: Socialism and the English Genius* (Secker & Warburg, 1941); miscellaneous essays, also referenced in Chapter 5.

Jeremy Paxman. *The English: Portrait of a People* (Penguin, 1998).

Michael Sandel. *The Tyranny of Merit: What's Become of the Common Good?* (Allen Lane, 2020); conversation with the author.

Connie Scott. Interview: 'Grandmother, 89, takes to the streets to protest the US firm that is shutting her GP surgery after 63 years', *Daily Mail*, 28 April 2018, https://www.dailymail.co.uk/news/article-5666929/Essex-grandmother-face-campaign-save-local-GP-surgery.html; conversations with the author.

Katy Shaw. *Hauntology: The Presence of the Past and in Twenty-First Century English Literature* (Palgrave Macmillan, 2018); conversation with the author.

Ali Smith. *Summer* (Penguin, 2020).

Adrian Wooldridge. *The Aristocracy of Talent: How Meritocracy Made the Modern World* (Allen Lane, 2021).

CHAPTER 2: CROSSING BORDERS

Perry Anderson. 'The Breakaway: Goodbye Europe', *London Review of Books*, January 2021, https://www.lrb.co.uk/the-paper/v43/no2/perry-anderson/the-breakaway. The comment by the former Dutch prime minister Ruud Lubbers, on the dishonesty of Britain's pro-EU elites, is from this essay.

BBC North West. 'Morecambe Bay Cockle Pickers Tragedy 10 Years On', *Inside Out*, 3 February 2014, https://www.youtube.com/watch?v=XaqYwGn75ro.

Philip Collins. 'David Lammy Has Shown What It Truly Means to be English', *New Statesman*, March 2021, www.newstatesman.com/politics/uk/2021/03/david-lammy-has-shown-what-it-truly-means-be-english.

David Goodhart. 'Too Diverse?', *Prospect*, February 2004, https://www.prospectmagazine.co.uk/magazine/too-diverse-david-goodhart-multiculturalism-britain-immigration-globalisation.

David Goodhart. *The Road to Somewhere: The Populist Revolt and the Future of Politics* (Hurst Publishers, 2017).

Matthew Goodwin and Roger Eatwell. *National Populism: The Revolt Against Liberal Democracy* (Pelican Books, 2018).

Ivan Krastev. 'Beyond the Great Disruption', *New Statesman*, February 2018, https://www.newstatesman.com/politics/uk/2018/02/beyond-great-disruption-confidence-finally-returning-europe.

Ivan Krastev. *After Europe* (University of Pennsylvania Press, 2017).

Ivan Krastev. *Is It Tomorrow Yet? Paradoxes of the Pandemic* (Allen Lane, 2020).

Robert Tombs. *The English and Their History* (Allen Lane, 2014).

George Walden. *New Elites: A Career in the Masses* (rev. edn, Gibson Square Books, 2020).

CHAPTER 3: THE TOWN THAT WEPT

General Sir Richard Dannatt. 'A Very Honest General', *Daily Mail*, 12 October 2006, https://www.dailymail.co.uk/news/article-410175/Sir-Richard-Dannatt – A-honest-General.html.

Dexter Filkins. *The Forever War* (Knopf, 2008).

Jeff Goldberg. 'The Obama Doctrine', *The Atlantic*, April 2016, https://www.theatlantic.com/magazine/archive/2016/04/the-obama-doctrine/471525/.

Jonathan Heaf. Interview with Warrant Officer Ken Bellringer: 'How Two British Surgeons Took on the Wounded Soldier's Last Taboo', *GQ*, May 2018, https://www.gq-magazine.co.uk/article/wounded-soldiers-taboo-british-surgeons.

Iraq Inquiry (Chilcot Report). The Report (2016), https://webarchive.nationalarchives.gov.uk/20171123122743/http://www.iraqinquiry.org.uk/the-report/.

John Keegan. 'England is a Garden', *Prospect*, November 1997, https://www.prospectmagazine.co.uk/magazine/englandisagarden.

Bruno Maçães. *Geopolitics for the End Time: From the Pandemic to the Climate Crisis* (Hurst, 2021).

V. S. Naipaul. *A Bend in the River* (Picador Classic, 1979).

Barack Obama. 'What Books Mean to Him', *New York Times* interview, January 2017, https://www.nytimes.com/2017/01/16/books/transcript-president-obama-on-what-books-mean-to-him.html.

Hew Strachan. 'The Town that Weeps', *RUSI Journal*, December 2010, https://www.tandfonline.com/doi/abs/10.1080/03071847.2010.54 2677.

Richard Watson. 'The Rise of the British Jihad', *Granta*, October 2008, https://granta.com/the-rise-of-the-british-jihad/. I worked on and edited this reported essay which provides background on the London bombings.

CHAPTER 4: THE IMAM OF FINSBURY PARK

Shamima Begum. Interview in *The Return: Life After Isis* (Sky Documentaries, 2020), https://www.sky.com/watch/title/programme/91d969d7-7d34-472a-a0d1-b867933a6e99.

Michel Houellebecq. *Soumission*; published in English as *Submission* (William Heinemann, 2015).

Ed Husain. *Among the Mosques: A Journey Across Muslim Britain* (Bloomsbury, 2021).

Andrew Hussey. *The French Intifada: The Long War Between France and Its Arabs* (Granta Books, 2014).

Anthony Loyd. 'How I Found Shamima Begum', *The Times*, 14 February 2019, https://www.thetimes.co.uk/article/how-i-found-isis-bride-shamima-begum-anthony-loyd-isis-bride-syria-n9vcmpkrf.

Shiraz Maher. *Salafi-Jihadism: The History of an Idea* (Hurst, 2016).

Azadeh Moaveni. *Guest House for Young Widows: Among the Women of Isis* (Bloomsbury, 2019). This book provides background on the lives of the Bethnal Green girls before they left for Syria.

Douglas Murray. *The Strange Death of Europe: Identity, Immigration, Islam* (Bloomsbury, 2017).

Zia Haider Rahman. *In the Light of What We Know* (Picador, 2015).

Three Girls, written by Nicole Taylor, directed by Philippa Lowthorne (BBC, May 2017), https://www.bbc.co.uk/programmes/bo8rgd5n. This three-part television drama series about the Rochdale grooming gang case is also cited by Gillian Duffy in Chapter 7 and others.

Graeme Wood. *The Way of the Strangers: Encounters with Islamic State* (Allen Lane, 2016); conversation with the author.

CHAPTER 5: THE BREXIT MURDER

New Towns Bill. Hansard, 8 May 1946, https://api.parliament.uk/historic-hansard/commons/1946/may/08/new-towns-bill.

Frederick Gibberd. Background on, and history of, Harlow, https://www.gibberd.com/projects/map

Thomas More. *Utopia* (Penguin Classics, 2004).

CHAPTER 6: STRETCHING THE FLAG

Jeremy Black. *English Nationalism: A Short History* (Hurst, 2018); conversation with the author.

Tony Blair. 'Tony Blair: Without Total Change Labour Will Die', *New Statesman*, May 2021, https://www.newstatesman.com/politics/2021/05/tony-blair-without-total-change-labour-will-die

Robert Colls. *This Sporting Life* (Oxford University Press, 2020).

John Denham. Speaker's Lecture, 30 June 2018: 'A Nation Divided? The Identities, Politics and Governance of England', https://englishlabournetwork.org.uk/2018/06/30/speakers-lecture-a-nation-divided-the-identities-politics-and-governance-of-england/.

Richard J Evans. *In Defence of History* (Granta Books, 1997).

Richard J. Evans. 'The History Wars', *New Statesman,* June 2020, https://www.newstatesman.com/international/2020/06/history-wars.

James Hawes. *The Shortest History of England* (Old Street Publishing, 2020); conversation with the author.

Nick Hornby. *Fever Pitch* (1992; Penguin Modern Classics, 2012).

Patrick Hutchinson. *Everyone Versus Racism: A Letter to My Children* (HarperCollins, 2020); conversation with the author.

Martin Jacques. 'The Shame in Spain', *Observer,* 8 May 2005, http://www.martinjacques.com/articles/the-shame-in-spain/.

Mark Perryman. *Ingerland: Travels with a Football Nation* (Simon & Schuster, 2006).

Raheem Sterling. 'It Was All a Dream', Players' Tribune, 2 June 2018, https://www.theplayerstribune.com/articles/raheem-sterling-england-it-was-all-a-dream.

Gareth Southgate. 'Dear England', Players' Tribune, 8 June 2021, https://www.theplayerstribune.com/posts/dear-england-gareth-southgate-euros-soccer.

CHAPTER 7: A VISITOR FROM THE FUTURE

The Casey Review: A Review into Opportunity and Integration (Ministry of Housing, Communities and Local Government, 2016), https://www.gov.uk/government/publications/the-casey-review-a-review-into-opportunity-and-integration.

Anoosh Chakelian. Interview with Simon Danczuk: 'On the Road with . . . Simon Danczuk', *Total Politics,* 21 February 2014, https://www.totalpolitics.com/articles/interview/road-simon-danczuk.

George Dangerfield. *The Strange Death of Liberal England* (Routledge, 1935).

Joan Didion. 'Insider Baseball', *New York Review of Books,* October 1988, https://www.nybooks.com/articles/1988/10/27/insider-baseball/

Andy Haldane. 'Ashington – A Speech', 24 September 2019, https://industrialstrategycouncil.org/ashington-speech-andy-haldane; conversation with the author while Haldane was chief economist at the Bank of England.

Alisa Henderson and Richard Wyn Jones. *Englishness The Political Force Transforming Britain* (Oxford University Press, 2020). This book includes comparative polling data on British citizens' changing views of national identity.

Darcus Howe. 'These Are Real Race Riots', *New Statesman*, June 2001, https://www.newstatesman.com/node/153537. The late Howe's political activism was dramatized in the first of the director Steve McQueen's film series *Small Axe*. The five films tell the stories of West Indian immigrants in London from the 1960s to the 1980s.

Boris Johnson. Speech at Manchester Science and Industry Museum, 27 July 2019, https://www.gov.uk/government/speeches/pm-speech-at-manchester-science-and-industry-museum.

Deborah Mattinson. *Beyond the Red Wall: Why Labour Lost, How the Conservatives Won and What Will Happen Next?* (Biteback, 2020).

CHAPTER 8 LOCKDOWN

David Brooks. *Second Mountain: The Quest For a Moral Life* (Allen Lane, 2019); conversation with the author.

Martin Fletcher. 'Britain and Covid 19: A Chronicle of Incompetence', *New Statesman*, July 2020, https://www.newstatesman.com/2020/07/britain-and-covid-19-chronicle-incompetence. This account of the British government's early responses to the Covid pandemic is compelling reading.

John Gray. *Feline Philosophy: Cats and the Meaning of Life* (Allen Lane, 2020); conversation with the author.

Bryan Magee. *Ultimate Questions* (Princeton University Press, 2017); conversation with the author.

Robert McCrum. *Every Third Thought: On Life, Death and the End Game* (Picador, 2017).

Alfred Lord Tennyson. *Selected Poems* (Penguin Classics, 2007).

Adam Tooze. *Shutdown: How Covid Shook the World Economy* (Allen Lane, 2021).

CHAPTER 9: UNTIED KINGDOM

Andy Beckett. 'Brexit May Spell the End of the Tabloid Version of Englishness: Can Labour Redefine It?', *Guardian*, 8 January 2021, https://www.theguardian.com/commentisfree/2021/jan/08/brexit-tabloid-englishness-labour-scottish-independence.

Tony Blair. 'Leaders' Speech, Brighton, 1995', British Political Speech, Speech Archive, http://www.britishpoliticalspeech.org/speech-archive.htm?speech=201; conversation with the author.

David Cameron. 'Scottish Independence Referendum: Statement by the Prime Minister', 19 September 2016, https://www.gov.uk/government/news/scottish-independence-referendum-statement-by-the-prime-minister.

Christophe Guilluy. *La France périphérique: Comment on a sacrifié les classes populaires*, (Flammarion, 2014).

Christophe Guilluy. *Le crépuscule de la France d'en haut* (Flammarion, 2016).

Tom Holland. *Athelstan: The Making of England* (Penguin Monarchs, 2016).

Krishnan Kumar. *The Making of English National Identity* (Cambridge University Press, 2006).

Charles Masterman. *The Condition of England* (1909; Faber and Faber, 2008).

James Robertson. *And the Land Lay Still* (Hamish, Hamilton, 2010).

Robert Tombs. *This Sovereign Isle: Britain In and Out of Europe* (Allen Lane, 2021); conversation with the author.

Adrian Wooldridge. 'The Disruptive Rise of English Nationalism', *The Economist*, 20 March 2021, https://www.economist.com/britain/2021/03/20/the-disruptive-rise-of-english-nationalism.

Gary Younge. 'Stormzy: "In my diction, in my stance, in my attitude . . . this is Black British"', *GQ*, February 2020, https://www.gq-magazine.co.uk/culture/article/stormzy-black-british.

EPILOGUE

Benedict Anderson. *Imagined Communities: Reflections on the Origins and Spread of Nationalism* (Verso, 1983).

Ruth Benedict. *Patterns of Culture* (1934; Houghton Mifflin 1989).

George Orwell. *Homage to Catalonia* (1938; Penguin Modern Classics, 2000).